ASIAN AMERICAN ISSUES

ASIAN AMERICAN ISSUES

MARY YU DANICO AND FRANKLIN NG

Contemporary American Ethnic Issues
Ronald H. Bayor, Series Editor

GREENWOOD PRESS
Westport, Connecticut • London

Library of Congress Cataloging-in-Publication Data

Danico, Mary Yu.
   Asian American issues / Mary Yu Danico and Franklin Ng.
      p.   cm. — (Contemporary American ethnic issues, ISSN 1543–219X)
   Includes bibliographical references (p.) and index.
   ISBN 0–313–31965–0 (alk. paper)
   1. Asian Americans—Social conditions. 2. Asian Americans—Ethnic identity.
   I. Ng, Franklin, 1947– II. Title. III. Series.
   E184.A75D36   2004
   305.895′073—dc22   2004016133

British Library Cataloguing in Publication Data is available.

Library of Congress Catalog Card Number: 2004016133
ISBN: 0–313–31965–0
ISSN: 1543–219X

First published in 2004

Greenwood Press, 88 Post Road West, Westport, CT 06881
An imprint of Greenwood Publishing Group, Inc.
www.greenwood.com

Printed in the United States of America

The paper used in this book complies with the
Permanent Paper Standard issued by the National
Information Standards Organization (Z39.48–1984).

10 9 8 7 6 5 4 3 2 1

To my partner Bryceton, who never ceases to amaze me with his love, generosity, patience, and steadfast support of my scholarship and work. To my beautiful "little divas," Kaira and Soleil, who continue to bring the warmth of the ocean and the freshness of the sun into my life every moment in the day.—Mary Yu Danico

To my wonderful wife, Lucia, whose love and support mean so much, and my children, Gavin and Margaret, who continue to share the joy of doing research with their dad.—Franklin Ng

CONTENTS

SERIES FOREWORD

Northern Ireland, the Middle East, and South Asia are just some of the places where ethnic/racial issues have divided communities and countries. The United States has a long history of such division that often has erupted into violent conflict as well. In America, a nation of immigrants with many ethnic and racial groups, it is particularly important to understand the issues that separate us from one another. Nothing could be more damaging to our nation of nations than the misconception of others' opinions on controversial topics.

The purpose of this series is to provide the means by which students particularly, but also teachers and general readers, can comprehend the contentious issues of our times. The diverse groups chosen for inclusion are the country's main ethnic/racial minorities. Therefore, the groups covered are African Americans, Native Americans, Asian Americans, Latino Americans, Jewish Americans, and Muslim Americans. Each book is written by an expert on that group, a scholar able to explain and discuss clearly in a narrative style the points of friction within the minority and between the minority and majority.

Each volume begins with the historical background of a contemporary issue, including court decisions and legislative action, that provides context. This introduction is followed by the pros and cons of the debate, various viewpoints, the opinion of notables, questions for discussion or paper topics, and recommended reading. Readers of this series will become conversant with such topics as affirmative action and reparation, Indian names and images in sports, undocumented immigrants and border control, intermarriage, separation of church and state, old-world ties and assimilation, and racial profiling. Knowledge of such concerns will help limit conflict, encourage discussion, and clarify the opinions of those who disagree with majority views. It is important, especially for students, to recognize the value of a different point of view.

Also of importance is realizing that some issues transcend ethnic/racial boundaries. For example, stereotypical images are concerns of both Native Americans and Asian Americans, affirmative action and reparations are more than black-white controversies, and separation of church and state affects Muslim as well as Jewish Americans. These subjects are perennial ones in American history and serve to illustrate that they need to be discussed in a way that brings attention to various views.

This type of series would have served a useful purpose during earlier years when Americans searched for answers and clarification for complex issues tied to race and ethnicity. In a nation that has now become more diversified and during a period once again of extensive immigration, it is time to look at our disputes and calmly appraise and discuss.

Ronald H. Bayor
Series Editor

ACKNOWLEDGMENTS

We feel privileged to write a book on Asian American Issues for this generation of knowledge seekers, as well as for the eyes of future generations. Sadly, neither one of us, growing up, had the opportunity to read books that outline issues facing Asian Americans. In fact, it was a challenge to find academic research, novels, or children's books that had Asian Americans as their focal point. Today, there are significant numbers of academic books, literature, plays, and so forth that address Asian American issues; however, much more dialogue is needed to weed out the various misperceptions our society has about Asian Americans. So when we were given the opportunity to write a book that would stimulate discussions on various issues, we jumped at it. While we were able to touch on many topics of interest, there are still many more that are not addressed in this book. We hope that more will be written to add to the growing collection of literature and scholarship on Asian Americans.

This book is the result of great collaboration between Franklin Ng and Mary Yu Danico. Through endless e-mails, phone calls, and virtual editing we successfully navigated the geographic boundaries and have produced a book that we hope will generate much discussion. Franklin Ng's calm, almost Zen-like persona made this project a joy to work on. His flexibility and openness to ideas make him an ideal collaborator.

We want to thank Wendi Schnaufer, editor at Greenwood Press, for her patience and warmth during the writing stages of the book, and Ronald H. Bayor for including our book in his series. We also thank our colleagues who have engaged in dialogue with us about the very issues we raise in this book. We thank Dean Alegado, Ibrahim Aoude, Rick Bonus, Yen Le Espiritu, Masako Ikeda, Davianna McGregor, Greg Mark, Jonathan Okamura, Franklin Odo, Gary Okihiro, Brett Stockdill, Gayle Sumida, Steve Sumida, Dana Takagi, and Linda Vo.

We also want to express our appreciation to our institutions and our departments for their continued support. Mary Yu Danico thanks Barbara Way, Dean of the College of Letters, Arts, and Social Sciences at Cal Poly Pomona for her continued support and mentoring. Mary Yu Danico would also like to acknowledge her research assistants, Irene Miyashiro and Kris Ruangchotvit, for their help on this project.

Finally, we thank our families for helping us to see the light at the end of the tunnel, and we especially thank our children, who bring out the bounce in our walk and the smiles on our faces.

INTRODUCTION

Living in the United States are many diverse ethnic groups with their own distinct culture, heritage, and history. Americans of Asian descent, often referred to as Asian Americans, have ancestral ties to a number of different Asian countries. They include countries as diverse as Cambodia, China, India, Indonesia, Japan, Korea, Laos, Pakistan, the Philippines, Thailand, and Vietnam. More than 11.9 million people of Asian descent live in the United States. As a result, they are the country's third largest minority group, after African Americans and Latino Americans.

The history of Asian immigrants in America spans more than 200 years. Official records document that early Chinese immigrants came from southeastern China, but other earlier, undocumented arrivals from the Philippines and China entered as early as the 1700s. In this long history of life in the United States, Asians have faced numerous challenges and hurdles in their desire to achieve the American Dream. From the anti-Chinese Immigration Law of 1882 to later antimiscegenation laws, Asian immigrants have experienced discrimination and antagonism from those who saw America as only being suitable for settlement by people of European descent. These people feared competition for jobs and, in some cases, even competition in social relationships. It was not until 1965 that all restrictions against Asian immigration were lifted. Today, their high rate of immigration makes the Asian American population one of this country's fastest growing minority groups.

According to the 2000 U.S. Census, about 4.5 percent of the total U.S. population is of Asian descent or Asian in combination with other races.[1]

Because Asia as a large continent contains so many countries, so the Asian American population of 12,504,636, which includes those of mixed ethnicity, consists of a rich variety of different ethnic and cultural groups.[2] Chinese Americans, including Taiwanese Americans, form the largest group with a population of 2,879,636.[3] Filipino Americans are the second largest group with about 2.36 million people.[4] The next largest groups are Americans of Asian Indian, Korean, Vietnamese, and Japanese ancestry. The languages of the many Asian American groups include Chinese, Hindi, Japanese, Vietnamese, Korean, Tagalog, Cambodian, Laotian, Hmong, and Thai. Among the major religions they practice are Buddhism, Christianity, Hinduism, Sikhism, Confucianism, Islam, Sikhism, and Shintoism. Asian Americans differ from each other in physical appearances, languages, and culture. They also have differences based on social class, religion, and gender. Furthermore, whether they are immigrants, refugees, or American-born may dictate if they have contrasting political and social experiences. In short, the issues facing Asian Americans are challenging and complex.

Today, many Asian Americans live in the western United States. According to the 2000 Census, only 19 percent of the general U.S. population lives in the West, but about 48 percent of Asian Americans reside in that region. Still, this is a smaller proportion than in the past. A brief chronological comparison may be helpful here. According to the 1860 Census, 100 percent of Asian Americans lived in the West. But by 1980, the level had dropped to 57 percent. As a result, Asian Americans are gradually dispersing throughout the United States, although there continues to be a geographical concentration in the West, particularly in California and Hawai'i. But the dispersal that has been occurring means that Asian Americans are increasingly visible in the Midwest and the South, beyond the West Coast and East Coast regions.[5]

With Asian Americans becoming noticeably prominent in all regions of the country and all walks of life, the issues in their communities take on a greater significance. While it is impossible to discuss all the pressing issues that affect Asian Americans, this book examines in successive chapters eight issues that have been the focus of much discussion among Asian Americans. An introduction provides the background to each issue that is the subject of debate. Because each issue has at least two sides, this volume provides contrasting perspectives to three central assertions that are related to each issue. By exposing readers to the differing viewpoints, readers can develop an understanding and appreciation for the complexity of issues in the Asian American community.

Chapter 1 examines the role of Asian American studies for Asian American communities and American society. Asians have a long history of migration to the United States, and they have helped to build the economy of the

American West. But this history of Asians has long been neglected, and Asians have been viewed as aliens or outsiders, rather than as Americans. Asian American studies, which developed out of the social and political movements of the 1960s and 1970s, sought to rectify that situation. Through education, research, and community involvement, Asian American studies was viewed as a means to promote understanding about Asian Americans. It would also engage in research and other activities to improve the status of Asian American communities. In the years since the 1960s and 1970s, there are questions about whether Asian American studies is still necessary and what its purpose should be.

Chapter 2 addresses the issue of whether Asian Americans are a model minority. Some people view Asian Americans as a successful minority that excels in education, succeeds in the workplace, and has won social acceptance by the larger society. This is quite a contrast from earlier periods in American history when Asians were marginalized, ostracized, and seen as undesirable immigrants or foreigners. Whether Asian Americans are indeed a model minority is a subject of debate. Many in American society, including Asian Americans themselves, believe that the term model minority is an apt description for Asians in the United States. Others, on the other hand, argue that there are flaws with that label and they claim that it spreads misunderstanding about Asian Americans.

Chapter 3 focuses on whether Asians in the United States have been sojourners or settlers. Sojourners are those who travel with the intention of returning to their homeland. In their history in America, many Asians have come as immigrants to America in search of work. Later, they returned to Asia to be reunited with their families and acquaintances. But this pattern of leaving the United States to go back to Asia can affect how Asians are perceived by the larger society. In addition, it can have an impact on the Asian American communities in the United States as well as the Asian homeland of the immigrants. Whether sojourning or settlement in America was harmful or beneficial to Asian Americans is an interesting question.

Chapter 4 turns the spotlight on Asian American literature. Cultural politics can be a sensitive and controversial issue in any community, and it is no less so in the Asian American community. The idea that art and literature should have a responsibility to a community is not easily negotiated with the idea of creativity and independence for artists and writers. Whether art and literature should have a social purpose at all is open to debate. Moreover, when there are questions about whether writing should promote a particular view of the community, there are concerns about social responsibility versus literary censorship. Furthermore, whether a particular piece of Asian American literature is representative of social reality and ethnic community and therefore "authentic" is a matter that can elicit much discussion. Asian Americans hold conflicting ideas about the purpose and scope of Asian American literature, for they can see how it might influence other people's perceptions about Asian Americans.

Chapter 5 delves into the subject of transnationalism among Asian Americans. In the contemporary world, transnationalism, or the movement of people, goods, and ideas, is a widespread occurrence. Many Asian Americans move back and forth between the United States and Asia because of their familial ties and business interests. Changes in transportation, communication, and the global economy have helped to promote transnationalism among Asian Americans. But whether transnationalism opens opportunities or presents dangers for Asian Americans is a topic of much discussion. With their knowledge of Asian cultures and languages, Asian Americans can see the rich potential and possibilities in trans-Pacific trade and commerce. On the other hand, potential exploitation of Asian Americans by governments and multinational corporations is certainly a concern. Asian Americans can certainly be a bridge for cross-cultural understanding. At the same time, by pursuing transnational activities, Asian Americans may be neglecting their communities in the United States. Transnationalism, in short, promises to be a subject for lively debate for some time among Asian Americans.

Chapter 6 looks at the phenomenon of Asian American panethnicity, a process by which different groups of Asian Americans forge a common identity. As a population, Asian Americans comprise numerous ethnic groups such as Koreans, Filipinos, Vietnamese, Japanese, Cambodians, Asian Indians, and Chinese. But some Asian Americans believe that developing a collective pan-Asian American consciousness is beneficial to the Asian American community as a whole. They can mobilize their resources to address mutual problems, promote interethnic cooperation, and represent the Asian American population more effectively. On the other hand, coalitions comprised of different ethnic groups always find it challenging to balance competing interests and different concerns.

Chapter 7 explores the topic of stereotypes. For Asian Americans, this is a subject that assumes great importance, for stereotypes about Asian Americans contributed to the harsh immigration laws of the late nineteenth and early twentieth centuries that excluded them from migrating to the United States. Stereotypes about Asians depicted them in negative terms as the bearers of disease and backward customs. Asians were seen by the press as a "yellow peril," a people who were economic competitors and a cultural menace to American society. With the advent of movies, Asians were presented to the public in stereotyped fashion as either sinister warlords, evil geniuses, exotic women, or nerdy geeks. Asian Americans today debate whether stereotypes about Asian Americans are still as negative and demeaning as in the past. Beyond that question, they engage in discussions about whether stereotypes affect them in their daily lives and their social relations with others.

The final chapter in this volume focuses on the subject of generational differences within the Asian American community. Because most of the Asian American populations are predominantly foreign born, except for the Japanese Americans, it is not unusual to hear about conflicts and divergences between the first and second generations, or, as it is frequently described, the cultural divide between the immigrant and American-born generations. But whether there are advantages or limitations in looking at Asian American communities through a generational lens is an issue that can be debated. There may be insights better derived from other sources, rather than looking at Asian Americans through a first, second, third, and fourth generation framework.

NOTES

1. Eric Lai and Dennis Arguelles, "Introduction," in *The New Face of Asian Pacific America,* eds. Eric Lai and Dennis Arguelles (San Francisco: AsianWeek and UCLA Asian American Studies Center, 2003), 1.

2. Ibid., 2.

3. Min Zhou, "Chinese: Once Excluded, Now Included," in Lai and Arguelles, 37.

4. Melany Dela Cruz and Pauline Agbayani-Siewert, "Filipinos: Swimming with and against the Tide," in Lai and Arguelles, 45.

5. Paul M. Ong and Loh-Sze Leung, "Demographics: Diversified Growth," in Lai and Arguelles, 10–11.

1

ASIAN AMERICAN STUDIES PROGRAMS

Asian American studies is an interdisciplinary field that examines the different aspects and experiences of Asian Americans. This includes the history of Asians in America, from the Filipinos or Manilamen, who came to Louisiana in the eighteenth century, to the Southeast Asians, who arrived after the end of the Southeast Asian conflict in 1975. It also includes topics that relate to contemporary Asian American communities, such as the issues of immigrant adjustment, bilingualism, religion, generational changes, employment, education, and community building. Furthermore, there are issues of social problems such as hate crimes, poverty, sexism, and homophobia in the Asian American communities to consider, as well. In addition, there is the matrix of race, ethnicity, gender, and class issues that relate to such matters as interethnic and interracial relations, interethnic marriage, mixed ethnicity identity, gender relations, and different sexual orientations. At the present time there are almost 50 universities and colleges with Asian American studies departments or programs throughout the United States, with another 11 offering Asian American studies courses.[1] And the number keeps growing. The first Asian American studies programs were founded in 1969 at San Francisco State University and the University of California, Berkeley, but today there are programs at elite private universities such as Stanford, Cornell, and New York University. Liberal arts institutions such as Loyola Marymount University, Oberlin College, Pomona College, and Occidental College offer instruction in Asian American studies. Public colleges and universities have responded to student interest, and there are now programs at institutions such as the University of Washington, the University of Illinois, the University of Michigan, the University of Wisconsin, and the state universities in California. Even some high schools, such as Berkeley High School, Milton Academy, and Brookline High School, have offered classes on Asian Americans to their students.[2]

BACKGROUND

Asian American studies programs emerged as a result of the civil rights movement of the 1960s and 1970s, which gave rise to the ethnic studies movement that included African American studies, Chicano and Latino studies, and Native American studies. It also encouraged an interest in the role of race and ethnicity in America and facilitated the development of Women's studies. The civil rights movement sparked not only the desire for racial equality in society, but raised concerns about equity and racial and ethnic representation in high schools and colleges around the nation. The question of whether schools and universities should reflect the diverse multicultural makeup of the nation's population emerged. Moreover, should not the curriculum foster understanding about this social reality and provide an education that might be relevant in addressing problems and issues in Asian American and other ethnic communities? San Francisco State College, now called San Francisco State University, gave birth to the ethnic studies movement. Community activists, scholars, and students had organized to demand an educational program that recognized the voices and history of their communities. They sought a Third-World college that could respond to the need for education about people of color and help to solve the problems that these communities faced.[3] In 1955 at the Bandung Conference in Indonesia, countries freed from colonial powers attempted to form a "third world" model through a policy of nonalignment with the United States and Soviet Union. The ethnic studies movement, like other liberation movements, chose this model demanding a college education free from oppression, such as racism, sexism, heterosexism, and colonialism. They pushed for self-determination and equality whereby students could be educated about their true history in the country through the development of autonomous programs that reflected the needs of each respective community.[4] The students' demands were not warmly received, however; in fact, students were forced to resort to acts of civil disobedience, such as protests, hunger strikes, and rallies. In response to this, "The authorities [in San Francisco] deployed up to ten thousand armed men almost every day for more than two months to crush the Third World strike, but the students prevailed—and Ethnic Studies was born."[5] As time passed, other campuses on the West Coast and on the East Coast joined the fight to demand courses that spoke to the experiences of ethnic minorities. The absence of these courses symbolized to many the lack of interest or concern about groups who had helped to shape the history and economy of the United States. While traditional departments such as anthropology, art studio, dramatic art, economics, English, film studies, history, political science, psychology, and sociology had offered courses on various minority groups, they often referred to them in the margins and not as the focal point of study. Consequently, students often received a disjointed picture of the experiences of Asian Americans versus a holistic picture of their experiences and their communities. Asian American studies programs, which had developed with other ethnic studies programs, were a response to remedy the situation. Asian American programs were devised to offer courses from many disciplines, but the courses dealt with Asian Americans as the central theme of study. Asian Americans would not be marginalized and confined to a single lecture or a passing remark.

The momentum of Asian American studies was drawn from student activists, many of whom were introduced to activism through their participation in the civil rights movement and protests against the Vietnam War. Inspired by the Black Panthers,[6] the American Indian movement,[7] and the Young Lords,[8] students of color criticized what they discerned to be the elitist universities' support of White supremacy on college campuses. As a broad coalition of students from different backgrounds—Asian Americans, African Americans, Native Americans, Hispanic Americans, and European Americans—they were "people of color" who had enlisted in the campaign to correct the situation. Activists of color saw the ethnic studies movement as part of the bigger picture to transform the racist educational system from the ground up. As a united front, a coalition of different ethnic groups demanded an education that reflected the struggles for racial justice at home and abroad. They also fought for programs that would encourage student and community organizing and welcomed the idea of interdisciplinary scholarship for and by people of color.[9] These programs included faculty and students working with community organizations and members, as well as conducting outreach to the community. In the 1990s, university campuses witnessed displays of activism by both students and faculty to establish new programs and sustain older ones. For example, between 1996 to 1998, students at Princeton, Northwestern, Columbia, Stanford, and the University of Maryland, to name a few, demanded institutional support for Asian American studies. They showed their concerns through sit-ins, occupation of administrative buildings, hunger strikes, and other public demonstrations.[10]

Some would argue that the Asian American studies movement in particular and the ethnic studies movement in general have transformed the academic culture. It has done so by redefining and reshaping the curriculum by in-cluding the histories and contemporary issues of the diverse Asian ethnic groups, by changing the nature of scholarship by researching the historical and contemporary issues and experiences of Asian Americans, by employing a more hands-on approach to the practice and methods of research, and by engaging communities through the use of interviews, oral histories, and ex-tensive field and participant observation. However, the pursuit of creating more Asian American studies programs on high school and college campuses can be undermined when educators and administrators cling to the "model minority" myth of Asian American educational success. The myth obscures Asian American interest in struggles for social justice. It gives the appearance, particularly when compared to African Americans and Latinos, that Asian Americans as a group are only concerned with maintaining the status quo, not making waves, and working diligently to achieve the American dream. If university administrators receive this false impression, they may act in ways that are detrimental to Asian Americans. Thinking that Asian Americans are assimilated and have no interest in ethnic programs, they may divert those scarce resources away from Asian American programs. Some may argue that there is no need for a major or a program in Asian American studies, since different disciplines may cover Asian American issues and experiences. For example, some would argue that in history classes, Asian American history is treated as a part of U.S. history, rather than being a field of its own. Moreover, in sociology courses, Asian Americans are often mentioned in race relations classes, but they are only examined briefly with other groups. The complex-ities of the group are overshadowed, with little attention paid to aspects of Asian history and how homeland developments affect the lives of Asian Amer-icans. All too frequently, the efforts to establish an Asian American studies program is often confronted by barriers put up by more established programs, which see a new program as a threat to their resources and territory. Instead of recognizing a new program as filling a void in the curriculum, established programs view Asian American studies programs as a threat that will compete with them for new faculty, classrooms, and other needed resources in colleges and universities.

There are questions as to whether ethnic studies programs in general, and Asian American studies programs in particular, have remained true to their original goals. Are these programs still rooted in community organization and activism, or have they become more professionalized and institutional-ized into the ivory tower by being more concerned about theory and schol-arship? While race and ethnic concerns have been addressed, what else has been ignored in the field? What about issues of gender, sexuality, and class? Are these issues reflected in Asian American studies or ethnic studies for that matter? As Asian American studies develops as a discrete field of academic inquiry, it is making important educational and intellectual contributions to American higher education, both in terms of pedagogy and in terms of research. However, some question the viability of specific ethnic programs. Does it promote an understanding of diverse Asian American ethnic communities or does it in fact create rifts and competition among these ethnic groups? While the battle for Asian American studies programs continues across the nation, there are still debates regarding whether these programs are really necessary. These are some of the propositions related to the viability of Asian American studies that are being discussed:

1. With Asian Americans drawing attention as the second fastest growing ethnic population in the nation, it is desirable that people should have a better understanding of Asian American communities.

2. Much has been omitted from U.S. history regarding the important role of Asian American men and women in the development of the United States. The history courses treat Asian American history as part of U.S. history, but they neglect aspects of Asian history and fail to show how homeland developments affected and continue to influence the lives of Asian Americans.

3. Asian American studies classes help students to acquire usable skills and to develop a sense of social responsibility. Since its founding, Asian American studies has placed great emphasis on training students to be of service both to their ethnic communities and to the larger society. Thus, educating all students in Asian American studies helps students to learn usable skills and to foster a sense of social responsibility. In addition, the program will help students prepare for employment in a multiethnic society.

SHOULD PEOPLE HAVE A BETTER UNDERSTANDING OF THE RAPIDLY GROWING ASIAN AMERICAN POPULATION?

For

Asian Americans are the second fastest growing ethnic group in the United States. For example, the 1990 census showed that California is now the nation's most racially diverse state with the largest percentage of Asian Americans (9.6% of the total California population). The state also has the largest percentage of Latino Americans (25.8%) in the country and the second largest number of African Americans (2.2 million, second only to New York's 2.9 million). Its population of Native Americans (242,164) is second only to Oklahoma's 252,420. Almost 3 million persons of Asian ancestry, representing about 40 percent of all such persons in the United States, live in California today. However, there are significant increases across the United States. Nationwide, Asian Americans consistently represent the second fastest growing ethnic population. With the increasing number of students leaving their home state for college, and graduates relocating to different states and sometimes different countries, it is important to address the experiences of this growing ethnic population. Given this demographic reality, students graduating with an interdisciplinary knowledge of Asian Americans, as well as with knowledge about other ethnic groups, will be well prepared for employment in many occupations. This could be business and management, education, social services, the health professions, law, high-tech industries, and other lines of work that involve interaction with coworkers and clients from diverse backgrounds.

Given the increasing visibility of Asian Americans in all walks of life, all students graduating from a college or university, and not just those of Asian ancestry, should know something about the history, communities, and cultures of Asian Americans who are an integral part of American society. Students who take classes in Asian American studies programs will have a better understanding about Asian American communities and experiences. Consequently, they will learn to see Asian Americans as active participants in the United States instead of subscribing to the various stereotypes of Asian Americans as "others" or foreigners.

Educating students about Asian Americans will sensitize them to diversity and cultural issues that often may impede interactions in everyday life. Furthermore, it will allow students of Asian ancestry to have a better understanding of their own history and culture, thereby promoting pride in their ethnic identity. One way in which students gain a sense of pride and belonging is by having faculty members who serve as role models. While students in four-year institutions regularly have Asian American faculty members in science, engineering, and math classes, they rarely see Asian American faculty members in the social sciences or humanities. As a result, those disciplines that serve as the core of general education do not present students with the opportunity to meet and establish relationships with faculty of Asian descent. Asian American faculty, besides being an asset to Asian American students, also provides an important source of mentorship for other ethnic minority and White students. While education is often gained in the classroom, meetings and social interactions outside of the classroom provide opportunities for informal learning. In fact, some may argue that students gain additional insight through these venues for advising and one-to-one meetings.

In addition to the classroom experience, there are growing efforts to make various Asian American businesses and retail centers more accessible to non-Asians. For example, the Los Angeles Koreatown has recently made efforts to make their commercial industry friendlier to non-Koreans. Many argue that signs written in the Korean language deter many potential customers from coming to their restaurants, retail stores, and other businesses. Instead of alienating non-Korean-speaking from Koreatown, there is a push to make it more accessible to all racial and ethnic groups. Asian American studies can help to promote a better cross-cultural and interethnic understanding. Knowledge of Asian Americans is essential in communities where Asian American populations are flourishing. However, it is just as important in areas where Asian Americans are a smaller percentage of the community. As more people recognize that America is a multicultural society, populated by people of different ethnic and racial backgrounds, it is essential that there be an attempt to acknowledge, recognize, and understand something about all those who live here. While there has been much written about the European American role in history, politics, and society, relatively little has been said or written about that of Asian Americans. This void in understanding and knowledge only makes Asian Americans distant objects rather than real people who are contributing to the vitality and dynamism of America today. The role of Asian American studies is integral to these efforts. In summary, not only is this field interested in educating students about both the historical and contemporary Asian American experience, but it also works closely with community organizations and groups. Through research and hands-on involvement, Asian American studies can reach out to both students and ethnic populations to strengthen the links between the universities and their neighboring communities.

Against

The 2000 U.S. Census highlights the fact that Asian Americans are a fast growing population in the United States. In almost every state, the public and the media are becoming increasingly aware that Asian Americans are an important part of the American mosaic. With this rapid demographic growth, there has been an accompanying expansion of university and college courses and programs in Asian American studies. Started at only a few colleges and universities in the 1960s and 1970s, Asian American studies today has its own professional organization, the Association for Asian American Studies (AAAS). The AAAS was founded in 1979 to advance excellence in pedagogy and research in the field of Asian American studies. The association also strived to promote better understanding between and among the various Asian ethnic groups who are studied in Asian American studies: Chinese, Japanese, Korean, Filipino, Hawaiian, Vietnamese, Hmong, Cambodian, Laotian, South Asian, Pacific Islander, and other groups. In addition, the association promotes the scholarly exchange among teachers, researchers, and students in the field of Asian American studies. Housed institutionally at Cornell University, the national organization has an Internet Web site, a national board and officers, a newsletter, and a publication entitled the *Journal of Asian American Studies*. Before the journal took form, the organization published an annual anthology, often with papers and essays drawn from its annual meetings at different sites across the country. As interest in Asian American studies increased, an East of California organization was formed "in the fall of 1991 on the campus of Cornell University, where representatives from twenty-three colleges and universities resolved to establish the network. Its purposes are: (1) to institutionalize Asian American studies; (2) to develop regional-specific research and publications; and (3) to provide mutual support to individuals and programs."[11] It meets twice annually, in the fall at a member campus and in the spring at the annual meeting of the AAAS. As a result of the East of California organizational efforts, the AAAS developed a directory of its members, as well as of universities with Asian American studies programs, certificates, and classes. Asian American studies has indeed prospered since its initial beginnings when it was taught at only a few institutions of higher learning.

While it is certainly desirable that the public should have a broader understanding of Asian Americans in the United States, it is less certain that Asian American studies is the proper vehicle for this purpose. In other words, it may not be that Asian American studies is the best mode of disseminating information about Asian Americans, for in many Asian American studies courses, the focus is on the largest Asian American populations. They concentrate predominantly on the Chinese and the Japanese. Perhaps this was because of the popular perception that these groups had arrived in this chronological order, and so the studies of these two groups are the most abundant. But it has meant that there is less attention to the Filipinos, Koreans, Asian Indians, Pakistanis, and Bangladeshis. The Southeast Asians who arrived at the end of America's war in the former French Indochina receive even less notice. The Vietnamese, Cambodians, Laotians, Hmong, Iu-Mien, Cham, and others are marginalized in Asian American studies. Groups such as the Thai, Malaysians, Indonesians, Singaporeans, Bhutanese, Nepalese, and Tibetans are in a similar predicament. In addition, there is little focus on Pacific Islanders and mixed Asian Americans or *hapas*.

Some Asian American studies programs also include coverage of Pacific Islanders and label themselves as Asian Pacific American studies programs. But this label of "Asian Pacific Americans" or "Asian Pacific Islanders," which is also sometimes used, has some difficulties. First of all, Pacific Islanders are a diverse population, encompassing Hawaiians, Samoans, Fijians, Chamorros from Guam, Tongans, Tahitians, and others. With the Asian American population itself being so diverse, it is uncertain that Asian American studies programs possess the capability or expertise to delve into the subject of Pacific

Islanders. Moreover, much of the attention might be devoted to Native Hawaiians, who have been linked to the Asian immigrant experience in Hawai'i. Second, if Asian American studies programs examined the Pacific Islander experience, it probably would be done in a limited fashion. Resources and attention probably would be focused first on the major East Asian American groups, such as the Chinese, Koreans, and Japanese and then second to Filipinos, South Asians, and Southeast Asians. For that reason, Pacific Islanders might well have reservations about programs that dubbed themselves Asian American/ Pacific Islander studies programs with such limited coverage of the Pacific Islander populations. Furthermore, some Native Hawaiian studies scholars and activists would argue that their experiences are more closely related to Native American experiences than Asian Americans. While Native Hawaiians have interacted with Asian Americans due to the role of the plantations and Asian laborers, their culture and traditions nonetheless resemble more of Native Americans. Therefore, the label with the words "Pacific Islander studies" would not describe the orientation of the program or department, and it would be misleading to students and others.

With so many Asian American groups represented in the American kaleidoscope, what should one do? How does one synthesize the information? Should there be a risk of academic division into smaller mutually hostile units? If Asian American studies courses take on a chronological approach, does that not mean that there will be greater coverage upon the Chinese, Japanese, Koreans, Filipinos, and Asian Indians, at the expense of the groups that arrived after the immigration changes of 1965? These are the many dilemmas that Asian American studies is still facing as it tries to be representative of its constituency and yet be educational in its objective. With Asian American studies bound by its activist roots in the Asian American movement struggles of the 1960s, and still wrestling with identity politics, perhaps the traditional academic disciplines, such as sociology, anthropology, history, and political science, can impart a more objective and impartial understanding of the role and place of Asian Americans in the United States.

DO ASIAN AMERICAN STUDIES CORRECT PAST OMISSIONS BY CLAIMING A PLACE FOR ASIAN AMERICANS IN U.S. HISTORY?

For

Ignorance, some say, is bliss. When race relations are discussed in the United States it is generally easier to not know about the experiences of groups with oppression, discrimination, racism, and even their successes. That way, the problems or successes of other ethnic groups are simply ignored.

Such is the case of those without knowledge of Asian American history. So many youths and young and old adults know very little about the history of Asian Americans in the United States. Unfortunately, it is not only non-Asians who can use "ignorance" as an excuse for being uninformed about Asian Americans. All too often, Asian Americans themselves are also not fully aware of the role that Asian American men and women have played in the building of modern America.

How is it that the accomplishments of Asian Americans in building railroads, developing the agricultural landscapes across the nation, fighting in wars involving the United States, and contributing to the success of the American nation are ignored or forgotten? Much of this has to do with the lack of education that is provided to students about the history of Asians in America. When we examine Asian American history, it is clear that the early Chinese laborers came to the United States with the intention of returning home. They were the sojourners who came to the United States in hopes of making it financially so that they could provide for their families in China. Wedded to their Confucian values, many believed that being away from their parents and family would not allow them to fulfill their family obligations and responsibilities. However, the economic reality caused many to realize that they would not be able to return home financially secure. In many ways, the early Chinese laborers recognized that it was more financially beneficial for their families at home if they remained in the United States, and sent money back to them. Many Asian immigrant workers, who followed the Chinese, encountered similar experiences. They met with racial and economic barriers in their path so that it was difficult to return home as a financial success. Instead, many stayed in the United States and managed to adapt so that they could help their families back home, while making just enough to sustain themselves.

While immigrants of European ancestry initially had a difficult time assimilating in America, their physical appearance allowed them to blend in with the dominant northern European groups. The Italians, the Jews, and the Irish, for example, endured discrimination and harsh working conditions because of their ethnicity. However, subsequent generations lost their accents and were able to integrate themselves into the fabric of White racial identity. For Asian Americans, assimilation was not an option. In fact, despite the second and later generations of Asian Americans losing their accents and undergoing religious and cultural changes, they were still seen as foreigners. Many of these perceptions had to do with racist ideologies that were prevalent prior to the civil rights movement. Antimiscegenation laws did not allow people of color to marry Whites in many states. Moreover, the laws of the United States prohibited first-generation Asian Americans from naturalizing to obtain citizenship. Not until World War II and after was it possible for immigrant Chinese, Filipinos, Asian Indians, Koreans, and Japanese to receive U.S. citizenship. Unfortunately, World War II also saw the removal of the Japanese from their West Coast communities and their forced removal into concentration camps euphemistically called war relocation centers.

The historical record shows that with so many legal restrictions and obstacles put upon them, Asian Americans could not participate in the everyday life of America. Not only could Asian immigrants not vote, but even their American-born children were instead regarded as foreigners. Predictably, such treatment and attitudes led Asian Americans to maintain close relationships with their families and friends back in Asia. But this, too, became the target of attack, as hostile critics argued that they had misplaced loyalties to Asia instead of America. As immigrants, they could work in the United States, but if they maintained ties with their homeland in Asia then they were seen as potential spies or threats. Asian Americans were in an unenviable position. Even if they tried to assimilate or acculturate in the United States, they were regarded as aliens and foreigners. And if they sought to maintain their filial ties to families back in their ancestral homeland, that only confirmed how alien and foreign they were.

Things changed for Asian Americans and other ethnic minorities in the United States after the passage of the Immigration Act of 1965. This measure permitted families divided on two sides of the Pacific Ocean to be reunited in America. The provisions of this act permitted a larger influx of Korean, Filipino, South Asian, and Chinese immigrants. While the pre-1965 immigrant groups had helped build the agricultural economy of the United States, the post-1965 immigrants were catalysts for transforming U.S. racial and ethnic relations. No longer could race relations be seen as a Black and White issue, for now it was obviously a matter of multiethnic/race relations. The growing numbers of Asians and Latinos entering the country signaled that a new era in racial and ethnic relations was opening in America.

The post-1965 women along with men entered the workforce. Asian American women in many instances had an easier time finding jobs in assembly lines, in computer companies, garment districts, and as domestic workers. In contrast, many Asian American men, who had professional degrees, had a more difficult time finding jobs for which they were qualified. Institutional barriers made it more difficult for the early immigrants to find positions they were qualified for. Their Asian accents, combined with how people viewed Asians with accents, contributed to their struggles. Specifically, the anti-immigrant sentiments expressed in the United States makes it difficult for anyone who is not "American" to establish themselves. Women, on the other hand, were hired for their "dainty" fingers being able to assemble small parts and components. Thus, sexism played a part in getting the women hired in the U.S. economy. This is one chapter in the labor history of Asian Americans, but many of the accomplishments and struggles of Asian Americans are still missing in U.S. history books. The glaring omission of a significant group of people who helped shape the U.S. economy, race relations, and culture has affected not only Asian Americans, but has helped to perpetuate the old stereotypes and fears about Asians as foreigners who do not truly belong in this country. In short, ignoring the role of Asian Americans in the curriculum only helps recycle racist ideologies that infer that America was founded and built by European Americans, and all others merely worked under their supervision.

Against

As one of the goals of the Asian American movement, Asian American studies has played an important role in showing how Asians played an important role in the history of the United States. *Roots: An Asian American Reader,* which was published by the UCLA Asian American Studies Center in 1971, was a pioneering anthology. In a single volume with contributions from many scholars and students, it gave coverage to Koreans, Filipinos, Chinese, Japanese, Hawaiians, and Asian women.[12] In the years that followed, other anthologies, compilations, and books followed to emphasize that Asians in America were not passive victims, but independent actors who charted new paths for themselves and their descendants. In the process, Asian Americans helped in the building of the economy of the United States, particularly in Hawai'i and the American West.

But a number of new developments have demonstrated that Asian American studies has limitations that have kept it from maintaining its pioneering stance of its early days. First of all, in the desire to claim America, to proclaim that Asians in the United States were Americans too, the field of Asian American studies failed to recognize the diasporic and transnational orientation of Asian immigrants. Publications by Asian American scholars and activists in the 1960s and 1970s were intent on proving that Asians were here to stay in the United States, despite arguments to the contrary. At the present time, scholars of immigration accept the position that many immigrants to the United States in the past were sojourners who stayed temporarily in the United States, with the hope of eventual return to their homeland. Other immigrants were sojourners who moved back and forth to several sites. Still other immigrants hoped to travel to their homeland, but were unable to make the trip due to various reasons, such as a lack of funds, a fear that they could not return to America, or a gradual realization that life in the United States offered the prospect of a better life.

Second, in their attempt to distinguish Asian Americans from Asians, the practitioners in the young field of Asian American studies of the 1960s and 1970s emphasized that they were interested in Asians in the United States, not Asians in Asia. At the time, they were trying to demarcate Asian American literature as different from Asian literature and trying to separate Asian American history from Asian history. But by arbitrarily separating Asian Americans from Asia, these early activists and scholars were missing the opportunity to show the complex relationships linking Asian Americans, Asia, and the United States. The fact that many of the activists and scholars of the era were not able to use Asian languages in their research probably contributed to this desire for separation. But, unfortunately, several decades later, in the twenty-first century, the situation has not changed very much. Asian American studies still focuses almost preponderantly on writings and literature in the English language by Asians in the United States. Writings by those Asians who reside in America as residents or citizens of the United States are ignored because of the lack of familiarity with Asian languages. By not being able to read Asian-language newspapers and publications in this country, or even to see and comprehend Asian language programs on television, many students in Asian American studies do not know what is happening in the immigrant or refugee communities. Chinese-language newspapers in the United States, for example, often have commentary about how Japan has failed to make amends and to apologize for its aggression during World War II.

Finally, Asian American studies still carries a great deal of its historical baggage from its activism of the 1960s and 1970s.[13] Formed out of an era when many were critical of America's involvement in the Vietnam War, suspicious about American capitalism and business, and distrustful of government, Asian American studies seems to be trapped in a time warp. For example, Asian American studies does not examine the history of Asian Americans in the military, although that is an important chapter in the experience of Asian Americans. Except for the obligatory reference to the participation of Japanese Americans during World War II, despite the removal of the Japanese on the West Coast to internment camps, there is little research on the participation in other wars, or the military experiences of other groups, such as the Filipinos, Chinese, Koreans, and Asian Indians. Related to this is a failure to study the history of Asian Americans, and this is not only the pioneers and leaders, in business, science, technology, and education. Only if there is the specter of discrimination and prejudice, such as a "glass ceiling" restricting the mobility of Asian Americans, is there some treatment of science and technology. Only if women are exploited in a garment factory or workers are joining a union is there any examination of Asian Americans and the economy. By having ideological blinders from its early origins, Asian American studies has missed the opportunity to have a more complete understanding of the role of Asian Americans in the history of the United States. Because of its stance on activism and resistance, Asian American studies fails to appreciate those Asian American men and women who have been pioneers and leaders in the military, in business and industry, in science, technology, and education, and even religion. By failing to move beyond its origins, Asian American studies is contributing to the omission of Asian Americans from many facets of American history.

BY EMPHASIZING SERVICE TO COMMUNITIES, DO ASIAN AMERICAN STUDIES PREPARE PEOPLE FOR LIFE IN A MULTIETHNIC SOCIETY?

For

Asian American studies was developed with the philosophy of using activism to help and to promote social change in ethnic communities. It was part of a vision that Asian American studies would serve its ethnic communities and the larger society. In the 1960s and 1970s, many ethnic studies programs initiated and supported innovative community organizing projects. These projects included cooperative garment factories, farmworker organizing, and fights for low-income housing. The Asian American studies programs also provided support for the protests against the Vietnam War and tried to advance the cause of civil rights.[14]

Today, some critics find fault with Asian American studies programs for losing sight of their original goals as they became professionalized and more academic in orientation. These critics argue that programs like Asian American studies are no longer connected with their grassroots constituencies, but rather have immersed themselves in the ivory tower. They formulate interesting theories about gender, sexuality, and racial hierarchies, but theories have little real impact on the lives and concerns of Asian American communities. While ethnic studies programs were once a part of an idealistic and service-oriented crusade, they have now become sites for professional jobs or careers. This is quite a turn of events, for initially Asian American programs welcomed student participation in governing, planning, and teaching. To have students intimately involved with Asian American studies programs was one of the basic assumptions of community activists. Today, however, few faculty members are closely involved with community organizations or ethnic community activities. The absence of Asian American faculty participation in community affairs gives credibility to the charge that the culture on college campuses perpetuates elitism and frowns upon community and grassroots organizing. However, these Asian American studies programs are still an avenue for political activism among people of color. Students continue to look to ethnic studies programs as the cornerstone of radical education change.

On college campuses, students of all ethnic backgrounds are often surprised to learn about the lack of exposure that campuses provide on ethnic minority experiences. This surprise often turns into frustration and anger as they realize that they are deprived of opportunities to learn about different segments of the American population. Consequently, in recent years, students of color have led mass protests, sit-ins, and hunger strikes at universities such as Washington, Maryland, Princeton, and Indiana. Some actions have been of a defensive nature to protect the integrity and viability of programs. For example, they have protested the issues of unfilled faculty positions, budget cuts, tuition hikes, the end of affirmative action, attempts to end remedial education, and the firing of popular teachers. Other battles have been offensive in nature. This includes fighting for the establishment of new ethnic studies programs, demands for the recruitment and retention of students and faculty of color, and for the establishment of gay-lesbian-bisexual support centers. For instance, student protests at Rutgers University in 1995 culminated in the takeover of the basketball court at the halftime of a televised game. The demands of the United Student Coalition were reminiscent of the 1960s. They asked for the resignation of the president; the rollback of tuition from $4,500 to $1,350 per semester; the elimination of SAT scores from admission requirements; the restructuring of the Board of Governors to a democratically elected board that reflects the student population; and the inclusion of minority and women's studies programs as part of the university's core curriculum. In 1996, Columbia University students organized the largest protests on that campus since the Vietnam War. They occupied a building and staged a 14-day hunger strike, demanding that Latino and Asian American studies be created to complement the existing African American Studies Center.

As students learn more about the Asian American experience and communities, they become more invested in the idea of serving as agents of social change. They learn how to build coalitions, organize meetings, present public statements, and work through the politics of the university system. These tools not only help in revealing the truths about the state of Asian American studies to the larger community, but they provide students with hands-on skills and the knowledge of how to ask, demand, and/or challenge the power elites for what they desire.

Besides political activism, students who are fortunate to have thriving Asian American studies programs on their college campuses have the opportunity to learn about communities in which they are likely to work, live, and have relationships. For the vast majority of students in the United States, it is inevitable that they will have professional, personal, and everyday interactions with Asian Americans. Despite the long legacy of Asian immigration, few people, including Asian Americans themselves, understand the complexities of this group. Understanding Asian American history and contemporary issues, as well as learning about the culture, will only enhance the relationships that are established and built among Asian Americans, as well as between non-Asian Americans. Given this demographic reality, students graduating with an interdisciplinary knowledge of Asian Americans, as well as with knowledge about other ethnic groups, will be well prepared for employment in many occupations—business and management, education, social services, the health professions, law, high-tech industries, and other lines of work that involve interaction with coworkers and clients from diverse backgrounds. They will also benefit by being prepared to participate and interact with their peers in a diverse and multicultural society.

Since its founding, Asian American studies has placed great emphasis on training students to be of service to both their ethnic communities and to the larger society. Asian American studies has always recognized and, wherever resources permitted, tried to strengthen links to Asian American communities. This includes attempts to develop students' language skills, both in English and in Asian languages. For by being bi- or multilingual, scholars can do community research, and students, as future social service providers, can learn how to offer more culturally sensitive services. In some Asian American courses, students have participated in community-based internships or learned to write funding proposals for projects that might help an Asian American constituency. Students are encouraged to think critically not only about the world around them but also to consider how that knowledge is generated, validated, or revised. Asian American studies faculty is very concerned about doing research in a socially responsible way to address the needs of American communities. Faculty members frequently ask themselves, and teach their students to ask, such pertinent questions as: For whom and for what purpose is this research being done? Who will benefit from the findings and in what ways will they benefit?

Against

From its inception, Asian American studies has sought to bridge the university and the community and to link scholarship to action. Given the context of the 1960s and the 1970s, when the United States saw heated debates about the Vietnam War, the civil rights movement, and the development of a counterculture, it is understandable that Asian American studies should have this concern. After all, Asian American studies was formed out of the struggle by students and community members for more relevant education that could address the issues in Asian American communities.[15]

Taking Asian American studies courses can help students gain useful skills and develop a sense of social responsibility. But students can also acquire the same skills and sense of purpose by taking courses in social work, health sciences, criminology, education, sociology, political science, anthropology, and economics. At the present moment, many universities are emphasizing voluntarism and service learning, the idea that students should learn to contribute to their society. By engaging in such community activity, the students can earn credit from their colleges and universities. And by participating in such course work, educators hope to restore what many feel is an ebbing sense of civic mindedness and to instill a willingness to volunteer for the social good of the community.

When Asian American studies was formed in the 1960s and 1970s, it was a new frontier and a new field. Drawing from many disciplines, the pioneers advancing this field of study were collecting bibliographies, generating new syllabi, and researching topics about Asian Americans, which had received little attention in the past. Challenging institutional apathy, if not resistance, by colleges and universities that did not embrace a new field of study, Asian American studies was born out of struggle and adversity. But the determination and commitment of early Asian American activists and scholars achieved success after several decades. Today Asian American studies programs, departments, and courses are available on many university and college campuses. Students, whether undergraduate or graduate, can enroll in Asian American studies courses. Scholars and faculty in other disciplines can elect to research or focus on subjects that are related to Asian Americans. Their university and community libraries also contain books, reference works, and other materials that are specifically about Asian Americans. The very success that Asian American studies attained has meant that the traditional disciplines have incorporated content about Asian Americans into their scholarship and instruction.

This acceptance of the validity of scholarship and instruction of Asian Americans as a legitimate subject for study and investigation has led other disciplines to focus their modes of inquiry and methodologies on Asian American topics. In many cases, they have developed more specialized knowledge about Asian American communities. As an illustration, students in social work may take courses that acquaint them with pressing issues with Southeast Asian Americans and how to assist with community-sensitive and culturally appropriate modes of intervention. Or, to take another example, students in nursing, psychology, and the health sciences can draw upon research from medical anthropology and cross-cultural psychology that has been focused on Asian American populations. To extend this further, political science courses can offer detailed analyses of the political behavior of Asian Americans as compared to other groups in the United States. Sociology courses can examine how Asian Americans are similar or different from other ethnic or racial groups in American society. They may even highlight the contrasting situations of Asian Americans in the continental United States with those who reside in the state of Hawaii.

The Asian American activists of the 1960s and 1970s deserve accolades for their determination and farsightedness in laying the foundation for Asian American studies. The momentum achieved by the formation of Asian American studies programs and courses generated important scholarship, community activism, and a broad awareness about Asians in the United States. The success of Asian American studies has meant that its insights and scholarship has been broadly disseminated and recognized. The victory that was won has meant that many of the agendas and concerns of Asian American studies have now been incorporated into other disciplines. As a result, it is no longer the only field in colleges and universities that can share information and knowledge about Asian Americans. Service learning that involves Asian Americans is now more readily available in other fields of study, so that the service component that was associated with Asian American studies is no longer unique and distinctive.

Undoubtedly, taking Asian American studies courses can still help students to be more prepared for life in a diverse, multicultural society. But students should also take courses to learn about other groups, such as African Americans, Hispanic Americans, Native Americans, and European Americans. An overemphasis on one group to the exclusion of others can lead to ethnocentrism, a bias in favor of one group over other groups. As American colleges and universities become much more multiethnic in their composition, hopefully students can become much more knowledgeable about their peers who are of diverse backgrounds. After all, much of a college education comes from outside the classroom when students engage in a dialogue with other students. But it also raises the interesting issue of whether ethnic studies programs, American studies programs, or programs in comparative American cultures should be the primary focus for universities and colleges. Instead of separate Asian American studies, African American studies, Native American studies, and Chicano/Latino studies programs, perhaps there should be an emphasis on multicultural, multiethnic programs that acknowledge the full diversity and complexity of American society. Many disciplines give attention to a broad range of racial and ethnic groups in the United States, unlike Asian American studies, which is primarily devoted to Asian American communities.

QUESTIONS

1. How fast is the Asian American population in the United States growing? As diversity in American society increases, what role can Asian American studies programs play?

2. Do specific ethnic programs like Asian American studies create rifts between ethnic groups or create more understanding? Explain your answer and discuss the implications on students if they did not have an ethnic specific program.

3. The civil rights movement was the catalyst for much change. However, has the movement progressed? Has the education system remained true to the initial vision of the civil rights movement or has it sold out to silence the few who still voice a desire for equality?

4. Students who major in Asian American studies will most likely be asked what they can do with that major. How would you answer this question?

5. Is it necessary to learn about Asian American communities in the new millennium? What are the advantages and disadvantages of taking courses on Asian American studies when interacting with people on a personal, professional, and social level?

6. What is Asian American studies and what is its focus?

7. How large is the Asian American population when compared with other ethnic groups in the United States? Which state has the greatest percentage of Asian Americans? Is this likely to be a trend with the other 49 states? Why or why not?

8. How might Asian American studies assume a greater significance because of population changes in the United States?

9. How has Asian American studies expanded as a field of study since the 1960s and 1970s?

10. What is the range of Asian groups in the United States that are included in Asian American studies programs? Have they been able to give comparable coverage in their courses to all these groups? Why or why not?

11. Should Asian American studies programs include coverage of Pacific Islanders in their courses? Why or why not?

12. Immigrants often face difficulties initially in adjusting to life in the United States. What differences or similarities were there for immigrants of European ancestry and those of Asian ancestry?

13. Were the activist roots of Asian American studies beneficial to its immigrant and ethnic constituencies? Has this led to Asian American studies ignoring or omitting important aspects of the Asian American experience? Explain.

14. Some critics have charged that Asian American studies has lost sight of its original goals of being closely connected to grassroots constituencies. Is that claim valid or not? Why?

15. How might Asian American studies prepare students for service in ethnic communities and in the larger society?

16. Are students in other disciplines without exposure to Asian American studies

likely to be just as successful working with immigrant and ethnic groups? Discuss.

NOTES

1. Eric Lai and Dennis Arguelles, *The New Face of Asian Pacific America: Numbers, Diversity and Change in the 21st Century* (San Francisco: AsianWeek, 2003), 206.

2. Ibid.

3. Bob Wing, "'Educate to Liberate!': Multiculturalism and the Struggle for Ethnic Studies," *ColorLines* 2, no. 2 (1999). www.arc.org/C_Lines/CLAarchive/story2_2_01.html.

4. Third World Forum, http://www.thirdworldforum.org/.

5. Ibid., 1.

6. Black Panther Party, http://www.blackpanther.org/.

7. American Indian Movement, http://members.aol.com/Nowacumig/backgrnd.html.

8. "The Young Lords Party 13-Point Program and Platform," *The Sixties Project,* http://lists.village.virginia.edu/sixties/HTML_docs/Resources/Primary/Manifestos/Young_Lords_platform.html.

9. Ibid., 1.

10. Eric Lai and Dennis Arguelles, "Introduction," in *The New Face of Asian Pacific America,* ed. Eric Lai and Dennis Arguelles (San Francisco: AsianWeek and UCLA Asian American Studies Center, 2003), 1.

11. Association for Asian American Studies, www.aaastudies.org/statement/statement.html.

12. Amy Tachiki et al., *Roots: An Asian American Reader* (Los Angeles: UCLA Asian American Studies Center, 1971).

13. John M. Liu and Lucie Cheng, "A Dialogue on Race and Class: Asian American Studies and Marxism," in *The Left Academy: Marxist Scholarship on American Campuses,* Vol. 3, ed. Bertell Ollman and Edward Vernoff (New York: Praeger, 1986), 139–163.

14. Wing, "Educate to Liberate!"

15. Karen Umemoto, "'On Strike!' San Francisco State College Strike, 1968–69: The Role of Asian American Students," *Amerasia Journal* 15 (1989): 3–41.

SELECTED WORKS

Chang, M. J., and P. N. Kiang. "New Challenges of Representing Asian American Students in U.S. Higher Education." In *The Racial Crisis in American Higher Education: Continuing Challenges for the Twenty-first Century,* ed. W. A. Smith, P. G. Altbach, and K. Lomotey. Albany: State University of New York Press, 2002.

Chang, Mitchell J. "Growing Pains." *Journal of Asian American Studies* (June 1999): 183–206.

Hirabayashi, L. R., and M. C. Alquizola. "Asian American Studies: Reevaluating for the 1990s." In *The State of Asian America: Activism and Resistance in the 1990s,* ed. K.A.-S. Juan. Boston: South End Press, 1994.

Hsia, J., and M. Hirano-Nakanishi. "The Demographics of Diversity: Asian Americans and Higher Education." *Change,* November/December 1989, 20–27.

Hune, S., and K. S. Chan. "Special Focus: Asian Pacific American Demographic and Educational Trends." In *Minorities in Higher Education,* ed. D. Carter and R. Wilson. Vol. 15, 39–107. Washington, DC: American Council on Education, 1997.

Kidder, William C. "Situating Asian Pacific Americans in the Law School Affirmative Action Debate: Empirical Facts about Thernstrom's Rhetorical Acts." *Asian Law Journal* 7, no. 29 (2000): 43.

Lai, Eric, and Dennis Arguelles, eds. *The New Face of Asian Pacific America: Numbers, Diversity & Change in the 21st Century.* San Francisco: AsianWeek, 2003, 206.

Liu, John M., and Lucie Cheng. "A Dialogue on Race and Class: Asian American Studies and Marxism." In *The Left Academy: Marxist Scholarship on American Campuses,* ed. Bertell Ollman and Edward Vernoff. Vol. 3, 139–163. New York: Praeger, 1986.

Orfield, G., and D. Whitla. "Diversity and Legal Education: Student Experiences in Leading Law Schools." In *Diversity Challenged: Evidence on the Impact of Affirmative Action,* ed. G. Orfield and M. Kurlaender. Cambridge, MA: Harvard Education Publishing Group, 2001.

Osajima, Keith. "Pedagogical Consideration in Asian American Studies." *Journal of Asian American Studies* (October 1998): 269–292.

Suzuki, B. H. "Asians." In *Shaping Higher Education's Future: Demographic Realities and Opportunities, 1990–2000,* ed. A. Levine. San Francisco: Jossey-Bass, 1989.

———. "Revisiting the Model Minority Stereotype: Implications for Student Affairs Practice and Higher Education." In *Working with Asian American College Students,* ed. Marylu K. McEwen, Corinne Maekawa Kodama, Alvin N. Alvarez, Sunny Lee, and Christopher T. H. Liang. New Directions for Student Services, no. 97. San Francisco: Jossey Bass, 2002.

Tachiki, Amy, et al. *Roots: An Asian American Reader.* Los Angeles: UCLA Asian American Studies Center, 1971.

Takagi, D. Y. *Retreat from Race: Asian-American Admissions and Racial Politics.* New Brunswick, NJ: Rutgers University Press, 1992.

Takeda, Okiyoshi. "One Year after the Sit-in: Asian American Students' Identities and Their Support for Asian American Studies," *Journal of Asian American Studies* 4, no. 2 (2001): 147–164.

Trueba, H., L. Cheng, and K. Ima. *Myth or Reality: Adaptive Strategies of Asian Americans in California.* Washington, DC: Falmer Press, 1993.

Umemoto, Karen. "'On Strike!' San Francisco State College Strike, 1968–69: The Role of Asian American Students," *Amerasia Journal* 15 (1989): 3–41.

Wang, L. Ling-chi. "Asian American Studies." *American Quarterly* 33, no. 3 (1981): 339–354.

Wing, Bob. "'Educate to Liberate!': Multiculturalism and the Struggle for Ethnic Studies." *ColorLines* 2, no. 2 (1999). www.arc.org/C_Lines/CLAarchive/story2_2_01.html.

2

ASIAN AMERICANS: A MODEL MINORITY?

In recent years, many people have viewed Asian Americans as a model minority. Among the many ethnic and racial groups in the United States, Asian Americans stand out. Newspapers, magazines, and television broadcasts often mention that Asians in the United States have achieved success in business, science, technology, education, and many other occupations. As students in schools, colleges, and universities, Asian Americans are lauded for their academic performance and contributions to America's competitiveness in the global arena. But is this popular perception truth or reality? Are there those in the Asian American community whose lives are not as successful as the media and others have made it out to be? Or is it the case that there is substance behind the image of Asian Americans as a model minority?

BACKGROUND

The term *model minority* is an interesting one. The phrase suggests that a minority group is somehow exemplary when compared with other groups. Its experience and performance contrast favorably when compared with that of other groups in American society. Sociologist William Petersen, writing in the January 9, 1966, issue of the *New York Times Magazine,* first introduced the idea of Japanese Americans as a model minority. In an article with the title "Success Story: Japanese American Style," he explained that the Japanese had suffered discrimination and adversity in the United States, but they had still managed to secure a better life for themselves and their children. During

World War II, over 110,000 Japanese living on the West Coast were forced to live in internment camps administered by the War Relocation Authority. With the claim of military necessity, the Japanese were uprooted from their homes and segregated in what were then called relocation centers. Despite this hardship, Japanese Americans, many of whom were Nisei,[1] or those born in the United States and of the second generation, were able to advance to the middle class.[2]

Several months later, the media conferred model minority status upon another Asian American group, the Chinese. In December of 1966, *U.S. News and World Report* carried a story with the Chinese Americans touted as an example of a successful minority group. Chinese Americans were described as a racial minority that had pulled itself "up from hardship and discrimination to become a model of self-respect and achievement in today's America."[3] They were characterized by low crime rates, strict discipline, a strong work ethic, a desire for education, commitment to family, and a low dependence on welfare. The story concluded that Chinese Americans were important contributors to their communities.

Aided by glowing accounts in the media, the perception that Asian Americans were a model minority steadily gained momentum. In 1982, for example, *Newsweek* featured a lengthy article with the heading "Asian-Americans: A 'Model Minority.'"[4] Moving beyond referring to only the Chinese and Japanese in America, *Newsweek* explained that the Asian American population was now more diverse and included Koreans, Taiwanese, Asian Indians, Vietnamese, and other Southeast Asians. Although many in this rapidly growing population were immigrants or refugees with limited fluency in the English language, they nonetheless were willing to work hard and emphasize education as the way to succeed in America. While there were formidable obstacles ahead, Asian Americans still believed that there was great potential to achieve success in the future.

Everyone likes a good Horatio Alger story, a tale of triumph against what seems to be great difficulty. Horatio Alger was a popular nineteenth-century author who wrote books about people who gained fame and wealth by the strength of their character and hard work. For many in the United States, Asian Americans, as the model minority, are like the heroes in Horatio Alger's books: they are the embodiment of self-reliance and perseverance. Indeed some Asian Americans welcome this positive portrayal of themselves, as they feel Asians in the United States have been stereotyped negatively long enough. But there are also those who are wary of the idea that Asian Americans are a model minority.

Some fear that the perception of Asian Americans as a model minority might trigger ill feelings with other ethnic and racial groups. As early as 1969,

Nicole Tan, shown here at the age of 12 in 2000 when she started her first day of classes at University of California, Davis, can be seen as an example of a model minority. AP/Wide World Photos.

Amy Uyematsu, an Asian American activist, had warned that other minorities resented the insinuation that they should imitate Asian Americans to become successful in American society. By allowing them to be portrayed as a model minority, Asian Americans were being used to deflect attention from societal problems and inequities.[5] Echoing this theme, *Time* magazine in 1993 cast a spotlight on "The Perils of Success" for Asian Americans. It reported that they had become "exemplary immigrants," but at a cost. No longer were Asian Americans merely restaurant owners or laundry operators. Instead Asian Americans had drawn upon their cultural values, which respected education and hard work to get ahead. But the very success they achieved had "bred resentment, envy, even backlashes of violence from other subnationalities as blacks and Latinos."[6]

Others worry that the model minority image might hurt Asian American communities. Community activists, those who work with social problems in the Asian American population, are concerned that a false perception might lead government officials and agencies to think that there are no difficulties in Asian American communities. But Asian Americans are quite diverse, and there are issues in their communities that are pressing and real. Refugee communities, with the Laotians, Hmong, Vietnamese, and Cambodians, which developed after the United States withdrew from Southeast Asia in 1975, face the problems of unemployment, poverty, juvenile delinquency, cultural conflict, and limited understanding of the English language. Their socioeconomic status is not the same as that of the fourth-generation Japanese Americans raised in the United States or the highly educated Taiwanese American professionals.

Still others maintain that Asian Americans are not really a model minority, for whether they are of the first or fourth generation, they continue to wrestle with issues of stereotyping and discrimination. Those who are native to the United States are often viewed as international students or foreign visitors. They are complimented on their fluency in English and asked when they plan to return to their homeland. In other words, Asian Americans are seen as perpetual strangers or eternal foreigners than as being an integral part of the American mosaic. Moreover, Asian Americans may have high levels of education and skill, but they are passed over for promotions. They encounter an invisible "glass ceiling," in which they are perceived to be not suitable for leadership or management in a firm or agency, and therefore are denied the opportunity to advance in a firm or governmental unit.

Whether Asian Americans constitute a model minority or not continues to be a topic of debate. Activists and social scientists feel that such an image has negative consequences for the Asian American community. On the other hand, others believe that there is substance to the perception that Asian Americans are a model minority. These are some of the propositions related to the model minority thesis that are being discussed:

1. Socioeconomic indicators show that Asian Americans rank highly in terms of income and education, which has a bearing on the quality of life and their status in American society.
2. The educational emphasis and cultural values of Asian Americans contribute to their success.
3. The image of Asian Americans indicates their social acceptance in the United States.

ASIAN AMERICANS RANK HIGHLY ON SOCIOECONOMIC INDICATORS SUCH AS INCOME AND EDUCATION

For

One way of understanding how a group is doing in American society is to compare its socioeconomic status with that of other groups. For example, the statistics for family income, housing, the status of families, and the level of education are ways of gauging how different ethnic and racial groups are faring in American society. When the 2000 U.S. Census data is analyzed, it is understandable why Asian Americans might well be considered a model minority. For example, in the category of median family income, Asian Americans rank the highest of any racial group at $59,324, compared to the national average of $50,046. The median family income for non-Hispanic White families was $54,698, for Latino families $34,397, and African American families $33,255.[7]

In terms of businesses and entrepreneurship, Asian Americans are noteworthy. The 1990 census noted that Asian American workers had a higher self-employment rate than the national average. About 12 percent of all Asian American workers between the ages of 25 and 64 were employed by themselves.[8] Many Asian Americans started their own businesses. Of all the Asian American groups, the 1997 U.S. Economic Census data indicated that Koreans had the highest tendency to enter into business ownership. According to Edward Chang, the Koreans are "entrepreneurs par excellence." Their rate of business ownership was 71 percent higher than their share of the population. For the Japanese, it was 47 percent higher, while for the Chinese, it was 41 percent higher. The Asian Indians ranked 34 percent higher, while the Vietnamese were 17 percent higher. For Hispanics, their rate of business ownership was 54 percent lower than their share of the population, while African Americans were listed at 68 percent lower.[9]

The extent of business activity by Asian Americans can be surprising. For example, Asian Indian Americans constitute less than 1 percent of the nation's population, but in the United States they own 46 percent of the economy hotels and motels.[10] Asian Americans are also heavily represented in the high technology, computer, and engineering industries. For example, the 1990 census indicated that Asian immigrants were over 20 percent of the scientists and engineers in Silicon Valley. The Chinese and Taiwanese were 51 percent of that group, while the Asian Indians were 23 percent.[11] In the 1990s, Asian Americans and Pacific Islander Americans in Silicon Valley owned and operated over 3,000 companies. They had sales of almost $17 billion, which was about 25 percent of all the Silicon Valley companies.[12] It was no wonder that Anna Lee Saxenian, a sociology professor at the University of California, Berkeley, observed, "When local technologists claim that 'Silicon Valley is built on ICs' they refer not to the integrated circuit but to Indian and Chinese engineers."[13]

In housing for their families, Asian Americans had the highest median value for housing units occupied by their owners at $199,300, while that for all owner-occupied units was $118,800. The median values of owner-occupied units for non-Hispanic Whites was $123,400, for Latinos it was $105,600, and for African Americans $80,600. For owners living in housing worth $200,000 or more, 49.8 percent were Asian Americans, 22.4 percent were non-Hispanic Whites, 14.6 percent were Latino homeowners, and 7.5 percent were African Americans.[14]

Asian Americans are widely regarded as having strong family values. This is supported by the recent 2000 census data. For example, families that are headed by a married couple, a husband and a wife, indicate the stability of families. Nationwide, 82.2 percent of Asian American families were headed by married couples, which was higher than the average of 76.7 percent for all families in the United States. Children born out of wedlock are children who did not have a married couple as their parents. In the United States, 15 percent of Asian American mothers gave birth to children while not being married. In comparison, the figures were 26 percent for non-Hispanic Whites, 30 percent for Latinos, and 62 percent for African Americans.[15]

Education is an important factor that can determine how well a group fares in employment in American society. According to the 2000 census, 44.1 percent of Asian Americans at the age of 25 or older received bachelor's degrees or higher degrees, such as master's degrees, doctoral degrees, law degrees, or other professional degrees. For non-Hispanic Whites, the figure was 27 percent, for African Americans, it was 14 percent, and for Latinos, it was 10.4 percent.[16] (Non-Hispanic White refers to those who are not Latinos and not from Spanish-speaking countries, such as Mexico, Cuba, Puerto Rico, and Central and South America.) From the educational data, Asian Americans are poised to do well in their future prospects in American society.

Against

The 1960s was a time of change, particularly in regard to race relations. Ethnic communities began to challenge a system that was based on European Americans holding much of the power and control in society, and insisted on fair and equal treatment for all people. During this time, the mass media developed a stereotype depicting Asian Americans as a model minority. In many ways, this was to offset the notion that racial equality did not exist. Society at large refused to acknowledge the social, political, and cultural inequities based on race by pointing to a group that "made it" both economically and academically. Clearly, the model minority stereotype was developed to silence the dissenting voices, as it seemed to argue that institutional racism was impossible given the success of Asian Americans. The message was that the model minorities were silent, uncomplaining, docile, and hardworking, which led to their success.

When statistics are examined, it is difficult to argue that many Asian Americans have made great strides in education, occupation, and housing. However, there are several aspects to this picture that need to be considered before people can truly understand the actual situation for Asian Americans. First of all, statistics after statistics seem to indicate how Asian Americans are doing better economically than even Whites. However, this picture is a distorted image of what Asian Americans are really experiencing in the labor market. One variable that household income does not take into account is the number of people living in the house. For many Asian American households, they have more than one breadwinner, which accounts for the higher income per household. In fact, in many instances, extended families live in the Asian households, thereby contributing to the inflated income of the households. Second, while it is true that Asian American families have strong family ties, there are other Asian American families that do not. When one examines the cultural investment in families, one could argue that African American and Latino families also hold strong family values. Yet, for Asian American families, the media and society at large portray them as unique and different from other ethnic groups. Popular images of the devoted and doting wife and polite and obedient children are prevalent.

Yet, what we do not see is that there is also a great deal of dysfunction in some Asian American households. For example, domestic violence is a problem that affects all racial and ethnic groups. However, the way in which each ethnic group deals with domestic violence varies depending on culture and class. Domestic violence includes physical or verbal abuse against a spouse, boyfriend or girlfriend, a partner, the elderly, and children. The idea of keeping such issues a family matter has been ingrained in the psyches of many Asian Americans. This is largely due to the idea that domestic violence was acceptable at one time. "The rule of thumb" comes from a European saying that a man could beat his wife or servant with a stick no wider than his thumb. Hence, the message has been that it is all right to abuse one's wife and children, for they are not seen as family, but rather like servants. For middle- to upper-class families, domestic violence incidents are often unreported to the police, but instead are handled in therapy or through the church. For working-class families, these options are not always available. Instead, nearby neighbors who hear domestic disputes may call the police, or the families themselves may not know of going to therapy. For Asian American families, there are cultural barriers that limit the reporting of domestic violence to police. The idea of keeping family affairs private is something that is practiced by many Asian immigrant and refugee families. Saving face or keeping face in the community is often all that the families are concerned about. The fear of shaming the whole family can affect whether one chooses to report a crime or not. Another barrier is language. For immigrant families who have limited English skills, they may have a difficult time reporting abuse in the household. Police officers who are not aware of cultural differences may not be attuned to body language and other signs that may actually be indicating that abuse is occurring. The problems in Asian American homes indicate that not all Asian American families live in middle-upper-class neighborhoods, drive nice cars, and wear designer clothes.

On the contrary, since 1970s, the United States has seen an influx of people from rural regions of countries such as mainland China, the Philippines, and India, as well as those escaping from political unrest in their homelands of Laos, Vietnam, Indonesia, and Cambodia. These people actually need and are given government assistance to get adjusted and settled in the United States. Unlike the Asian immigrants who came after 1965, many of these refugee groups are uneducated, illiterate, and have little to no social support in the United States. Consequently, they have more difficulties in acquiring jobs that provide an adequate income for their families.

One of the hurdles that Asian Americans face is society's tendency to categorize all of the groups as being the same. Despite the vast diversity of the Asian American communities, and even within specific ethnic groups, Asian Americans are seen as a homogeneous group. For example, many people may not be aware of the differences between immigrants and refugees. The immigrant experience is a stark contrast to the refugee experience. Whereas the first group migrated voluntarily, the latter were forced out of their homelands and placed in refugee camps before coming to the United States. These families often had limited social support and financial resources. Consequently, all the adult family members were often compelled to enter the workforce, leaving the young children to fend for themselves. Moreover, while education is prized and valued in Asian countries, for those leaving countries devastated by war, the opportunity to receive an education was disrupted. Forced to work in order to help their families survive, these refugees frequently cannot resume their education, and therefore relegate themselves to a lower tier in the labor market.

A reason that leads many to the illusion that Asian Americans are well off is the high value of their homes. Most of the regions where Asian Americans are living are located in metropolitan areas where the cost of living is much higher. For example, an Asian American family living in San Francisco, California, will pay more in rent or in purchasing a home than someone living in Iowa. The cost of living in urban areas is more expensive than rural areas. Thus the dollar does not go as far for those living in urban areas, and they may require more financial resources. Clearly, one must look at the many assumptions and limitations of this model minority stereotype before assuming its truth. In short, statistics can only present part of a picture; they need to be interpreted within a general context.

DO THE EDUCATIONAL EMPHASIS AND CULTURAL VALUES OF ASIAN AMERICANS CONTRIBUTE TO THEIR SUCCESS?

For

Higher education opens the doors to future jobs and careers. It provides the opportunities for professional success and a comfortable income in later life. Asian Americans have undoubtedly drawn notice in this category. For example, for Asian Americans at the age of 25 or over, 44.1 percent of them have received bachelor's degrees, master's degrees, doctoral degrees, or professional degrees. In comparison, the figures were 27 percent for non-Hispanic Whites, 14 percent for African Americans, and 10.4 percent for Latinos.[17]

The desire to pursue higher education is so pronounced as a cultural value among Asian Americans that they are represented at many colleges and universities in proportions far greater than their percentage in the total population in the United States. For example, at Harvard University in 2002, Asian Americans comprised 17 percent of its Class of 2006.[18] African Americans were 7 percent, while Mexican Americans, Puerto Ricans, and other Hispanics also amounted to 7 percent. Native Americans were 1 percent.[19] At the University of California, Berkeley, Asians and Asian Americans who were citizens or immigrants represented 42 percent of its undergraduate enrollment for 2001, while Caucasians were 31.7 percent.[20] The large representation of Asian Americans at universities is so well known that MIT (Massachusetts Institute of Technology) is referred to as "Made in Taiwan," while UCLA University of California, Los Angeles) is labeled "United Caucasians Living among Asians."

Because Asian Americans win admission in such large numbers to colleges and universities, their ethnicity has sometimes become a hindrance. Although their presence is touted as contributing to the diversity of those campuses, they are not included in affirmative action programs like Latino, Native American, and African American students. They are not seen as being underrepresented and are not targeted for outreach programs. They are excluded from minority fellowship programs and do not receive extra instructional assistance in programs helping minorities in engineering, science, mathematics, and other fields. Instead, a general impression exists in university admissions offices that Asian Americans emphasize education and will have high grade point averages (GPA) by doing well in their schoolwork. Asian Americans are also expected to perform well on their standardized tests, such as the Scholastic Assessment Tests (SAT), ACT Assessment Tests, and Advanced Placement Tests. Just to ensure that this will be the case, many Asian American parents send their children to the equivalent of cram or examination preparation schools. Particularly in the West Coast, but also in other areas with high Asian American populations, educational institutes or centers have arisen that promise to prepare students to do well on these standardized tests that are required for college admissions. Targeting Asian American parents, they claim that their workshops or programs of instruction will lead to higher test scores that can pave entrance to an Ivy League university, a prestigious liberal arts school, or the University of California system. Despite the high cost for this additional instruction, Asian American parents are all too willing to pay the fees. They believe that this added emphasis on education serves their children and will help to win admission to a very selective and prestigious university. This, in turn, helps their children to attain professional and higher incomes after they complete their studies.

Against

Asian Americans as a group have experienced many socioeconomic successes. A higher percentage of Asian Pacific Islanders than Hispanic Whites over the age of 24 years had a bachelor's degree or higher in 1999, and Asian Pacific Islanders received 10 percent of the doctorates conferred by colleges and universities in the United States Although these are successes, they are based on consolidated statistics related to many ethnically diverse peoples, such as Americans of Chinese, Japanese, Indian, Vietnamese, and Polynesian ancestry, all of whom are included in the category of Asian Americans. Again, the propensity to lump Asian Americans as a homogeneous group clouds the true picture of mixed educational success for Asian Americans. For example, while only 5.6 percent of Japanese Americans have only an elementary education or less, 61 percent of Hmong Americans fall into this category.[21] Although the poverty rates for Japanese Americans and Filipino Americans are 3.4 percent and 5.2 percent, respectively, 24 percent of Vietnamese Americans, 42 percent of Cambodian Americans, and 62 percent of Hmong Americans live below the poverty line.[22] Educated, English-speaking, wealthy professional Chinese Americans from Hong Kong will have different experiences and needs for their children in the United States than will poorly educated, non-English-speaking, financially troubled laborers from the countryside in China.[23]

Among Southeast Asian parents, many have difficulty understanding the American school system.[24] "The parents' lack of education leads to a lack of role models and guidance. Without proper direction, youth can turn to delinquent behavior and in some very extreme cases, join gangs instead of devoting themselves to education."[25] And for some families, they have to choose between education and work, and with limited economic support, there is little alternative for these families. In particular, Southeast Asian students and their families, such as the Vietnamese, Laotians, Cambodians, and Hmong, may fit in this category. Their backgrounds may include war trauma, relocation experiences, family separations, and education disruptions. They will have different psychological and academic needs from Asian immigrants who came to America voluntarily.

Research shows that while some Asian Americans do fare better educationally than their White counterparts and have fewer delinquent behaviors, Asian American youth reported more depressive symptoms, withdrawn behaviors, and social problems. They also had poorer self-images and reported more dissatisfaction with their social support.[26] Furthermore, Asian American students report that they are often the target of racial discrimination from their peers and complain that others are often "mean" or unfriendly to them. Finally, as a result of Asian American youth buying into the model minority myth, those who are more acculturated may themselves discriminate against newly arrived immigrants or refugees. For example, Korean students were seen as distancing themselves from Southeast Asian students because they did not want to be associated with or perceived as "welfare sponges." This is a form of ethnic misidentification.[27] Thus, Asian American youth may internalize racist sentiments and discriminate against those who are seen as an embarrassment to their ethnic group.

The data also shows that there have been an increased number of suspensions of Filipino and Southeast Asian students for fighting at schools. In fact, the proportion of suspensions for this group was higher than for Whites, Latinos, and African Americans. The pressure to be the model minority takes its toll on Asian American youth, but it is more severe for Southeast Asian youth who are unable to conform to the unrealistic expectations of their parents. They have the highest high school dropout rates in the country. For example, among them, Vietnamese Americans only have a college degree attainment rate of 18 percent, only about one-quarter the rate for other Asian American ethnic groups. Laotians, Cambodians, and Khmer are even worse, for they only have rates that are around 5 percent.[28]

While Asian Americans are well represented in bachelor's degrees earned, there are barriers when they enter the workforce. For example, there has been a growth in Asian Americans obtaining entry level positions in law firms, but they later experience obstacles in promotional opportunities. The perceptions of Asian Americans as lacking in leadership qualities arise from stereotypes that foist impressions of docility, passivity, and rigidity upon them.[29] Thus, the perception that Asian Americans have attained economic and educational success hides the existence of a "glass ceiling," a barrier in occupational status that Asian Americans have yet to break. Aside from legal employment, in four-year universities and colleges there are a significant number of Asian American students, yet the faculty and administration does not mirror the student body. Furthermore, there are few Asian American faculty members in the pipeline for executive and administrative posts, positions that ultimately will create and implement policies for the universities.[30]

In corporations, the situation is not much better. The representation of Asian Americans in upper-level management and management in general is below their actual representation in society. For instance, the U.S. Equal Employment Opportunity Commission reported that of 38,000 companies submitting a report in 1991, 5 percent of all professionals were Asians, which is well above the 2.9 percent of Asians in the population.[31] But only 2 percent of the officials and management were Asian Americans. Asian Americans have a higher pool of well-educated citizens than the rest of society, yet at the same time they are being passed over for roles as managers and officials. Hence, while there are a large number of Asian Americans achieving success, there are equally a large number of Asian Americans who are not in this situation. For the most part, they are invisible to the mainstream public, but they do not enjoy the educational, economic, or social success that is popularly attributed to Asian Americans.

DOES THE IMAGE OF ASIAN AMERICANS INDICATE THEIR SOCIAL ACCEPTANCE IN THE UNITED STATES?

For

Asian Americans are a diverse population and are not uniformly in the middle- or upper-class segments of American society. Many Japanese Americans, for example, are in the second, third, or fourth generation. As a group, they are predominantly American-born, are more acculturated, and speak English flawlessly. But whether they are immigrants, refugees, or natives born in the United States, Asian Americans have attained an enviable record of success. From the Vietnamese refugees who braved the South China Sea to escape communism after the fall of South Vietnam in 1975 to the South Asian immigrants who work in Silicon Valley with their H-1 visas, America presents a land of opportunity in which Asian Americans have been able to enjoy a life more comfortable than that which they could have in their homelands. In fact, in 1997 South Asians were only 0.3 percent of the U.S. population, but they were estimated to be providing 4 percent of all the physicians in the country.[32]

The popular image of Asian Americans today is favorable. For example, the success of Asian Americans in academic studies is already well known, as they annually win recognition at the high school level as National Merit scholars or Intel Science Talent Search (STS) Competition (formerly Westinghouse Science and Technology Competition) winners. From their later accomplishments in higher education, they become leaders in science, technology, and other fields. David Ho won the honor of being *Time* magazine's "Man of the Year" in 1996 because of his prominent role in the fight against AIDS (acquired immune deficiency syndrome). Coming from Taiwan as a young child, Ho learned to speak English, graduated from California Institute of Technology, and earned a medical degree from Harvard University. Jerry Yang, as another example, went from his graduate studies in engineering at Stanford University to starting Yahoo!, a pioneering online navigational guide to the Web. The experiences of David Ho and Jerry Yang could be duplicated many times, as Asian Americans have gone on to record achievements in education, science, technology, and business.

Asian Americans have also become highly visible in politics and popular culture. It used to be that Asian Americans shied away from participating in politics, but that is no longer the case. For example, Norman Mineta and Elaine Chao served as the Secretary of Transportation and the Secretary of Labor in the cabinet of President George W. Bush. George Ariyoshi, a Japanese American, served several terms as governor in Hawai'i in the 1970s and 1980s. Benjamin Cayetano, a Filipino American, has also served several terms as a governor of Hawai'i in the 1990s and 2000s. Outside of Hawai'i, where Asian Americans are not as large a percentage of a state's population, Asian Americans have nonetheless been able to win high political offices. Thus, Gary Locke, a Chinese American, has been elected governor of the state of Washington. In Oregon, David Wu, a Chinese American, has won several terms as a Congressman. Gary Locke and David Wu join others who were able to win high political posts outside of Hawai'i. They follow political leaders such as Dalip Singh Saund, an Asian Indian from California who was the first Asian American elected to serve as a Congressman in 1956, and S. B. Woo, a Chinese American who was elected lieutenant governor of Delaware in 1984.

In popular culture, readers know about the writings of authors Maxine Hong Kingston, Amy Tan, and Bharati Mukherjee. In sports, the exploits of figure skaters Kristi Yamaguchi and Michelle Kwan, the success of Olympic swimmer Sammy Lee and golfer Tiger Woods are well known. There are also football and baseball players like Dat Nguyen, a Vietnamese American, and

Benny Agbayani, a Filipino American. Architects I. M. Pei, designer of the East Wing of the National Gallery of Art, and Maya Lin, designer of the Vietnam Veterans Memorial, have received critical acclaim for their work. In the motion picture and television industry, journalists Connie Chung and Ann Curry, Lucy Liu (*Charlie's Angels*), Jason Scott Lee (*Map of the Human Heart*), Keanu Reeves (*The Matrix*), George Takei (*Star Trek*), Pat Morita (*The Karate Kid*), and Tia Carrere (*Relic Hunter*) are among those who have gained recognition in the public eye. As film directors and producers, those who have drawn attention include Christine Choy, Steven Okazaki, Janet Yang, and Chris Lee.

Against

Asian Americans have enjoyed some economic success in the United States, and the model minority stereotype has created some favorable images for Asian Americans. However, the model minority myth ignores the group differences regarding degrees of acculturation, and variations in social, political, economic, and educational backgrounds. By focusing on the successes, and

MTV VJ Suchin Pak, left, plays for the camera with actor Parry Shen at a 2003 party in New York for the stars of the movie *Better Luck Tomorrow*. Shen is one of the stars of the movie, which portrays affluent Asian American teens who turn to crime in a Southern California suburb. AP/Wide World Photos.

generalizing it to all Asian Americans, the model minority myth does not take into consideration the large number of students and families who suffer from poverty and illiteracy.[33] Furthermore, the images of Asian Americans, while favorable in some cases, have also been offset by portrayals of Asian Americans as the perpetual foreigners.

The successful Asian American is seen as someone who lives in a middle- to upper-class neighborhood, drives a luxury car, and works as a professional. Yet, when keeping in mind that not all Asian Americans are the same, many in the public would be surprised to find that in California, 40 percent of all Vietnamese Americans are on public assistance. However, they do not receive much help, and their financial resources are severely taxed due to government officials' acceptance of the model minority myth that Asian Americans do not need assistance. Despite the problems associated with grouping Asian Americans together, Southeast Asian refugees are still categorized with other Asian Americans for research and funding purposes. When the experience of Southeast Asian refugees in the United States is closely examined, the statistics show high levels of high school dropouts and large numbers on welfare. Surprisingly, it is similar to the situation of the poorest members of the "non-model" minority groups, such as African Americans, Latinos, and Native Americans. Southeast Asians, Latinos, and African Americans also share the commonality of having a high percentage of single-parent families. Largely due to the horror of the "Killing Fields," nearly one-quarter of Cambodian households are headed by single women. The "Killing Fields" is a reference to the genocidal policies of Pol Pot. Also known as Saloth Sar, he led his Communists, known as the Khmer Rouge, into implementing policies that decimated the Cambodian population. Because he distrusted Cambodians who associated with the West, were educated, and had lived in cities, he forced many into harsh labor camps where they died or were executed.

Another group that has not fared well is the Korean immigrants. While many of them immigrated with professional degrees and a high level of education, many are not able to obtain high-paying jobs. Instead they are left to work as janitors, waiters, busboys, or forced to go into business for themselves. For those who have opened small businesses, they are able to make profits, due to working long hours or having family members work most or all of the shifts.[34] Furthermore, the image of Korean merchants during the 1992 Los Angeles uprisings did not help their public image. The Los Angeles uprising, also referred to as the "LA riots," was one of the largest acts of civil disobedience since the Watts riots of the 1960s. Rodney King, an African American motorist, was stopped by the Los Angeles police for speeding. A bystander videotaped five Los Angeles police officers beating Rodney King after he was physically down and restrained by them. Despite the videotape documenting the beating, all of the police officers were acquitted of all wrongdoing on April 29, 1992. This date, 4–29–92, is often referred to by the Korean American community as *Sa-I-Gu*, which means 4–29 in the Korean language. Prior to the beating there were other incidents of the criminal justice system discriminating against African Americans. Latasha Harlins, a sixteen-year-old African American girl, was caught on a liquor store's surveillance camera stealing a bottle of orange juice. What followed on film was a Korean female cashier shooting the girl in the back as she was leaving the store. Despite the evidence, the Korean woman was found guilty but sentenced to parole, not having to serve any time in prison. These two incidents, combined with years of police harassment and racial profiling of African Americans, led to the public's reaction to the Rodney King verdict. With the exception of a few Korean Americans, most were seen as foreigners who were at "war" with the local African American community. The perpetuation of the stereotype of Asian Americans as perpetual foreigners is not new. There is no denying that Asian Americans have played an integral part in building the United States. Yet regardless of the length of time that many generations of Asian Americans have been in this country, they are still questioned about their loyalty to the United States. The most outstanding example was during World War II, when thousands of Americans of Japanese descent were interned under the rationale of military necessity. Despite the fact that there were Japanese Americans who had enlisted as soldiers in the U.S. Army before 1941, they were still not trusted or treated as Americans.

At the beginning of 1941, there were approximately 3,500 Japanese Americans in the military, but many were discharged or classified by the Selective Service as 4-F, a designation for those who are unfit physically, mentally, or morally. Later, however, they were more accurately reclassified as 4-C, or unfit due to nationality or ancestry. After some time the War Department permitted the formation of the first all Japanese American Nisei military unit called the 100th Battalion. This unit, comprised mostly of Japanese Americans, trained at Camp McCoy, Wisconsin, and Camp Shelby, Mississippi. They adopted the phrase "Remember Pearl Harbor" as their motto. Not too long thereafter in 1943, recruiters went to the Japanese relocation camps asking for volunteers to form a new Japanese American combat unit to be called the 442nd Regimental Combat Team. Those numbers were bolstered by an additional 12,500 men from Hawai'i who had volunteered. The new Nisei volunteers joined the Japanese Americans still in the military and were sent to Camp Shelby, Mississippi, for combat training. At Camp Shelby, the 442nd Infantry Regiment was formed, consisting of three battalions plus support companies, the 522nd Artillery Battalion, and the 232nd Combat Engineers. The unit designation was the 442nd Regimental Combat Team and most of its officers were Caucasians. The 442nd chose the slogan "Go For Broke," a Hawaiian slang term from the dice game craps. "Go For Broke" meant to risk everything, or to give everything you have—all or nothing!

The 442nd Regimental Combat Team and the 100th Battalion sustained casualties of 9,486 wounded and over 600 killed. It suffered the highest casualty rate of any American unit during the war. For their heroism, the men of the 442nd/100th won 52 Distinguished Service Crosses, 560 Silver Stars, and 7 coveted Presidential Unit Citations. The men in the 100th Battalion alone had earned 900 Purple Hearts, 36 Silver Stars, 21 Bronze Stars, and 3 Distinguished Service Crosses.[35] Besides the contributions of Japanese Americans in the European theater, some also fought in the Pacific theater. Some second-generation Japanese Americans, or Nisei, had lived or studied in Japan before 1941. With their fluency in the Japanese language, these Nisei served in the Military Intelligence Service as translators. They interpreted Japanese messages that had been intercepted and provided a valuable contribution to America's war effort against Japan. At the end of the war, some of them continued their military service by serving as translators during the United States's occupation of Japan. But despite the patriotism and military service of the Nisei, the War Relocation Authority camps continued to intern Japanese Americans until the end of the war in 1945.

A more recent example of Asian Americans being treated as foreigners was in 1998, when American figure skater Tara Lipinski beat fellow American Michelle Kwan to capture the gold medal at the Nagano Winter Olympics in Japan. A headline announcing the upset victory on the MSNBC Web site read, "American Beats Out Kwan." Four years later, in Salt Lake City, Utah, Kwan—again favored to win gold—lost out to fellow American Sarah Hughes and Russian skater Irina Slutskaya. The day after the women's figure skating finals in Salt Lake City, the *Seattle Times* sports headline read, "American outshines Kwan, Slutskaya in skating surprise." Despite the fact that Kwan competed for the American team, her Chinese heritage overshadowed her national affiliation. These two incidents involving the press and media demonstrate that there are those who still do not consider someone who is not of European ancestry to be American. While the press and the media are supposed to be much more informed about such matters, it evidently is not always the case.

The perpetual foreigner image has haunted Asian Americans, even though it is contrary to the model minority or honorary White image that is also associated with Asian Americans. Unfortunately, Asian Americans have the dubious honor of having both stereotypes. The subconscious message is that if you don't make waves, do as we say, then you will not be harassed as much. Taking into consideration that the model minority stereotype emerged at the height of the civil rights movement, Asian Americans often had to choose between being affiliated with African Americans or White Americans. However, not all Asian Americans have embraced this false choice and instead have challenged the White domination that pits minority groups against each other. What is clear is that when people talk about citizenship or being American, they are really talking about institutionalized racism in the United States that continues to elevate European Americans to the top and that relegates everyone else to the bottom. Institutional racism is racism that is imbedded in the social and political structure of the United States, in policies and laws that favor White Americans over ethnic minorities. White privilege is so ingrained that it is difficult to see, but it also means that Whites do not have to explain themselves or wonder if they will be favored in situations that involve race. Often Asian Americans are touted as the ones in-between, yet such sentiments ignore those who are disadvantaged in our society much like the "non-model" minorities.

Most recently, the 1996 political election contribution scandal resurfaced as an issue in the 2000 campaign, with investigations targeting Asian Americans. During the two elections, Asian Americans were depicted as those who raised campaign funds without legal compliance to rules and regulations. Then there was the Wen Ho Lee case, in which espionage allegations prompted the idea of the new enemy being mainland China. Wen Ho Lee was a Los Alamos scientist who was suspected and tried of downloading classified data. Asian Americans have been questioned for their loyalty since they immigrated in the nineteenth century, yet these questions continue today. An April 16, 2001, *Business Week* article said that a Gallup survey found that more than 80 percent of Americans believed that China was "dangerous." Some may wonder how negative impressions of China or other parts of Asia may affect the perceptions of Asian Americans. But the reality is that the loyalties of people of Asian descent are still questioned when there are international tensions, political conflicts, or economic friction between the United States and Asia. At those times, Asian Americans can be the targets of hate crimes and unpleasant incidents. For example, on September 11, 2001, hijackers took control of four airplanes and crashed two of them into the Twin Towers in New York, one crashed into the Pentagon in Washington, D.C., and one crashed in the wooded grounds of Pennsylvania after passengers confronted the hijackers.[36] This day was quickly referred to as "9/11" and associated with acts by terrorists. After 9/11, Americans of Asian and Arab descent were seen as potential terrorists and as threats to national security. The numbers of hate crimes after 9/11 made it clear to people of Asian descent that they are still seen as outsiders in their own country.[37] Following the U.S. spy plane incident in 2001, in which an American plane was downed on Hainan Island off Mainland China, a local radio talk show host in Springfield, Illinois, said that people should boycott all Chinese restaurants. He went on to say that all Chinese should be sent home to "their country." Another commentator suggested the creation of a Chinese detention camp for the Chinese. The announcer's phoning of people with Chinese last names and harassing them followed this remark. Most recently the Severe Acute Respiratory Syndrome (SARS) scare in Asia has impacted Asian American businesses across the nation. SARS is a respiratory illness that has been reported in Asia, North America, and Europe. This is largely fueled by the media's exaggeration of the danger of SARS, despite that more people die of car crashes or influenza. The SARS disease has now become the Asian disease. Chinese restaurants and grocery stores in many communities have suffered as a result of public perception that someone at these Chinese business establishments may be afflicted with SARS. In summary, while the public image of Asian Americans is positive in some ways, the negative perceptions still continue to cause problems. Just as the positive image of docile, hardworking, family-oriented Chinese laborers existed in the 1880s, so did another one about them being the devious, manipulative, and foreign yellow peril. While the social, political, and cultural climate has changed since that time and improved for the better, in some ways, much has remained the same in terms of negative stereotypes. Physical and cultural differences continue to be used in American society to distance and separate Asian Americans as foreigners.[38]

QUESTIONS

1. What is the definition of a model minority? If one accepts the idea of a model minority, are there other groups besides Asian Americans that can qualify as model minorities? Why or why not?

2. If one does not accept the concept of a model minority, what problems might there be with that idea? What about the assertion that while the concept of a model minority has a few flaws, nevertheless, on the whole, the idea is a useful one?

3. Asian Americans is a term that refers to many different ethnic groups. Are there variations among these groups so that not all of them fit into the category of a model minority? Which groups might these be? On the other hand, are there some groups that fit into the category of a model minority? Which groups would you place in that category?

4. What is the history behind the view that Asian Americans are a model minority? How did that idea develop through time?

5. Can the case be made that there was greater validity to the idea of Asian Americans being a model minority in the past than in the present? Or is it more true today than in the past?

6. Who was Horatio Alger and how can the notion of a model minority be linked with him?

7. What are the benefits and costs of Asian Americans being perceived as a model minority?

8. The media is often credited with promoting the image of Asian Americans as a model minority. Does the media really have that much influence? Or is the model minority status more a reflection of actual economic achievement and academic success? How does one define media, and does the media sometimes operate at cross-purposes to cancel itself out? Or is there a single result?

9. Does the media present a uniformly positive image of Asian Americans as a model minority? Or have there been cycles and changes? Are there negative consequences for Asian Americans being viewed as a model minority? Can international relations affect the image of Asian Americans as a model minority?

10. What are socioeconomic indicators and why are they important? Do the socioeconomic data indicate that Asian Americans are a model minority? What data or information are necessary to establish that a group is a model minority? Besides income level and quality of housing, what other criteria might one include?

11. Do Asian Americans value education and succeed in their studies more than other groups? Is it due to their cultural values? Do immigrant students come with more academic skills than their American-born counterparts?

12. What are cram schools? Why do Asian American parents send their children to these schools? Can you think of some other preparation courses that are similar in function to cram schools?

13. For the amount of education that Asian Americans have, do they have a similar level of earning power compared with other ethnic groups?

14. What are the poverty rates for Asian Americans? How do they compare with the levels for other groups?

15. How do Asian Americans do in management and upper-level leadership positions? What is the significance of their numbers at this level?

16. Does the perception of Asian Americans being a model minority affect their relations with other groups such as African Americans or Hispanic Americans? How about their relations with European Americans?

NOTES

1. Japanese for second generation.

2. William Petersen, "Success Story: Japanese American Style," *New York Times Magazine*, 9 January 1966, 26ff.

3. "Success Story of One Minority Group in the United States," *U.S. News and World Report*, 26 December 1966, 73–76.

4. Martin Kasindorf, with Paula Chin, Diane Weathers, Kim Foltz, Daniel Shapiro, and Darby Junkin, "Asian Americans: A 'Model Minority,'" *Newsweek*, 6 December 1982, 39ff.

5. Amy Uyematsu, "The Emergence of Yellow Power in America," in *Roots: An*

Asian American Reader, ed. Amy Tachiki, Eddie Wong, and Franklin Odo (Los Angeles: UCLA Asian American Studies Center, 1971), 9–13.

6. James Walsh, "The Perils of Success: Asians Have Become Exemplary Immigrants, but at a Price," *Time*, Fall 1993, 55–56.

7. Joyce Nishioka, "Socioeconomics: The Model Minority?" in *The New Face of Asian Pacific America: Numbers, Diversity & Change in the 21st Century*, ed. Eric Lai and Dennis Arguelles (San Francisco: AsianWeek, 2003), 32.

8. Min Zhou and Carl L. Bankston, III, "Entrepreneurship," in *The Asian American Almanac*, ed. Susan Gall and Irene Natividad (Detroit: Gale Research, 1995), 511–512.

9. Edward Taehan Chang, "Koreans: Entrepreneurs par Excellence," in *The New Face of Asian Pacific America*, ed. Eric Lai and Dennis Arguelles (San Francisco: AsianWeek and UCLA Asian American Studies Center, 2003), 61.

10. Gelly Borromeo, "Born for Business," in *The New Face of Asian Pacific America*, ed. Eric Lai and Dennis Arguelles (San Francisco: AsianWeek and UCLA Asian American Studies Center, 2003), 41.

11. Eric Lai, "Business and Hi-Tech," in *The New Face of Asian Pacific America*, ed. Eric Lai and Dennis Arguelles (San Francisco: AsianWeek and UCLA Asian American Studies Center, 2003), 236.

12. Ibid., 239.

13. Ibid.

14. Nishioka, "Socioeconomics: The Model Minority?" 31.

15. Ibid., 30–32.

16. Ibid., 31.

17. Ibid., 32.

18. *Harvard College: A Tradition of Excellence* (Cambridge: Admissions and Financial Aid, Harvard College, 2003), 13.

19. Ibid.

20. University of California, Berkeley, Office of Undergraduate Admissions, "Undergraduate Student Profile," 3 November 2002, http://admissions.berkeley.edu/undergraduateprofile.htm (accessed 25 May 2003).

21. S.-F. Siu, *Asian American Students at Risk: A Literature Review*. Report No. 8. Baltimore, MD: Johns Hopkins University, Center for Research on the Education of Students Placed at Risk, December 1996.

22. X. H. Yin, "The Two Sides of America's 'Model Minority,'" *Los Angeles Times*, 7 May 2000, part M, 1.

23. Siu, *Asian American Students at Risk*.

24. Noy Thrupkaew, "The Myth of the Model Minority," *The American Prospect Online*, 8 April 2002, http://www.prospect.org/print/V13/7/thrupkaew-n.htm/.

25. Ibid., quoting Narin Sihavong, director of SEARAC's Successful New American Project.

26. Angela Kim and Christine J. Yeh, *Stereotypes of Asian American Students*. Eric Digest (New York: ERIC Clearinghouse on Urban Education, 2002).

27. Stacey J. Lee, *Unraveling the "Model Minority" Stereotype: Listening to Asian American Youth* (New York: Teachers College Press, 1996).

28. "The Model Minority Image," *Asian Nation*, http://www.asian-nation.org/model_minority.shtml.

29. Lily Liu, "All Asian Asians Are Good At . . . ," *Diversity and the Bar*, May 2001, http://www.mcca.com/site/data/inhouse/minoirtyattorneys/asianamerican.htm.

30. Bob Suzuki, "Revisiting the Model Minority Stereotype: Implications for Student Affairs Practice and Higher Education," in *Working with Asian American College Students,* ed. Marylu K. McEwen, Corinne Maekawa Kodama, Alvin N. Alvarez, Sunny Lee, and Christopher T. H. Liang. New Directions for Student Services, no. 97. San Francisco: Jossey-Bass, 2002.

31. Malcolm Yeung, "The Raging Buddha," in *Model Minority: A Guide to Asian American Empowerment,* 1994, www.modelminority.com/history/primer.htm.

32. Ann Morning, "South Asia," in *Encyclopedia of American Immigration,* ed. James Ciment (Armonk, NY: M. E. Sharpe, 2001), 1212.

33. Educational Testing Service, "Stereotyping Shortchanges Asian American Students," 1997, http://modelminority.com/academia/ets.html; Siu, *Asian American Students at Risk;* Yin, "The Two Sides."

34. "The Model Minority Image," *Asian Nation,* http://www.asian-nation.org/model_minority.shtml.

35. The 100th Battalion/442nd RCT, http://www.kent.k12.wa.us/KSD/SJ/Nikkei/442RCT.html.

36. September11News.com, "Attack Images and Graphics," http://www.september11news.com/AttackImages.htm.

37. Post 9/11, "Hate Crimes," http://gbgm-umc.org/umw/legislative/hatecrimes.html.

38. Elaine Kim, "Perpetual Foreigners," (keynote address at conference on the Changing Status of Asian Pacific Americans at Berkeley, California, November 17–23, 1999).

SELECTED WORKS

Barringer, Herbert R., Peter Xenos, and David T. Takeuchi. "Education, Occupational Prestige, and Income of Asian Americans." *Sociology of Education* 63 (1990): 27–43.

Bonacich, Edna. "A Theory of Middleman Minorities." *American Sociological Review* 38 (1973): 585–594.

Bonacich, Edna, and John Modell. *The Economic Basis of Ethnic Solidarity.* Berkeley: University of California Press, 1980.

Borromeo, Gelly. "Born for Business." In *The New Face of Asian Pacific America,* ed. Eric Lai and Dennis Arguelles, 240–243. San Francisco: AsianWeek and UCLA Asian American Studies Center, 2003.

Chan, S., and L. Wang. "Racism and the Model Minority: Asian-Americans in Higher Education." In *The Racial Crisis in American Higher Education,* ed. P. G. Altbach and K. Lomotey. Albany, NY: SUNY Press, 1991.

Chang, Edward Taehan. "Koreans: Entrepreneurs par Excellence." In *The New Face of Asian Pacific America,* ed. Eric Lai and Dennis Arguelles, 57–66. San Francisco: AsianWeek and UCLA Asian American Studies Center, 2003.

Crystal, David. "Asian Americans and the Myth of the Model Minority." *Journal of Contemporary Social Work* 70, no. 7 (1989): 405–413.

Fong, Timothy P. *The Contemporary Asian American Experience: Beyond the Model Minority.* Englewood Cliffs, NJ: Prentice Hall, 1998.

Gardiner, Debbie. "Donuts Anyone? Cambodians Own Some 90 Percent of Califor-

nia's Donut Shops." *Asian Week,* 22–28 June 2000. www.asianweek.com/
2000_06_22/bix1_cambodiandonut.

Harvard College: A Tradition of Excellence. Cambridge: Admissions and Financial Aid,
Harvard College, 2003.

Hing, Bill Ong, and Ronald Lee, eds. *The State of Asian Pacific America: Reframing
the Immigration Debate.* Los Angeles: LEAP Asian Pacific Public Policy Institute and UCLA Asian American Studies Center, 1996.

Kasindorf, Martin with Paula Chin, Diane Weathers, Kim Foltz, Daniel Shapiro, and
Darby Junkin. "Asian Americans: A 'Model Minority,'" *Newsweek,* 6 December
1982, 39ff.

Kim, Angela, and Christine J. Yeh. *Stereotypes of Asian American Students.* Eric Digest.
New York: ERIC Clearinghouse on Urban Education, 2002.

Kim, Elaine. "Perpetual Foreigners." Keynote address at conference on the Changing
Status of Asian Pacific Americans at Berkeley, California, November 17–23,
1999.

Kim, Kwang Chung, and Won Moo Hurh. "Korean Americans and the 'Success' Image: A Critique." *Amerasia Journal* 10, no. 2 (1983): 3–21.

Kitano, Harry, and Stanley Sue. "The Model Minorities." *Journal of Social Issues* 29,
no. 2 (1973): 1–10.

Kotkin, Joel. *Tribes: How Race, Religion, and Identity Determine Success in the Global
Economy.* New York: Random House, 1993.

Lai, Eric. "Electric Dreams: APAs in Hi-Tech." In *The New Face of Asian Pacific
America,* ed. Eric Lai and Dennis Arguelles, 235–239. San Francisco:
AsianWeek and UCLA Asian American Studies Center, 2003.

Lee, Stacey J. *Unraveling the "Model Minority" Stereotype: Listening to Asian American Youth.* New York: Teachers College Press, 1996.

Lien, Pei-te, Christian Collet, Janelle Wong, and Karthick Ramakrishnan, "Asian
Pacific-American Public Opinion and Political Participation." *PS: Political Science & Politics* 34, no 3 (September 2001): 625–630.

Light, Ivan Hubert. *Ethnic Enterprise in America: Business and Welfare among Chinese, Japanese, and Blacks.* Berkeley: University of California Press, 1972.

Liu, Lily. "All Asian Asians Are Good At . . . ," *Diversity and the Bar,* May 2001, http://
www.mcca.com/site/data/inhouse/minorityattorneys/asianamerican.htm.

Morning, Ann. "South Asia." In *Encyclopedia of American Immigration,* ed. James
Ciment, 1207–1214. Armonk, NY: M. E. Sharpe, 2001.

Nakanishi, Don. "A Quota on Excellence? The Asian American Admissions Debate."
In *The Asian American Educational Experience,* ed. Don Nakanishi and Tina
Yamamoto Nishida. New York: Routledge Kegan Paul, 1995.

Nishioka, Joyce. "Socioeconomics: The Model Minority?" In *The New Face of Asian
Pacific America: Numbers, Diversity & Change in the 21st Century,* ed. Eric
Lai and Dennis Arguelles, 29–35. San Francisco: AsianWeek and UCLA Asian
American Studies Center, 2003.

Petersen, William. "Success Story: Japanese American Style." *New York Times Magazine,* 9 January 1966, 26ff.

Rose, Peter I. "Asian Americans: From Pariahs to Paragons." In *Clamor at the Gates:
The New American Immigration,* ed. Nathan Glazer. San Francisco: Institute
for Contemporary Studies Press, 1985.

Saito, Leland T. *Race and Politics: Asian Americans, Latinos, and Whites in a Los
Angeles Suburb.* Champaign: University of Illinois Press, 1998.

Siu, S.-F. *Asian American Students at Risk: A Literature Review*. Report No. 8. Baltimore, MD: Johns Hopkins University, Center for Research on the Education of Students Placed at Risk, December 1996.

Smith-Hefner, N. J. "Language and Identity in the Education of Boston-area Khmer." *Anthropology and Education Quarterly* 21, no. 3 (1999): 250–268.

Suzuki, B. H. "Asian Americans as the 'Model Minority': Outdoing Whites? Or Media Hype?" *Change*, November/December 1989, 2–19.

———. "Revisiting the Model Minority Stereotype: Implications for Student Affairs Practice and Higher Education." In *Working with Asian American College Students*, ed. Marylu K. McEwen, Corinne Maekawa Kodama, Alvin N. Alvarez, Sunny Lee, and Christopher T. H. Liang. New Directions for Student Services, no. 97. San Francisco: Jossey-Bass, 2002.

Thrupkaew, Noy. "The Myth of the Model Minority." *The American Prospect* 13, no. 7 (2002). www.prospect.org/print/v13/7/thrupkaew-n.html.

Trask, Haunani-Kay. "Settlers of Color and 'Immigrant' Hegemony: 'Locals' in Hawai'i." *Amerasia Journal* 26, no. 2 (2000): 1–24.

United States Commission on Civil Rights. *Civil Rights Issues Facing Asian Americans in the 1990s*. Washington, DC: United States Government Printing Office, 1992.

U.S. Department of Commerce, Economic and Statistics Administration. U.S. Census Bureau. Asian and Pacific Islanders, 1997 Economic Census, Survey of Minority Owned Business Enterprises, Company Statistics Series. May 2001.

Uyematsu, Amy. "The Emergence of Yellow Power in America." In *Roots: An Asian American Reader*, ed. Amy Tachiki, Eddie Wong, and Franklin Odo, 9–13. Los Angeles: UCLA Asian American Studies Center, 1971.

Walsh, James. "The Perils of Success: Asians Have Become Exemplary Immigrants, but at a Price." *Time*, Fall 1993, 55–56.

Woo, Deborah. *Glass Ceilings and Asian Americans: The New Face of Workplace Barriers*. Walnut Creek, CA: AltaMira Press, 2000.

Yamanaka, Keiko, and Kent McClelland. "Earning the Model Minority Image: Diverse Strategies of Economic Adaptation by Asian American Women." *Ethnic and Racial Studies* 17 (1994): 79–114.

Yin, X. H. "The Two Sides of America's 'Model Minority.'" *Los Angeles Times*, 7 May 2000, part M, 1.

Yong-Jin, Won. "Model Minority Strategy and Asian Americans' Tactics." *Korea Journal* 57 (1994).

Yun, Grace, ed. *A Look beyond the Model Minority Image: Critical Issues in Asian America*. New York: Minority Rights Group, Inc., 1989.

Zhou, Min, and Carl L. Bankston, III. "Entrepreneurship." In *The Asian American Almanac*, ed. Susan Gall and Irene Natividad, 511–512. Detroit: Gale Research, 1995.

and the Chinese in New York, had come to America before the gold rush in California in the mid-nineteenth century, that pivotal event helped to shape perceptions of the Chinese and other Asians. Like the other Argonauts or Forty-niners who descended upon California and the American West, the Chinese were also soldiers of fortune who sought to improve their lives by searching for gold. But while California accepted the waves of migrants from around the world who had been attracted by the prospect of quick riches, only the Chinese were singled out for discriminatory treatment. Various foreign miners' taxes were enacted by the Sacramento legislature, but only the Chinese were targeted for payment by tax collectors. This practice gave currency to the idea that the Chinese were extracting wealth from California in order to return to China, so the state had a right to tax them. Whether the Chinese were building railroads, laboring in agriculture, fishing, or working in factories, they were viewed as temporary visitors in America, staying long enough until they had accumulated the wealth necessary to buy land, start a business, or help their families. This view that the Chinese were transients was sometimes extended to encompass the Japanese, Filipinos, Koreans, and Asian Indians, but it was primarily associated with the Chinese.

The Chinese were seen as sojourners, or temporary residents, those who went to another land for economic reasons, but who hoped someday to journey back to their home country. However, the reasons why the Chinese returned to China were complex. Some returned because of cultural practices or ties to their family or homeland. For example, the wives of many Chinese men resided with their husbands' families. Others wanted to start businesses or return to farming in their homeland. Still others yearned to return so that they could live with their countrymen and be joined again with a culture that they knew best. Reinforcing the tendency to return to China was the discriminatory climate that the Chinese faced in the United States. Until 1943, the Chinese in America were not permitted to naturalize and become citizens of the United States. They were also beset by laws that discriminated against them and even permitted school segregation in parts of California and the South.[1] There were alien land laws that prevented Chinese immigrants from owning land if they were not citizens. Moreover, in California and several other states, there were antimiscegenation laws that did not allow them to enter into interracial marriages.[2] The impact of the antimiscegenation laws was exacerbated because exclusionary immigration policies against China severely restricted Chinese female immigration to the United States. The result was that until the 1960s, American Chinatowns were primarily bachelor societies, with a larger ratio of men to women. For many Chinese immigrant men in the United States, their wives could not join them due to the exclusionary laws and those who did not have wives would not have the opportunity to marry and start families.

The idea of Chinese immigrants as sojourners began to receive more systematic study with Paul Siu's article, "The Sojourner," published in the *American Journal of Sociology* in 1952.[3] His doctoral dissertation at the University of Chicago with the title, "The Chinese Laundryman: A Study of Social Isolation," which he finished the next year, also dealt with the subject.[4] It studied the lives of Chinese immigrants who worked in laundries in Chicago. Siu explained that the sojourner was one who went abroad to perform a job with the intent of returning quickly. The individual did not assimilate to the host society, but maintained the idea of traveling back to the homeland. The sojourner might then stay there, or return back to the host country, or even make several trips back and forth. Siu stated that sojourner attitudes could be found not only among the Chinese, but also among foreign businessmen, diplomats, international students, foreign journalists, foreign missionaries, and anthropologists doing fieldwork abroad. After the publication of his article, the term *sojourner* became increasingly popular, but it was predominantly applied to the Chinese and not to other groups he had mentioned.

When the Asian American movement started in the 1960s and 1970s, those associated with it sought to develop a new identity for Asians in the United States.[5] Asians in this country were Asian Americans who accepted the United States as their home, not Asia. In trying to establish that they were part of the American mosaic, activists emphasized that Asian Americans had helped to build the economy of the nation, but their contributions had been ignored in the history books. Furthermore, since the nineteenth century, they had established homes and communities in the United States, but the public continued to see them as not of this country and stereotyped them as foreign. In attempting to stake a claim to America, activists said that Asian Americans were not sojourners or temporary residents of the United States. Despite the discriminatory laws and treatment directed at them, Asians in the United States had remained and had established roots in America. Some Asian American activists wanted to change the popular view that Asian immigrants of the past had come to work, but not to stay.

The activists were acutely aware that because Asian immigrants in the past were perceived as sojourners, Asian Americans were seen as peripheral to American history. In contrast, European immigrants were seen as remaining in the United States after their arrival and staying to make valuable contributions to American society. The United States was regarded as a nation of immigrants, but it was immigrants from Europe. In addition, the important entry to the United States was Ellis Island with its Statue of Liberty, and not Angel Island. Angel Island in San Francisco Bay was the receiving site for immigrants coming to the West Coast, for the period from 1910 to 1940. Most Americans today are familiar with Ellis Island, but few have heard of Angel Island or know about its role as an immigration station.[6]

Although many Asian American activists have been concerned about the perception that Asian immigrants of the past were sojourners, recent historical scholarship has been following three different paths. First of all, researchers have discovered that European immigrants were also sojourners who returned to their home countries. Because immigration statistics tended to emphasize arrivals and ignored departures, the impression was left that Europeans had a different outlook than the sojourning Asians. But until World War I, large numbers of sojourning immigrants from Italy, Poland, Greece, and other countries returned to their homeland.[7] Second, researchers have found that most Chinese immigrants until World War II, when China fell under Communist control, were indeed sojourners. They intended to return to their land of origin, although circumstances sometimes prevented that from happening, or they decided to stay in the United States.[8] Many Japanese migrants were also sojourners, and they were called *dekaseginin*, which means one who goes out to earn money.[9] As demographers and scholars learned that migrants often returned to their homelands, they used several terms as synonyms for sojourning, such as return migration, reverse migration, or remigration.

Finally, in the contemporary era, researchers acknowledge that migration and the movement of people is a widespread practice. Transnationalism, with the crossing of national borders by migrants, has been facilitated by global capitalism which seeks economic advantage through efficient use of land, capital, labor, and other resources. Are sojourners—or their modern counterparts, transnational migrants—desirable as a group to the country to which they have emigrated? Where do their loyalties lie? Are there certain benefits or costs to themselves? There are several propositions that continue to be the subject of debate:

1. Asians who came to the United States became settlers instead of sojourners. If there had not been any exclusionary immigration policies and discriminatory laws aimed at Asians, these individuals and their communities would have offered a different vision of an Asian American community before World War II.

2. Asian migrants who settled in the United States were better able to help their communities in their homelands and won the acceptance of other Asian Americans within the larger society.

3. Settling in one society confers benefits upon Asian Americans, while there are distinct disadvantages to those who are sojourners or transnational migrants.

DID ASIANS COME TO THE UNITED STATES AS SOJOURNERS INSTEAD OF SETTLERS, DUE TO EXCLUSIONARY LAWS?

For

The term sojourner has had an unfortunate effect on Asian Americans and their history in the United States. Historian Sucheng Chan aptly observes that "with the single word sojourner, some oft-quoted scholars have banished Asians completely from the realm of immigration history."[10] However, research by historians has uncovered the existence of several Asian American communities, indicating that there were Asians who indeed had elected to settle in the United States instead of traveling back to their homeland. One well-documented example is that of the Point Alones village in California. Another historian noted that the village situated in the Monterey Bay region comprised Chinese men, women, and children. From the 1850s to the turn of the century, the Chinese here earned a living fishing with sampans, catching fish and abalone. The formation of Chinese families here on the Pacific Coast indicated a desire to remain in the United States instead of returning to China.[11]

Another example is that of the Chinese town of Locke in California, although its residents were those already in America after the passage of the Chinese Exclusion Act of 1882. Located in the San Joaquin Valley along the Sacramento River, Locke was a rural community started in 1915 by Cantonese from the Zhongshan district of southern China's Guangdong province. Despite the existence of the Alien Land Law of 1913 in California, which was aimed at preventing the ownership of land by those who did not possess citizenship in the United States, the Chinese had secured permission from businessman George Locke to build there. In the next few decades, a lively Chinatown arose on the site with restaurants, stores, and other businesses. In the 1950s, the population of the small town began to decline, but it has been designated a historic landmark and efforts have been made to preserve the site.[12]

The Japanese who settled in the Yamato Colony in central California in the early 1900s also had decided to remain in the United States. Their leader, Kyutaro Abiko, was a Christian who believed that the sojourner idea should be abandoned. If Japanese abandoned the *dekasegi* ideal of working elsewhere with the intent of returning home, they could have a better life in the United States. He was convinced that permanent settlement should be the future. With that in mind, the Yamato Colony in Livingston, California, was an agricultural cooperative based on farming. It was believed that farming would give the Japanese immigrants an economic stake in the United States. He

U.S. flag display forms a backdrop to a statue of the ancient Chinese philosopher Confucius at a flag-raising ceremony on July 4, 2001, in Boston's Chinatown, which was holding its first-ever formal observation of Independence Day. AP/Wide World Photos.

also encouraged marriages so that a stable family life could be established for the members of the Yamato Colony.[13] From the examples of Point Alones village, the rural community of Locke, and the Yamato Colony in Livingston, there is ample evidence that there were Asian immigrants who were not sojourners and who planted roots in the United States.

In recent years, a greater interest in women's history has developed. In various varieties of history, but especially social history or cultural history, the trend is to examine issues of gender, class, and race. In immigration history and Asian American history as well, there is an emphasis on placing women at the center instead of concentrating only on the men as in the past. Yet the task is not easy to accomplish. As historian Gary Okihiro observed, "recentering Asian women in American history is a particularly thorny problem, because of the demographics of Asian migration." He points out that women "were barely present in the bachelor society that typified much of the early period of Asian American history."[14] The movement to recenter women into history is useful, for it also explains why many immigrants returned to their homelands. Without women and families, first-generation arrivals to this country felt obliged to return to their homeland to be with their wives and kin.

Against

There is no question that many people of Asian ancestry ended up as settlers in the United States. The percentage of people of Asian descent who returned to Asia was not more than the English who returned to England.[15] For many early immigrants or migrant workers, their intent was not necessarily to settle but to return to their homeland. However, it was not the original intent of many Asian laborers who came to the United States and Hawai'i as indentured servants. Like early Europeans, Asian laborers came to America in hopes of enhancing or improving their economic situation and in turn sending their success back home. As it is for any group, it is often difficult to leave one's home where family, culture, and tradition have been such an integral part of their identity. For people of Asian ancestry, it is particularly difficult to leave a culture where family ties and maintaining one's culture is such an important aspect of their upbringing. Thus, many of the early Asian workers came to the United States and Hawai'i with the idea of eventually returning home to fulfill their family obligations and responsibilities to their parents. But the economic, political, and social situation in the United States and in Hawai'i made it difficult for the early laborers to return to Asia. The low pay on the plantations, gold mines, and railroads, combined with the high cost of lodging, food, and travel back to Asia, made it nearly impossible for many to return home.

The discriminatory laws played a significant role in determining the status of Asian American communities today. For example, the Chinese Exclusion Act of 1882 affected the Chinese population in America in two ways. For those who were already here, the law forced them to make a choice of continuing work in America or going home to Asia, knowing that their chances of returning to America were slim. For those who returned to China to visit family members, they were not allowed to voyage back to America.

The 1882 Exclusion Act also played a vital role in drawing the next wave of Asian laborers. The economic needs of the United States, combined with the poor economic conditions in parts of Asia, pulled and pushed Japanese and Korean laborers to Hawai'i and America. Much like the Chinese laborers, the Japanese workers who toiled in the Hawaiian sugar plantations planned to eventually return home. In fact, they remained in constant communication with the Japanese embassy and sometimes gained significant support from it when they were mistreated on the plantations. The Korean workers, on the other hand, were in a different political situation. With the Japanese takeover and colonization of Korea and the ensuing turbulent political climate, many Koreans were displaced from their homeland. They were simultaneously escaping political corruption, famine, and poverty. For many, the choice to remain in the United States was not a real choice, but rather an economic necessity. Furthermore, the rhetoric from American business owners was attractive to Asian laborers, who believed that they would be able to make it rich in the land of opportunities. Thus the promise of the American dream was planted in Asian workers, much as it had been planted in the early European immigrants.

The crux as to why Asian immigrants were perceived as sojourners is the racist ideologies held by the dominant White group. The early European immigrants were able to hide their ethnicity by changing their names and creating a new identity. However, Asian immigrants were seen as perpetual foreigners because they were brought to Hawai'i and the continental United States to meet the demands for labor. But their skin color singled them out as different. Prominent U.S. leaders held the view that the United States should be preserved for Whites. Benjamin Franklin questioned: "Why should we darken the people of America? Now there is an opportunity to increase the lovely White by excluding the black and tawney."[16] Jefferson also advocated the removal of blacks from the United States, for he wanted the country to be a sanctuary for Whites and immigrants from Europe.

The idea that the early immigration policies and laws impacted Asian American communities cannot be disputed. However, racist policies and laws continued to haunt Asian immigrants in the United States many years later. For example, during the Jim Crow era of the 1950s, people of Asian ancestry had to choose between being White or Colored. While a few chose to be with the "colored" group, most opted to choose the group that had the most privileges bestowed upon them. Consequently, this has resulted in Asian Americans being perceived as honorary Whites. This perception has ostracized them from other ethnic minority groups, and at the same time made them invisible to White America. Moreover, the power exercised by the dominant White groups did not only affect Asian immigrants, but all immigrants who were seen as threats to their control. Consequently, this form of racism divides ethnic minority groups against each other and thereby creates rifts between ethnic minorities, but still elevates the positions of Whites.

DID ASIANS WHO SETTLED IN THE UNITED STATES HELP THEIR HOMELANDS AND WIN ACCEPTANCE IN THE LARGER SOCIETY?

For

Migrants who decide to remain in the United States are in a better position to help their communities. By rooting themselves in the country to which they have emigrated, they are able to build the institutions that can help their community. Thus, they can publish newspapers to disseminate useful information to the immigrant community. They can start schools, hospitals, associations, and other endeavors for themselves, which ultimately can improve the quality of life for their immigrant community. There can be an institutional completeness, in which whole litanies of services are available for the benefit and welfare of the overall group of immigrants and their offspring.[17]

Moreover, by developing connections with their neighbors and being rooted to the host country, immigrants present a favorable image of themselves and ease their acceptance by the larger society. By residing in the United States, for example, immigrants and their children nurture an appreciation for the receiving country that has offered them economic opportunities. As they understand the values and dynamics of the host society, they may prefer its strengths as compared to that of their former homeland. They may choose to serve in the armed forces of the United States and affirm their loyalty to America. The instances of military service among Asian Americans are many. Japanese Americans, for example, served with distinction in World War II. They joined the 100th Battalion and the 442nd Regimental Combat Team, which fought in Europe, and their record of patriotism and courage helped to convince many that the internment of Japanese Americans had been a mistake. Chinese Americans, Korean Americans, and Filipino Americans also enlisted during World War II and contributed to the Allied effort to defeat the Axis powers of Germany, Italy, and Japan.[18]

By settling in the United States, migrants and their children can win American citizenship. It is true that American law denied Asian immigrants citizenship before World War II. Chinese immigrants could not be naturalized until 1943, and Filipino and Asian Indian immigrants were denied that opportunity until 1946. For the Korean and Japanese immigrant generation, naturalization came even later in 1952. But by winning citizenship through naturalization or gaining it through birth in this country, Asian Americans could play a more important role in improving the status of Asians in the United States. For example, in 1895, Chinese Americans in San Francisco formed an organization called the Native Sons of the Golden State, which later became the Chinese American Citizens Alliance in 1915. With many lodges established in Los Angeles, Fresno, Oakland, San Diego, Boston, Chicago, Pittsburgh, Detroit, Portland, and elsewhere, the organization focused on the civil rights of Chinese Americans. It monitored immigration legislation and fought bills that would be detrimental to the Chinese in America. They worked to repeal Chinese exclusion in 1943, and they also lobbied for the McCarran-Walter Act of 1952, which admitted Chinese aliens and granted them permanent resident status.[19] For example, Dalip Singh Saund, a native of India, lobbied in Washington, D.C. for the right of Asian Indians to naturalize. He helped to organize the India Association of America in 1942 to pursue this goal. After victory was achieved, he became a citizen in 1949, and won election as a congressman from California in 1956. He served until 1962 and had the distinction of being the first Asian American to serve in Congress.[20] With American citizenship, Asian Americans in political office are in a better position to enact policies that can help their communities. Furthermore, they can elevate the visibility of Asian Americans in public life to a greater degree.

Against

Migrants who settled in the United States did contribute greatly to their immediate communities. Yet, whether their accomplishments were recognized or valued by the larger society is questionable. History has shown that Asian Americans who ended up settling in the United States helped build what is now America. From building the agricultural landscape to the railroads and the promotion of arts and sciences, Asian Americans contributed a great deal to this nation, but have not been credited with much until recently.

In thinking about their communities, many assume that Asian Americans are a homogeneous group, all coming from similar socioeconomic backgrounds, religious affiliations, political ideologies, and cultural traditions. It is only when Asian American communities are examined closely that the intraethnic differences, for example, between different groups of Asian Americans, such as those of Chinese, Japanese, and Vietnamese backgrounds, are revealed. There are also interethnic differences; for example, there are numerous dialects in China and diverse religious sectors in Korea, which ultimately affect the way people from the same ethnic group interact with each other. Hence, some groups who settle in the United States are able to help their communities if they have the social support, capital, and experience to build a community. Those who come from economically depressed backgrounds have difficulty sustaining themselves, let alone helping their communities. Furthermore, while there are various locations where there are sizable Asian American communities, such as Hawai'i, New York, Chicago, and California, there are also those with fewer Asian Americans.

When Asian Americans settle in communities and support them, public opinion sometimes works against them. Instead of viewing the Asian American population as one that helps to support the local economy, a perception of Asian Americans as being exclusive, insular, and cliquish emerges. Instead of gaining support from the larger society, they are often criticized for supporting only Asian issues, and their loyalty to American society and its culture is questioned. When the community of Monterey Park, near Los Angeles in southern California, experienced an influx of Chinese immigrants, local White residents began to complain about the foreign presence in their community. Specifically, the residents complained about the Chinese signs on businesses. They objected to the use of a foreign language that they could not read, and these concerns fueled an "English only" campaign advocating the use of the English language.[21] The Monterey Park case shows that the mere idea of having an increasingly visible Asian American community can foster resentment and hostility from the larger society. For Asian Americans who immigrate and settle in America, the battle to be accepted continues, for they are frequently still viewed as outsiders.

DO ASIANS SETTLING IN AMERICA BENEFIT, WHILE THOSE WHO ARE SOJOURNERS OR TRANSNATIONAL MIGRANTS ARE DISADVANTAGED?

For

Being a sojourner has its benefits and costs. As sojourners, migrants can accumulate money that can help their family members and themselves. Moreover, as modernizing agents, they can transfer knowledge and skills that can help their homeland. But there are also disadvantages in being sojourners. One disadvantage that may occur is a lack of fluency in English. Because they believe that their stay in the United States is temporary, or because they make multiple trips back and forth to their homelands, sojourners can have less facility with the English language, which may hurt their employment prospects.

Another disadvantage is that sojourning means that migrants have a limited physical presence in two or more different locations. This dilutes their opportunities to network and develop the intense social ties that can benefit their employment opportunities. It can also mean that they can be manipulated by two or more different governments in the several countries to which they travel. Because they do not commit themselves to a single country and government, their allegiance may be suspect and they may been seen as disloyal. Not seen as reliable citizens or residents, sojourners may be exploited by governments, businesses, and others as well. They are seen as expendable, vulnerable, and unreliable. They are perceived as sojourners who never reside in one place.

Finally, sojourners or transnationals can exact a toll on their families and themselves. Straddling between several societies may mean encounters with different value systems, so sojourning families are likely to experience cultural conflict. There may be cultural confusion and problems in intercultural communication. The gender roles for males and females can be different as well and can cause marital and family conflict. It is possible that there will be generational conflict between the parents and their children who may be of the 1.5 or second generation.[22] The parents have one notion of what is desirable behavior to be practiced within the family, but the children favor another mode of behavior that they have learned from peers. The problems that can occur in child rearing, socialization, and generational conflict ultimately can be very challenging and painful for parents and their children.

Against

The growing global economy has created more diasporic communities around the world. Modern technology has made air travel and phone calls more affordable, and Internet access has opened new doors for people to maintain ties and create new relationships around the globe. In order to be competitive in today's market, it is vital to recognize the interconnectedness between countries. The global village is much more interdependent than it once was. While there are obvious benefits to settling in one place, the emergence of transnational corporations as well as the growing number of people working and living in various parts of the world has made transnational/diasporic communities more viable.

Jobs around the world have created a diasporic working community where individuals ranging from employers to laborers find that there are more economic opportunities outside the United States. For immigrants, the economic recessions in America have made the establishment of business ventures outside the United States more attractive. Whether it is opening up new businesses in Asia, Mexico, or South America, or joining the growing number of migrant workers, working outside of the United States has made it more feasible for many to pursue jobs that they would otherwise not find in America. For those who are able to find jobs in the United States, they find that they are often traveling abroad anyway to work with companies in other parts of the world. This is not a new phenomenon. Since the beginning of the United States, companies from Europe have invested in American companies and businesses, thereby creating transnational ties with Europe. For example, British companies have opened up businesses in the United States and have become an integral part of American pop culture. Thus, Burger King and BP gas (British Petroleum) have become household names in the United States. Furthermore, this creates connections and ties to Britain that might not otherwise exist. The same can be said for Chinese companies who have invested in local real estate by buying malls and buildings. Investment in the United States not only helps the local economy by employing people here, but it also creates new relationships with people in other parts of the world.

Education has also helped to foster diasporic communities. Because of the American belief in the value of education, nearly everyone in the United States can obtain access to education. In fact, some argue that compared to other countries, it is easier to get a college education in the United States. With community colleges, state universities, liberal arts colleges, and Ivy League universities to select from, there is a place for those who seek higher education. This ideological commitment to accessible education is not true in other parts of the world. For example, in Asia the educational culture makes it very difficult for many to enter college unless they score well on entrance examinations and rank in the top percent of their high schools. If students fail to obtain high entrance examination scores, they have no opportunity for a college education in their country. This creates pressure and stress for youths and young adults in Asia. Without a chance to receive a higher education, those who are not admitted into universities feel helpless. In their status-conscious countries, they will experience limited options when it comes to employment.

Consequently, the push for educational attainment has created a different diasporic group in the form of foreign exchange students. This population comes to the United States so they can obtain the education that is not readily available to them in their homeland. However, it is not only at the college level that students begin to migrate. The recent phenomenon of *parachute kids* has seen an increase in the number of youths in junior high schools or high schools who live in the United States while their families remain in their homelands. Prior to Hong Kong's reunification with China, families who were uncertain of the political and economic climate after the change began purchasing homes in the United States. They sent their children to the neighborhoods with the best schools at the middle school or high school level, with supervision or guardianship being provided by one parent, relatives, or family friends. For example, San Marino, California, is one of the most affluent neighborhoods in southern California, and is considered to have one of the best school districts in California. As a result, its schools have witnessed this phenomenon of parachute kids. As a result, parachute kids and other youths with diasporic identities, can take advantage of the education system in the United States while maintaining close connections to their families in Asia. As a result, they are not only educated about U.S. culture and education, they are able to navigate the global borders. This unique position posits youths in a world where they are able to adjust to diverse settings, and communicate with people from around the globe.

QUESTIONS

1. What is the definition of a sojourner? What are some of the explanations as to why there was sojourning among the Chinese?

2. Who is Paul Siu and what is his connection with the term sojourner? What were the attributes that he assigned to the sojourner?

3. According to Paul Siu, was it only the Chinese who were showing sojourning attitudes? Have other Asians also been associated with sojourning?

4. Why are Asian American activists so concerned about the identification of the Chinese with sojourning? Is their concern a valid one?

5. What are some of the negative images associated with sojourning? Are there any positive images?

6. What were the consequences of Asian immigrants being associated with sojourning, while European immigrants were not? Do you know of any examples of sojourning among Asian Americans in your community?

7. Have European immigrants to the United States also been sojourners? Why or why not?

8. How is transnationalism linked to sojourning? Are there other terms that are similar in meaning to sojourning?

9. In what ways did American laws and attitudes encourage sojourning or return migration among Asian immigrants.

10. Can a case be made that Asian immigrants were settlers instead of sojourners? If so, what evidence could be cited?

11. Were the sojourners more likely to be men or women? Or are there no differences? What evidence could be cited?

12. What are the benefits of transnationalism or sojourning? Are there costs or disadvantages? Explain.

13. Are settlers better able to help their immigrant and ethnic communities? Why or why not?

14. Are there problems associated with sojourning families? Explain the reasons for the answer.

15. What is the relationship of globalization and the world economy to the development of diasporic communities?

NOTES

1. Victor Low, *The Unimpressible Race: A Century of Educational Struggle by the Chinese in San Francisco* (San Francisco: East/West Publishing Company, 1982); Eiichiro Azuma, "Interethnic Conflict under Racial Subordination: Japanese Immigrants and Their Asian Neighbors in Walnut Grove, California, 1908–1941," *Amerasia Journal* 20 (1994): 29; Malik Simba, "*Gong Lum v. Rice:* The Convergence of Law, Race, and Ethnicity," in *American Mosaic: Selected Readings on America's Multicultural Heritage,* eds. Young I. Song and Eugene C. Kim (Englewood Cliffs, NJ: Prentice Hall, 1993), 265–276.

2. Megumi Dick Osumi, "Asians and California's Anti-Miscegenation Laws," in *Asian and Pacific American Experiences: Women's Perspectives,* ed. Nobuya Tsuchida (Minneapolis: Asian/Pacific American Learning Resource Center, University of Minnesota, 1982), 1–37.

3. Paul C. P. Siu, "The Sojourner," *American Journal of Sociology* 58 (July 1952): 34–44.

4. Paul C. P. Siu, *The Chinese Laundryman: A Study of Social Isolation,* ed. John Kuo Wei Tchen (New York: New York University Press, 1987).

5. William Wei, *The Asian American Movement* (Philadelphia: Temple University Press, 1993).

6. Him Mark Lai, Genny Lim, and Judy Yung, eds., *Island: Poetry and History of Chinese Immigrants on Angel Island, 1910–1940* (San Francisco: Hoc Doi, 1980).

7. Roger Daniels, *Coming to America: A History of Immigration and Ethnicity in American Life* (New York: HarperCollins Publishers, 1990), 25–28 and 287–289.

8. Yong Chen, *Chinese San Francisco, 1850–1943: A Trans-Pacific Community* (Stanford, CA: Stanford University Press, 2000), 262–267; Ronald Skeldon, "The Chinese Diaspora or the Migration of Chinese Peoples?" in *The Chinese Diaspora: Space, Place, Mobility, and Identity,* eds. Laurence J. C. Ma and Carolyn Cartier (Lanham, MD: Rowman and Littlefield Publishers, 2003), 52, 54–56, and 60–61; Adam McKeown, review of *Becoming Chinese, Becoming Chinese American* by Shehong Chen, *American Historical Review* 108 (April 2003): 536–538.

9. Yuji Ichioka, *The Issei: The World of the First Generation Japanese Immigrants, 1885–1924* (New York: Free Press, 1988), 3–6; Lane Ryo Hirabayashi, Akemi Kikumura-Yano, and James A. Hirabayashi, eds., *New Worlds, New Lives: Globalization and People of Japanese Descent in the Americas and from Latin America in Japan* (Stanford, CA: Stanford University Press, 2002), xiii, xv–xvi, 19, and 179–186.

10. Sucheng Chan, "European and Asian Immigration into the United States in Comparative Perspective, 1820s to 1920s," in *Immigration Reconsidered: History, Sociology, and Politics,* ed. Virginia Yans-McLaughlin (New York: Oxford University Press, 1990), 38.

11. Sandy Lydon, *Chinese Gold: The Chinese in the Monterey Region* (Capitola, CA: Capitola Book Company, 1985).

12. Jeff Gillenkirk and James Motlow, *Bitter Melon: Stories from the Last Rural Chinatown in America* (Berkeley, CA: Heyday Books, 1987).

13. Ichioka, *The Issei,* 146–150.

14. Gary Y. Okihiro, *Margins and Mainstreams: Asians in American History and Culture* (Seattle: University of Washington Press, 1994), 6.

15. Asian/Japanese immigration to Hawai'i 1886–1924: 55 percent returned to

Japan; English immigration to United States 1895–1918: 40–50 percent returned to England.

16. Benjamin Franklin, "Observations Concerning the Increase of Mankind, Peopling of Countries, & c." (1751), *The Writings of Benjamin Franklin: Philadelphia, 1726–1757,* www.historycarper.com/resources/twobf2/increase.htm.

17. Raymond Breton, "Institutional Completeness of Ethnic Communities and the Personal Relations of Immigrants," *American Journal of Sociology* 70 (September 1964): 193–205.

18. Carina A. del Rosario, ed., *A Different Battle: Stories of Asian Pacific American Veterans* (Seattle: Wing Luke Asian Museum and University of Washington Press, 1999).

19. Sue Fawn Chung, "Fighting for Their American Rights: A History of the Chinese American Citizens Alliance," in *Claiming America: Constructing Chinese American Identities during the Exclusion Era,* eds. K. Scott Wong and Sucheng Chan (Philadelphia: Temple University Press, 1998), 98, 101–102, and 110–111.

20. Jane Singh, "Dalip Singh Saund (1899–1973): Congressman, Farmer, Politician," in *Distinguished Asian Americans: A Biographical Dictionary,* ed. Hyung-chan Kim (Westport, CT: Greenwood Press, 1999), 312–315.

21. Tim Fong, *The First Suburban Chinatown: The Remaking of Monterey Park, California* (Philadelphia: Temple University Press, 1994).

22. The phrase "1.5 generation" was popularized by Korean Americans and refers to those who were born abroad but came to America at an early age and were educated mostly in the United States. The second generation refers to those who were born in the United States from immigrant parents and who hold American citizenship. Elaine H. Kim and Eui-Young Yu, eds., *East to America: Korean American Life Stories* (New York: New Press, 1996), 375.

SELECTED WORKS

Azuma, Eiichiro. "Interethnic Conflict under Racial Subordination: Japanese Immigrants and Their Asian Neighbors in Walnut Grove, California, 1908–1941." *Amerasia Journal* 20 (1994): 27–56.

Breton, Raymond. "Institutional Completeness of Ethnic Communities and the Personal Relations of Immigrants." *American Journal of Sociology* 70 (September 1964): 193–205.

Chan, Sucheng. "European and Asian Immigration into the United States in Comparative Perspective, 1820s to 1920s." In *Immigration Reconsidered: History, Sociology, and Politics,* ed. Virginia Yans-McLaughlin. New York: Oxford University Press, 1990.

Chen, Yong. *Chinese San Francisco, 1850–1943: A Trans-Pacific Community.* Stanford, CA: Stanford University Press, 2000.

Chung, Sue Fawn. "Fighting for Their American Rights: A History of the Chinese American Citizens Alliance." In *Claiming America: Constructing Chinese American Identities during the Exclusion Era,* ed. K. Scott Wong and Sucheng Chan. Philadelphia: Temple University Press, 1998.

Daniels, Roger. *Coming to America: A History of Immigration and Ethnicity in American Life.* New York: HarperCollins Publishers, 1990.

del Rosario, Carina A., ed. *A Different Battle: Stories of Asian Pacific American Vet-*

erans. Seattle: Wing Luke Asian Museum and University of Washington Press, 1999.

Fong, Tim. *The First Suburban Chinatown: The Remaking of Monterey Park, California.* Philadelphia: Temple University Press, 1994.

Gillenkirk, Jeff, and James Motlow. *Bitter Melon: Stories from the Last Rural Chinatown in America.* Berkeley, CA: Heyday Books, 1987.

Hirabayashi, Lane Ryo, Akemi Kikumura-Yano, and James A. Hirabayashi, eds. *New Worlds, New Lives: Globalization and People of Japanese Descent in the Americas and from Latin America in Japan.* Stanford, CA: Stanford University Press, 2002.

Ichioka, Yuji. *The Issei: The World of the First Generation Japanese Immigrants, 1885–1924.* New York: Free Press, 1988.

Kim, Elaine H., and Eui-Young Yu, eds. *East to America: Korean American Life Stories.* New York: New Press, 1996.

Lai, Him Mark, Genny Lim, and Judy Yung, eds. *Island: Poetry and History of Chinese Immigrants on Angel Island, 1910–1940.* San Francisco: Hoc Doi, 1980.

Low, Victor. *The Unimpressible Race: A Century of Educational Struggle by the Chinese in San Francisco.* San Francisco: East/West Publishing Company, 1982.

Lydon, Sandy. *Chinese Gold: The Chinese in the Monterey Region.* Capitola, CA: Capitola Book Company, 1985.

McKeown, Adam. "The Sojourner as Astronaut: Paul Siu in Global Perspective." In *Re-Collecting Early Asian America: Essays in Cultural History,* ed. Josephine Lee, Imogene L. Lim, and Yuko Matsukawa. Philadelphia: Temple University Press, 2002.

———. "Review of *Becoming Chinese, Becoming Chinese American* by Shehong Chen." *American Historical Review* 108 (April 2003): 536–538.

Ng, Franklin. "The Sojourner, Return Migration, and Immigration History." In *Chinese America: History and Perspectives.* San Francisco: Chinese Historical Society of America, 1987.

Okihiro, Gary Y. *Margins and Mainstreams: Asians in American History and Culture.* Seattle: University of Washington Press, 1994.

Osumi, Megumi Dick. "Asians and California's Anti-Miscegenation Laws." In *Asian and Pacific American Experiences: Women's Perspectives,* ed. Nobuya Tsuchida. Minneapolis: Asian/Pacific American Learning Resource Center, University of Minnesota, 1982.

Peffer, George Anthony. *If They Don't Bring Their Women Here: Chinese Female Immigration before Exclusion.* Urbana: University of Illinois Press, 1999.

Simba, Malik. "*Gong Lum v. Rice:* The Convergence of Law, Race, and Ethnicity." In *American Mosaic: Selected Readings on America's Multicultural Heritage,* ed. Young I. Song and Eugene C. Kim. Englewood Cliffs, NJ: Prentice Hall, 1993.

Siu, Paul C. P. "The Sojourner." *American Journal of Sociology* 58 (July 1952): 34–44.

———. *The Chinese Laundryman: A Study of Social Isolation,* ed. John Kuo Wei Tchen. New York: New York University Press, 1987.

Skeldon, Ronald. "The Chinese Diaspora or the Migration of Chinese Peoples?" In *The Chinese Diaspora: Space, Place, Mobility, and Identity,* ed. Laurence J. C. Ma and Carolyn Cartier. Lanham, MD: Rowman and Littlefield Publishers, 2003.

Wei, William. *The Asian American Movement.* Philadelphia: Temple University Press, 1993.

Yanagisako, Sylvia. "Transforming Orientalism: Gender, Nationality, and Class in Asian American Studies." In *Naturalizing Power: Essays in Feminist Cultural Analysis,* ed. Sylvia Yanagisako and Carol Delaney. New York: Routledge, 1995.

Yang, Philip Q. "Sojourners or Settlers: Post-1965 Chinese Immigrants." *Journal of Asian American Studies* 2 (February 1999): 61–91.

Yu, Henry. *Thinking Orientals: Migration, Contact, and Exoticism in Modern America.* New York: Oxford University Press, 2001.

4

ASIAN AMERICAN LITERATURE: A MIRROR OF COMMUNITY CONCERNS?

Asian American literature today is an exciting arena for artistic creativity. Asian American writing encompasses many categories ranging from fiction to non-fiction, prose to poetry, adult literature to children's literature, and novels and stories to plays and dramas. When Asian American literature as a phrase was coined in the 1960s and 1970s, it was commonly misunderstood. Some people thought that writings about Asia comprised Asian American literature, while others believed that writings by Asians in Asia were part of Asian American literature. The misunderstanding stemmed from the belief that people of Asian descent living in America were no different from Asians in Asia. In reality, there is a large body of writing by Asian American authors, poets, and playwrights that is acknowledged as Asian American literature. But as the amount of Asian American writing increases, there are occasional debates as to the purpose of Asian American literature. Should Asian American literature mirror community issues and concerns? Or should it be a vehicle for personal expression and artistic creativity?

BACKGROUND

A goal of the Asian American movement in the late 1960s and 1970s was to claim a space in America for people of Asian descent. Feeling that Asian Americans had been stereotyped as well as misunderstood, activists in the movement sought to heighten their visibility in the United States. While one way was to show greater participation in politics, another way was to capture public attention through literature and the arts. As people living in the United States, Asian Americans needed a literature that described their lives and feelings. Literature and the arts were vehicles for expression and creativity, modes of demonstrating that Asian Americans had their own cultural identity and artistic sensibility. But in carving out a space for Asian American literature and Asian American arts, these activist pioneers did not seek the marginalization and isolation of Asian American literature. Rather, they argued that Asian American literature was also part of American literature, an integral part of the rich heritage of the United States.

The Asian American movement was fueled by students and community activism at San Francisco State University and the University of California, Berkeley, in the 1960s and 1970s. As university administrators agreed to offer courses that taught about Asians in the United States, questions about how to organize those classes began to appear. Jeffery Paul Chan, one of those who pushed for Asian American studies, recalls that at San Francisco State University, campus officials suggested that courses on Asian American literature could be taught. When Chan and his friends were alone, they asked each other, "What Asian American literature?"[1]

In a way, Chan and his fellow activists were present at the creation of Asian American literature. In his words, they had to "scramble around and find some [Asian American literature]."[2] Browsing in libraries and foraging in bookstores, they discovered books, diaries, stories, poetry, and other works written by Asian Americans. With each new discovery, there was a sense of excitement and exhilaration. They learned that there had been earlier, pioneering writers who had developed an Asian American consciousness, an awareness that verified that there were Asians living in America. In 1974, with Lawson Inada, Frank Chin, and Shawn Wong, Chan edited an anthology with the unusual title, *Aiiieee! An Anthology of Asian-American Writers.*[3] They were screaming to attract notice from the public to recognize that there was a body of writing known as Asian American literature. They wanted people to know that there were talented Asian American writers who had produced a body of creative work that was drawn from the lives and experiences of Asian Americans.

During this early phase of trying to define and develop Asian American literature, there were many questions that had to be addressed. Could literature written by Asians who were noncitizens in the United States be considered Asian American literature? American laws, after all, had denied naturalization to first-generation Chinese immigrants until 1943. For Filipinos and Asian Indians of the first generation, they had not been allowed naturalization until 1946. As for Japanese, Koreans, and other Asians of the immigrant generation, they were not eligible for naturalization until the

McCarran-Walter Act of 1952.[4] On the other hand, many workers also intended to return to their home country, but because fortune dictated otherwise, they remained in the United States. Conversely, what about Asian Americans who lived in Asia and elsewhere? Should their writings be considered Asian American literature? What actually constitutes Asian American literature? While some may think of Asian American literature as linked to Asians in America, there are also Asian Americans who have lived in Asia and around the globe who are a part of the Asian diaspora. Are their writings considered Asian American literature? What if the writings in the United States or Asia were written in Asian languages instead of English? Then, too, if the writers were of *hapa*, or mixed ethnicity background, should they be included in Asian American literature? An example might be Edith Maud Eaton (1865–1914), also known as Sui Sin Far,[5] who was of Eurasian, or European and Asian, ancestry.[6] Issues pertaining to gender, class, diversity, and transnationalism also became key concerns.

Since the late 1960s, activists have tried to create an Asian American movement.[7] They hoped to promote understanding of Asians in the United States and to empower their communities. They sought to project a positive image of Asian Americans by destroying stereotypes. They did not want Asian Americans to be seen as always speaking broken English with foreign accents. Nor did they want Asian Americans to be viewed as the perennial enemy soldiers, evil warlords, and criminal gangsters, as was often the case in novels, Hollywood movies, and television programs. In short, they were concerned about the issue of representation, or how Asian Americans were depicted in the media, literature, and popular culture. Activists also focused on the issue of authenticity. They were all too aware of characterizations of Asian Americans that were distorted and unrealistic.

Some activists believe that Asian American literature should be a mirror of the community and serve its people. This can be accomplished if Asian American literature has a positive portrayal of the Asian American community and helps to puncture negative stereotypes. But others differ and believe that writing itself is a creative and artistic act, and that Asian American literature should not be constrained by social goals. Moreover, they believe that the questions of what is representative and what is authentic are hard to determine and difficult to resolve. The issue of the scope and purpose of Asian American literature can thus be quite complex. These are some of the propositions that are being debated:

1. Asian American literature should have a responsibility to the community by serving its people. It should have an activist vision and a social purpose.

2. Literature should promote Asian American panethnicity and harmony, which

would project a positive image of the community that would benefit Asian Americans.

3. Asian American literature should be based on what is authentic in order to represent and serve the Asian American community effectively.

SHOULD ASIAN AMERICAN LITERATURE HAVE AN ACTIVIST VISION AND SOCIAL PURPOSE TO SERVE THE COMMUNITY AND ITS PEOPLE?

For

Books that tackle race relations in the United States have historically faced some controversy. There have been high schools that have restricted certain books from the classroom to other books being used as examples of American life. For example, one can think of efforts to exclude Mark Twain's well-known classic, *Huckleberry Finn*, which is used as an example of early American life but also is about the harsh realities of white racism. Yet it is difficult to expect literature to represent the lives of a group of people who are so diverse and vast. Some activists would argue that Asian American literature has a responsibility to the community by serving its people. While there is an awareness of the issue of responsibility, the commitment to serve people is less certain. Since Asian Americans are a heterogeneous group because of their culture, class, and gender, it is difficult for one piece of literature to address the experiences of this diverse group.

So the question arises, what does it mean to serve the Asian American community through literature? There are several possible answers to this. Asian American literature can create a historical connection with people, whereby community members can see their own lives and the lives of their ancestors reflected in those pages. Here oral histories can aid in providing Asian American writers with rich insights into the experiences of people from myriad walks of life. Asian American literature can also reveal a social consciousness when the experiences of discrimination, racism, and politics are embedded in it. It can serve the community on a personal basis, discussing issues of individual identity, community formation, and cultural politics that are all reflective of the lives of Asian Americans in the United States. One question, however, surfaces in the midst of these possibilities. Does serving the community restrict a writer's freedom to write what they wish to write? It is important to allow creativity to thrive, and most cannot put down a book when the pages are filled with passion and depth. Readers are eager to turn the pages of books to which they have a connection, relation, or interest. Thus, the scope for literature that is discussed here is very complex. The community has multiple needs, but there is room for literature to address the complexities of the Asian American community.

Shouldering the responsibility to serve a community can be a difficult task. Thus, it is important to have an activist vision and a social purpose. But what constitutes an activist vision? When we think of activists, images of protestors holding up signs or individuals challenging the system may come to mind. However, activists come in various shapes and sizes serving different social purposes. With any issue or movement, there are at least two sides. For example, the topic of bilingual education in schools has its supporters and opponents. Each side has its activists working for what they feel is the social purpose, but each looks at the issue from a different perspective. Furthermore, an activist can be laissez-faire or radical in action. Promoting issues in a nonconfrontational manner can be just as effective as those who are in one's face. Regardless of the type of activism, what the activists have in common is a passion for social justice. However, one can debate their definition of justice.

Against

When activists tried to promote an awareness of Asian American identity in the late 1960s and 1970s, they saw literature as an important resource. They looked to earlier writings in poetry, fiction, autobiographies, plays, and songs that explored the theme of being Asian in America. Because they were developing the idea of an Asian American sensibility, they were looking for literary predecessors who had been thinking about how to chart a path between being neither Asian nor assimilated American, or suffering from cultural schizophrenia. Edith Maud Eaton assumed the pen name of Sui Sin Far and wrote stories about Chinese and Eurasians in the United States, without avoiding reference to the prejudice and discrimination that they experienced. Although she was of English and Chinese ancestry, the editors of *Aiiieeee! An Anthology of Asian-American Writers* (1974) commented that Eaton "was one of the first to speak for an Asian-American sensibility that was neither Asian nor white Americans." They noted that in her work there was "no cultural conflict between East and West." Rather, that was "a modern invention of whites and their yellow goons—writers who need white overseers to give them license to use the English language."[8] Louis Chu's *Eat a Bowl of Tea* (1961) was cited as "the first Chinese-American novel set against an unexoticized Chinatown—the kind of Chinatown that has been duplicated wherever large numbers of Chinese emigrants settle."[9] Toshio Mori's *Yokohama, California* (1949) was mentioned as one of several works that could "see through the phoniness of the concept of the dual personality and reject it."[10] Asian Americans who wrote about their lives without seeing a tension, crisis, or dilemma were seen as being irrelevant, indifferent, or selling out to assimilation. Those authors who touched upon the theme of being Asian in the United States, but resolved the issue by choosing to fit into the dominant American society were thought to be guilty of self-hatred and devoid of pride in their Asian American identity.

Because the Asian American movement wanted to raise ethnic consciousness, instill pride in identity, and encourage political activism, they valued political action and community activism as a strategy to change society. They emphasized the importance of responsibility to the community and working on behalf of the community. Some thought that merely creating and studying literature like an academic exercise was frivolous, self-indulgent, and irresponsible when people of color and ethnic movements were being challenged by conservative opponents. They believed culture and art should be linked to politics in order to serve the people, to serve the community; art and literature should have a political and educational function to raise awareness about the need for social change, which would ultimately serve the community. One way of doing this, for example, would be to describe the living and working conditions of Chinese American laborers in a Chinatown, Filipino American cannery workers in Alaska, or Vietnamese American fishermen in the Gulf of Mexico. Informed about social and economic problems, the public could then try to find ways to improve the conditions of these workers.

But some believe that Asian American literature should not be sociology, and it should not be reduced to an ideology of social realism. They argue that literature should be diverse in its purposes and directions, just as writers, poets, and artists are different in temperament and personality. They accept that there is a role for political writing. Some examples of Asian American literature do have the power to educate and move their readers. Thus, Carlos Bulosan's *America Is in the Heart* (1974) gave a personalized account of the experience of Filipino immigrants in the United States during the depression era, who had to struggle to survive and had to be able to cope with the cruel racism and discrimination that faced them. His book highlights the divergence between the promise of America and the harsh reality that confronted the Filipinos in their attempt to make a home in the United States.[11] Another example is Milton Murayama's *All I Asking for Is My Body* (1975), which depicts life on a sugar plantation in Hawai'i. It describes how the plantation owners were able to dominate their workers and intimidate critics who challenged their control.[12] While some individuals may choose to be politically minded in their work (although with varying degrees of directness), it hardly seems appropriate to require all writers and artists to be political in their work. Such uniformity of purpose in writing would not be conducive to creativity and would not capture the interest of readers. To require Asian American literature to have a social function would confine Asian American writers and readers in a prison of the mind, a kind of mental gulag, where a single school of thought was valued above all else. It would be boring if every piece of writing about Japanese Americans had to have an obligatory reference to the Japanese American internment during World War II, or that every work about Chinese Americans had to mention Chinatown or immigration exclusion until 1943. It would be, in fact, a strange turn of events if the Asian American movement that had been struggling for autonomous cultural expression were to now require a regime of conformity.

SHOULD ASIAN AMERICAN LITERATURE PROMOTE PANETHNICITY HARMONY, AND A POSITIVE IMAGE TO BENEFIT ASIAN AMERICANS?

For

Asian American literature has only recently begun to address the pan-Asian American issues that have arisen in the new millennium. This is largely due to the fact that various ethnic groups in Asian American communities are still underrepresented in literature. There has been an attempt among writers to fill the void by bringing out the voices of neglected Asian ethnic groups. As an example, there has been a welcome trend among Asian American writers, like Helen Zia, who discuss issues of pan-Asian American ethnicity and multiracial identity and what it means to become Asian American. She writes about the diverse Asian American struggling with identity, sexuality, and generational issues among other issues. In various books, like *Charlie Chan Is Dead: An Anthology of Contemporary Asian American Fiction* (1993), edited by Jessica Hagedorn, the previously silenced Asian Americans are finally heard through poetry, short stories, and prose. Marie Hara and Nora Okja Keller also bring forth the voices of *hapa* women, showing that there are also Asian Americans of mixed ancestry who add further complexity to issues of diversity.[13] These writers bring forth the complexities of Asian America and its people.

It is amazing to see how little pan-Asian American ethnicity is represented in literature. Instead, one still sees Asian Americans mistaken for Asians. Some may wonder about the benefits of promoting pan-Asian ethnicity. For example, non-Asian Americans are not the only group with a limited understanding of Asian Americans. Asian Americans themselves often fail to discern the similarities among themselves. Literature, however, that provides a picture of how various Asian ethnic groups interact with each other can create dialogue and discussion among the groups. Doing this, however, can stir controversy and cause conflict between various groups. As an illustration,

Lois-Ann Yamanaka's *Blu's Hanging* (1997) was a book surrounded by controversy.[14] Yamanaka depicted the lives of local Asian Americans and Hawaiians, but she was criticized by some for a seemingly racist portrayal of Filipinos. While her work was of a fictional nature, some people in Hawai'i and Filipino Americans were offended by her depiction of Filipinos as sexual predators and pedophiles. While the concerns of the community are important, what did this book do to promote harmony? Some may say very little; in fact, many would argue that this controversy ripped the community apart. But in reality, the book provided an opportunity for people in the community to talk about race relations and confront issues of colonization, racism, and interethnic divisions that exist in Hawai'i. In order to achieve harmony and understanding, discussions must precede it.

When panethnic issues are addressed, it can create hostility as well as solidarity. But what is crucial is that issues are finally aired. One might wonder if shedding light on conflicts and struggles is less desirable than spotlighting harmony and successes. But the Asian American community's willingness to expose favorable as well as unfavorable images of the community only benefits it. It takes Asian Americans away from the stereotypes of them as a model minority, foreigners, and martial art experts, to being a group that is more complex and multidimensional. Literature has an amazing way of getting readers involved in a story and humanizing its characters. With increasing numbers of pan-Asian American stories, plays, and poems, readers can begin to gain the image of Asian Americans as a group that is human; no two are alike, yet they are accessible and very understandable to so many readers. This is a positive step forward that will ultimately promote harmony not only among Asian Americans, but with other racial and ethnic groups as well.

Against

In trying to promote an awareness of Asian American identity, many activists believe that literature can be an asset. It can help people feel proud of their identity and cultivate a sense of solidarity in the community. Should literature promote unity and harmony among Asian Americans in order to present a favorable image of the community? Literature is not bound by such assumptions; in fact, it can have a destabilizing effect. One example is Frank Chin's work. His plays, *The Chickencoop Chinaman* (1973) and *The Year of the Dragon* (1974), along with his other work, gave a raw and powerful insider's view of the Chinese American experience.[15] He painted the seamy side of American Chinatowns and was uncompromising in showing the conflict between the immigrant generation and their American-born children. He emphasized that assimilation and deracination had stripped Chinese Americans of their identity. He saw his work as a means of getting Chinese

Americans to reclaim their heritage and distinguish between the "real" and the "fake" Asian American culture. For example, he believed that the conversion to Christianity by Asian Americans had led to cultural amnesia and a devaluing of the Asian heritage. For some, it had even led to their believing in racist stereotypes about Asians and had fostered self-contempt and self-hatred. But in drawing attention to the less flattering side of the Chinese American experience, critics who saw him as being bombastic and iconoclastic attacked him.[16]

Another example is the controversy that arose several years ago over Lois-Ann Yamanaka's novel *Blu's Hanging* (1997).[17] An author in Hawai'i, Yamanaka's book caused controversy because of its portrayal of life among Asian immigrants in the islands. A well-known writer who has won prestigious awards for her work, Yamanaka described some of the unflattering views about Filipinos in Hawai'i. While these views were based upon widely known stereotypes that circulated in the islands, critics argued that she had offended the Filipino community. Moreover, by mentioning the stereotypes, she was reinforcing racism and discrimination against this Asian American group. Her supporters defended her by saying that she was acknowledging the existence of stereotypes in order to tell a story. Far from condoning the stereotypes or ignoring their existence, she was forcing her readers to confront the harsh world of her characters who must live with these negative images. In this context, Yamanaka's work might be the needed catalyst to make people face up to the prejudices that they hold.[18]

While Asian American panethnicity and harmony might seem to be desirable goals for Asian American literature, an exclusive focus on these themes actually limits the artistic creativity of writers and artists. By failing to shade in the rough-and-tumble side of life, the less than idyllic aspects of human interaction, Asian American writers would be describing a Pollyannaish world divorced from reality. By failing to recognize the stereotypes that circulate in society and the conflicts that may result, Asian American authors would be depicting a false utopia that does not really exist. On the other hand, if Asian American writers were free to confront the complex realities of interethnic friction and competition with the whole universe of human emotions, a much more sophisticated and compelling literature would be presented before a broad audience.

SHOULD ASIAN AMERICAN LITERATURE BE AUTHENTIC TO REPRESENT AND SERVE THE COMMUNITY EFFECTIVELY?

For

In the late 1970s, activists questioned whether Asian Americans were accurately portrayed in literature. Asian Americans were indistinguishable, for they were depicted in the same manner regardless of their ethnic background. Moreover, literature continued to focus on Asian experiences without consideration for contemporary experiences of Asian Americans. Today there is a growing body of literature covering the experience of Chinese and Japanese, but others such as Filipinos, Koreans, and Southeast Asians still receive little attention. This neglect is important, for it is related to the question of representation and authenticity. This is crucial today with the continuing influx of Asian immigrants to the United States and the changing face of the Asian American community. With the potential for misleading stereotypes and misunderstanding, some activists argue that it is important to represent Asian Americans in literature as authentically as possible. Yet one must consider that such criticism evokes the question of what is authentic? If one does not experience something, does that make it less real? Asian American literature has addressed the life of Asian American communities throughout the years. Authors often choose to write about the social, cultural, and political events related to their communities. For example, Edith Maud Eaton (Sui Sin Far), the first Asian American writer of short fiction, wrote about Sino phobia, a fear of Chinese people that was later extended to all Asians from the 1870s until the Immigration Act of 1965. Sui Sin Far's short story *In the Land of the Free* recounts the high cost of racist immigration restrictions when they are enforced without regard to human feelings. Younghill Kang's autobiography, *East Goes West,* recounts the trials of a Korean student who worked as a domestic servant in an American home, but in reality, the book exposes the limited choices open to an Asian immigrant and the feminization of foreign Asian young men. There are another set of authors who write about the experiences of being interned as a result of Executive Order 9066, which forced 110,000 Japanese Americans from their West Coast homes to inland desert camps encircled with barbed wire. John Okada's *No-No Boy* traces the psychological scars of draft resisters and the subsequent war at home. Later on, the works of Maxine Hong Kingston and Janice Mirikitani reflect the ramifications of the civil rights and women's liberation movements of the 1960s and 1970s. These writers display an affirmation and assertion of the self as an amalgam of the specificities of race, culture, gender, and class.

More recently, contemporary writers have written about issues of social justice, ethnic identity, racial politics, and the everyday interactions and lives of Asian Americans. Jessica Hagedorn's anthology *Charlie Chan Is Dead* consists of poems and short stories from Asian American writers that illustrate the challenges faced by Asian Americans. There is also a group of authors who revisit the past in order to better understand the present. For example, Nora Okja Keller's *Comfort Women* reveals the harsh conditions under which Korean women were forced into prostitution during the Japanese colonization. This work of fiction, poignantly describing the pain caused by this experience, is calling for social justice for those Korean women whose lives were ripped and stolen by the Japanese. The edited volumes *Making Waves* and *Making More Waves* have a number of stories written by Asian American women, all challenging patriarchy and racism through the eyes of women.

While Asian American issues have been the center of attention, there has also developed a growing body of literature in Hawai'i that treats not only Asian American but Pacific Islander experiences as well. As a result, what has emerged is an exploration of mixed-race identity, or as it is described in Hawai'i, *hapa* identity. Maria Murphy Hara, along with Nora Okja Keller, writes in *Intersections* about the lives of *hapas* and their complex identity because of their mixed ethnic heritage. While all of these books and anthologies reflect a different set of realities, they are all authentic and represent experiences of different groups who are situated in a particular place and time. When readers become aware of the varying lifestyles and situations, they begin to realize the diversity and richness of these authentic experiences, and they are then able to recognize the needs of the community. Only then are they able to effectively serve the community in which they live.

Against

One of the major concerns of the Asian American movement was to educate the public about Asians in the United States. By attacking stereotypes and presenting what was authentic about Asian Americans, Asian American literature would be furthering that goal. But what was authentic? Was something that had been written actually representative of the Asian American community or the social reality of an Asian American group? These questions surfaced as writings by Asian Americans began to increase, but Asian Americans themselves did not agree in their responses to different works by Asian American writers.

One example was Maxine Hong Kingston's *The Woman Warrior: Memoir of a Girlhood among Ghosts* (1976).[19] Born in Stockton in the Central Valley of California, Kingston studied English literature at the University of California, Berkeley. When she wrote *The Woman Warrior*, which was her first novel, she drew upon her personal experience, her acquaintance with Chinese myths and practices, and her knowledge of Asian and Asian American history. From these different strands, she fashioned a powerful, entrancing story with feminist, mythical, and autobiographical elements. While many readers and reviewers praised her work as an imaginative tour de force, others have raised questions about the value of her work. Some objected to her stance as a woman warrior to attack Chinese patriarchal attitudes, which saw men and boys as more desirable than women or girls. While some of her critics agreed that such attitudes did exist, they felt that it was not politic and desirable to disclose so openly some of the negative aspects of their community to the general public. Still others saw her novel as autobiographical and criticized her for what they believed to be exaggerations and distortions of her experience. Moreover, when Kingston creatively blended myth and fiction in her book, some critics argued that she had misunderstood the Chinese myths and legends.[20]

Another example was Amy Tan's *The Joy Luck Club* (1989).[21] The novel, which sensitively explored mother-daughter relationships, appealed to the public and enjoyed a tremendous success in sales. Film director Wayne Wang produced a film version of *The Joy Luck Club* in 1993, and it met with tremendous commercial success at movie theaters nationwide. While most readers, book reviewers, and film critics praised her work, some in the Chinese American community thought that her novel was inauthentic and that it was too detached from reality. Some said that it had been written to pull on the heartstrings of her readers and movie-going audience. Still others mentioned that the book portrayed Chinese men as being patriarchal, cruel, and insensitive. Consequently, Tan scored points with feminists, women, and others who were critical of Chinese patriarchy and the continual devaluing of women in China; however, critical acclaim came at the expense of Chinese and Chinese American men, who were then stereotyped as insensitive, cold, and sexist.[22]

The controversies over the work by Kingston and Tan are hardly isolated cases. C. Y. Lee's novel, *The Flower Drum Song* (1957), which became a Broadway musical in 1958 and a motion picture in 1962, has also faced criticism over the question of authenticity and accuracy. To some Asian Americans of a later generation, the depiction of Americanization or acculturation among the American-born Chinese was objectionable and not credible. On the other hand, many Chinese Americans believed *The Flower Drum Song* accurately reflected their reality while they were growing up, and they were pleased to see Hollywood produce a film about their Chinese American experiences. For David Henry Hwang, a Chinese American playwright, *The Flower Drum Song* has historical and cultural value; he revised it for a Broadway production in 2002 and 2003.[23]

The debates over literary work underscore how seriously Asian Americans are concerned with their cultural heritage and identity.[24] Is Asian American literature depicting Asian American culture accurately? Are the writings of Asian American authors authentic or contrived? What image does the Asian American work project to the larger public? Does it represent the Asian American community well? All of these questions are important, but care should

Author Amy Tan, 2002. AP/Wide World Photos.

be taken to give room for individual creativity and artistic license to Asian American writers. Literature is not sociology, and it should not have the burden of retracing history or narrating what is in the news.

Nor is there necessarily one common Asian American experience or reality. Asian Americans may be of Filipino, Korean, or Asian Indian descent. They or their predecessors may have come from various regions in the ancestral homeland, and they may know different customs or languages. Furthermore, their experiences and outlooks may be distinctive due to their gender, class, religion, generation, personality, and place of residence. They may also be of mixed ancestry, with a family heritage stemming from several ethnic backgrounds. As a result, it is erroneous to think that there can be a single version of that which is authentic, accurate, or representative of an Asian American community or group.

Too often, Asian American readers have complained that the situation described in a book or story is not similar to their experiences. But the experience of one Asian American in New Orleans, Louisiana, may not be the same as that of an Asian American living in Los Angeles, California. Nor is the experience of an Asian American living in Appleton, Wisconsin, likely to be similar to that of an Asian American residing in Honolulu, Hawai'i. Asian Americans are not a monolithic group, and they do not have a singular collective experience. From this vantage point, literary battles waged over the question of whether literature is a mirror for the community, associated with the issues of authenticity and representation, are likely to be vexing and counterproductive. Asian American authors should be judged on the literary merits of their work, and their artistic independence and autonomy should be accepted.

QUESTIONS

1. What is the Asian American movement and what were its goals? What is its relationship to Asian American literature? Is Asian American literature the same as American literature? Why or why not?

2. Before you read this chapter, what did you think qualified as Asian American literature? What had you read before that you thought was Asian American literature? Has your opinion changed after reading this chapter?

3. How and why did activists try to create a category known as Asian American literature? Why did an early anthology of Asian American literature have the unusual title of *Aiiieeee!*?

4. Imagine you are one of the activists who is trying to discover and create Asian American literature. Would you include Asians who were writing while staying in America even if they had resided here for only three years? How about those Asian writers who were deemed "foreigners" because the U.S. government had determined that foreign-born Asians could not naturalize for citizenship until after World War II? Would this affect your thinking on whom to include and whom to exclude?

5. As activists attempted to decide which works could be considered Asian American literature, what were some of the questions they had to address? Can you think of other questions that ought to be considered?

6. How has the scope of Asian American literature been altered by immigration and social change? How might an author who is foreign-born think differently from one who is American-born? Is that always the case?

7. What is the role of oral history in a community? Should this be considered a category of Asian American literature? Explain.

8. Should Asian American literature be written to serve individuals or the community? Must a writer have a responsibility to the needs and expectations of the community? How should responsibility be defined?

9. Should literature be written as a creative exercise, or as "art for art's sake"? Or should literature expand the thoughts of its readers?

10. Is it desirable for literature to be a sociological representation of a community or ethnic group? Select a work written by an Asian American writer. How does he or she deal with this issue?

11. Can writers successfully mix art and politics in their work? Do both aspects need to be included in Asian American literature?

12. Who was Edith Maud Eaton and what is her role in Asian American literature?

13. Should Asian American literature promote the goal of panethnicity, the idea that Asian Americans are a community with common interests?

14. Is it desirable for Asian American literature to present a positive image of Asian Americans to the general public? What might be the benefits and problems in adopting such an approach to Asian American literature?

15. Should Asian American literature be written with a goal of maintaining or promoting cooperation and harmonious relations among the different Asian American groups? How does this relate to the controversy over Lois-Ann Yamanaka's work?

16. How would someone determine if literature is authentic and representative of the Asian American community? If readers find an essay or a book that does not comport with their own experiences or memories, is that work inaccurate or misleading? If writers are free to exercise artistic creativity, could they misrepresent an ethnic group or a community and cause harm?

NOTES

1. Jeffery Paul Chan and George J. Leonard, "Asian American Literary Pioneers," in *The Asian Pacific American Heritage,* ed. George J. Leonard (New York: Garland Publishing, 1999), 396.

2. Ibid.

3. Frank Chin, Jeffrey Paul Chan, Lawson Fusao Inada, and Shawn Wong, eds., *Aiiieee! An Anthology of Asian-American Writers* (Washington, DC: Howard University Press, 1974).

4. For historical background, see Ronald Takaki, *Strangers from a Different Shore: A History of Asian Americans* (Boston: Little, Brown and Company, 1989); Sucheng Chan, *Asian Americans: An Interpretive History* (Boston: Twayne Publishers, 1991); Harry H. L. Kitano and Roger Daniels, *Asian Americans: Emerging Minorities* (Englewood Cliffs, NJ: Prentice Hall, 1995); and Gary Y. Okihiro, *Margins and Mainstreams: Asians in American History and Culture* (Seattle: University of Washington Press, 1994).

5. Her name is spelled as Sui Sin Fah here, but the more frequent rendering is Sui Sin Far. Chin et al., *Aiiieee!*, xxi.

6. Annette White-Parks, *Sui Sin Far/Edith Maude Eaton: A Literary Biography* (Urbana: University of Illinois Press, 1995).

7. William Wei, *The Asian American Movement* (Philadelphia: Temple University Press, 1993); Steve Louie and Glenn Omatsu, eds., *Asian Americans: The Movement and the Moment* (Los Angeles: UCLA Asian American Studies Center Press, 2001); Fred Wei-han Ho, ed., *Legacy to Revolution: Politics and Culture of Revolutionary Asian Pacific America* (San Francisco: AK, 2000).

8. Chin et al., *Aiiieee!*, xxxi.

9. Ibid., xxxiii.

10. Ibid.

11. Carlos Bulosan, *America Is in the Heart* (Seattle: University of Washington Press, 1974).

12. Milton Murayama, *All I Asking for Is My Body* (San Francisco: Supa Press, 1975).

13. Marie Hara and Nora Okja Keller, *Intersecting Circles: The Voices of Hapa Women in Poetry and Prose.* Honolulu, HI: Bamboo Ridge, 1999.

14. Lois-Ann Yamanaka, *Blu's Hanging* (New York: Farrar, Straus and Giroux, 1997).

15. Frank Chin, *The Chickencoop Chinaman and The Year of the Dragon: Two Plays* (Seattle: University of Washington Press, 1981).

16. Xiao-huang Yin, *Chinese American Literature since the 1850s* (Urbana: University of Illinois Press, 2000), 229–231.

17. Yamanaka, *Blu's Hanging.*

18. Candice L. Fujikane, "*Blu's Hanging:* The Responsibilities Faced by Local Readers and Writers," *Hawaii Herald,* 16 January 1998, A9–A11; Jamie James, "This Hawaii's Not for Tourists," *Atlantic Monthly,* February 1999, 90–94.

19. Maxine Hong Kingston, *The Woman Warrior: Memoirs of a Girlhood among Ghosts* (New York: Alfred A. Knopf, 1976).

20. King-Kok Cheung, "*The Woman Warrior* versus *The Chinaman Pacific:* Must a Chinese American Critic Choose between Feminism and Heroism?" in *Conflicts in Feminism,* ed. Marianne Hirsch and Evelyn Fox Keller (New York: Routledge, 1990), 234–251; Yin, *Chinese American Literature,* 234–239.

21. Amy Tan, *The Joy Luck Club* (New York: Putnam's Sons, 1989).

22. Yin, *Chinese American Literature,* 235–237, 241–242.

23. C. Y. Lee, *Flower Drum Song* (New York: Farrar and Cudhay, 1957).

24. C. Y. Lee, "The Short Story That Changed My Life," in *Yellow Light: The Flowering of Asian American Arts,* ed. Amy Ling (Philadelphia: Temple University Press, 1999), 11–18; Chan and Leonard, "Asian American Literary Pioneers," 402–404. See, for example, Amy Ling, "Introduction: What's in a Name," in Ling, *Yellow Light,* 1–8.

SELECTED WORKS

Alquizola, Marilyn. "Subversion or Affirmation: The Text and Subtext of *America Is in the Heart.*" In *Asian Americans: Comparative and Global Perspectives,* ed. Shirley Hune, Hyung-Chan Kim, Stephen Fugita, and Amy Ling. Pullman: Washington State University Press, 1991.

Beauregard, Guy. "Reclaiming Sui Sin Far." In *Re-collecting Early Asian America: Essays in Cultural History,* ed. Josephine Lee, Imogene L. Kim, and Yuko Matsukawa. Philadelphia: Temple University Press, 2003.

Bulosan, Carlos. *America Is in the Heart.* Seattle: University of Washington Press, 1974.

Chan, Jeffery Paul, and George J. Leonard. "Asian American Literary Pioneers." In *The Asian Pacific American Heritage,* ed. George J. Leonard. New York: Garland Publishing, 1999.

Chan, Sucheng. *Asian Americans: An Interpretive History.* Boston: Twayne Publishers, 1991.

Cheung, King-Kok, ed. *An Interethnic Companion to Asian American Literature.* New York: Cambridge University Press, 1997.

———. "*The Woman Warrior* versus *The Chinaman Pacific*: Must a Chinese American Critic Choose between Feminism and Heroism?" In *Conflicts in Feminism,* ed. Marianne Hirsch and Evelyn Fox Keller. New York: Routledge, 1990.

Chin, Frank. *The Chickencoop China man and The Year of the Dragon: Two Plays.* Seattle: University of Washington Press, 1981.

Chin, Frank, Jeffrey Paul Chan, Lawson Fusao Inada, and Shawn Wong, eds. *Aiiieee! An Anthology of Asian-American Writers.* Washington, DC: Howard University Press, 1974.

Fujikane, Candice L. "*Blu's Hanging*: The Responsibilities Faced by Local Readers and Writers." *Hawaii Herald,* 16 January 1998, A9–A11.

Hara, Marie, and Nora Okja Keller. *Intersecting Circles: The Voices of Hapa Women in Poetry and Prose.* Honolulu, HI: Bamboo Ridge, 1999.

Ho, Fred Wei-han, ed. *Legacy to Revolution: Politics and Culture of Revolutionary Asian Pacific America.* San Francisco: AK, 2000.

James, Jamie. "This Hawaii's Not for Tourists." *Atlantic Monthly,* February 1999, 90–94.

Ketrak, Ketu H. "South Asian American Writers: Geography and Memory." *Amerasia Journal* 22 (1996): 121–138.

Kim, Elaine H. *Asian American Literature: An Introduction to the Writings and Their Social Context.* Philadelphia: Temple University Press, 1982.

Kingston, Maxine Hong. *The Woman Warrior: Memoirs of a Girlhood among Ghosts.* New York: Alfred A. Knopf, 1976.

Kitano, Harry H. L., and Roger Daniels. *Asian Americans: Emerging Minorities.* Englewood Cliffs, NJ: Prentice-Hall, 1995.

Lee, Rachel C. *The Americas of Asian American Literature: Gendered Fictions of Nation and Transnation.* Princeton: Princeton University Press, 1999.

Lim, Shirley Geok-lin, and Amy Ling, eds. *Reading the Literatures of Asian America.* Philadelphia: Temple University Press, 1992.

Ling, Amy, ed. *Yellow Light: The Flowering of Asian American Arts.* Philadelphia: Temple University Press, 1999.

Louie, Steve, and Glenn Omatsu, eds. *Asian Americans: The Movement and the Moment.* Los Angeles: UCLA Asian American Studies Center Press, 2001.

Murayama, Milton. *All I Asking for Is My Body.* San Francisco: Supa Press, 1975.

Okihiro, Gary Y. *Margins and Mainstreams: Asians in American History and Culture.* Seattle: University of Washington Press, 1994.

Sumida, Stephen H., and Sau-ling Cynthia Wong, eds. *A Resource Guide to Asian American Literature.* New York: Modern Language Association of America, 2001.

Takaki, Ron. *Strangers from a Different Shore: A History of Asian Americans.* Boston: Little, Brown and Company, 1989.

Tan, Amy. *The Joy Luck Club.* New York: Putnam's Sons, 1989.

Wei, William. *The Asian American Movement.* Philadelphia: Temple University Press, 1993.

White-Parks, Annette. *Sui Sin Far/Edith Maude Eaton: A Literary Biography.* Urbana: University of Illinois Press, 1995.

Yamanaka, Lois-Ann. *Blu's Hanging.* New York: Farrar, Straus and Giroux, 1997.

Yin, Xiao-huang. *Chinese American Literature since the 1850s.* Urbana: University of Illinois Press, 2000.

5

ASIAN DIASPORA/
TRANSNATIONALISM

Transnationalism is a phenomenon of our times. Diaspora, the movement of people, goods, information, and ideas from one country to another is occurring everywhere in response to the demands of the global economy. This extensive movement across borders has been made easier by changes in communication, transportation, and technology. This has brought people into the United States from India, Pakistan, South Korea, China, Taiwan, Hong Kong, Vietnam, Laos, Cambodia, Thailand, and elsewhere. It has also led to the coining of a term, transnationalism, which refers to people who maintain simultaneous contact with several lands, such as their country of origin and the country to which they have gained entry. This complex involvement with several countries at the same time has consequences, for it means that there are different ways of viewing space and cultural identity. But does transnationalism create problems for Asian Americans? Or is it something they should welcome?

BACKGROUND

In the traditional view, migration was a process in which people left their countries due to considerations that pushed them from their homes, or attractions that drew them to another land, or a combination of these push-and-pull factors. Once the migrants had left their homeland and moved to the host country, they had to grapple with problems of cultural differences, language differences, the struggle to make a living, and the need to save their earnings. The earnings might pay for remittances to family members in the homeland, and for some, it could also finance the passage back home at a later date. In the traditional view, many others were never able to return to their land of origin. Instead, they ruptured their ties to their homeland, adapted to the new circumstances, and finally assimilated into the country to which they had migrated. As sociologist Robert E. Park described it, it was a process of contact, competition, accommodation, and assimilation.[1]

More recently, however, many view migration as a widespread phenomenon responding to the demands of global capitalism and the restructuring of the world economy. This extensive movement of people from one country to another has been labeled transnationalism, a term that denotes that the migrants are maintaining their ties to several nations, including the site of origin from which they left. Transnationalism suggests that the migrants are crossing borders, seeing nations as spaces without boundaries, as they engage in economic activities. The discussion of transnationalism is often paired with reference to diasporas, defined as the dispersal of people whether due to voluntary or involuntary causes. The involuntary causes behind diasporas might be political reasons, such as a communist takeover, religious conflict, or ethnic violence.

Transnationalism and diasporas as concepts have transformed the way many people view international migration. The world is seen as an arena for the fluid and mobile movement of peoples in response to different conditions. The boundaries of nations are seen to be more porous and permeable as people become transnational migrants. In an age of globalization fostered by modern communication, transportation, and technology, these transnational migrants, sometimes called transmigrants, can simultaneously maintain affiliation with several geographical sites. The ease of telephone usage, air travel, and Internet linkage means that people are continuously connected to family, friends, and others all across the globe. With satellite television, teleconferencing, use of the Internet, fax machines, and phones, people feel that they are in close contact with relatives and acquaintances.

Asians in the United States are especially noticeable as transmigrants. These are transnational migrants who are linked in a global circuitry with different geographical sites at the same time. Businessmen originally from Hong Kong and Taiwan, for example, are often referred to as "astronauts." Possessing American citizenship they travel extensively to China, Hong Kong, Taiwan, and other parts of Asia to pursue business opportunities. They may even live for extended periods in Asia and have "parachute children" in the United States, children who live under the care and supervision of wives, other relatives, or even friends.[2] Many Asian Indians work in the United States, but they frequently return to India to visit relatives and acquaintances. Moreover,

Asian Indian men may read newspapers and return to India to arrange marriages with women.

So extensive is the movement of Asians around the globe that they are viewed as diasporic in their dispersal. Writers refer to a Chinese diaspora, as Chinese are scattered in communities throughout Asia, the Americas, Oceania, and Europe. Others refer to a South Asian diaspora, referring to the South Asian peoples formerly belonging to the British Empire, for example, those in India, Pakistan, and Bangladesh who can be found in South Africa, Fiji, England, Canada, Australia, and the United States. Still others talk about a Japanese diaspora, a Korean diaspora, and a Filipino diaspora. When South Vietnam fell to the Communist forces in 1975, there was a Vietnamese diaspora, as *Viet Kieu* or overseas Vietnamese communities became established in the United States, Canada, France, Australia, and French Guiana. When Laos was taken over by the Communists in 1975, there was a Hmong diaspora, as this ethnic group from the mountains of Laos also formed communities in the United States, Canada, France, Australia, and French Guiana.

The transnational flow of peoples has important implications for multiculturalism and cultural diversity. As many different ethnic groups mingle and interact with each other, they alter the cultural landscapes of the places where they are located. The residents of these locales can become more international, more cosmopolitan, and more cross-culturally aware. They have the opportunity to become familiar with different customs, practices, foods, behaviors, and language expressions. They know how to eat sushi (rice balls) and sashimi (sliced raw fish); they can drink boba tea (a beverage with tapioca balls), sing karaoke songs, and rent a Hong Kong martial arts or Asian Indian Bollywood (the Indian version of Hollywood) video. They can learn kung fu (martial arts), practice ikebana (flower arrangement), or learn about yoga (meditation). There is the conjuring of hybridity in cultural identity due to the mixing of cultures, interracial marriage, mixed ethnicity offspring, and transracial adoptions.[3]

But this practice of moving from one country to another, with ties to several nations, also draws mixed reactions. Not everyone celebrates the results of globalization, transnationalism, diasporas, and multiculturalism. Some wonder what this practice augurs for the notion of the nation-state, the idea that people belong to one political entity with accompanying political allegiance. They think that the idea of a common national culture is being eroded. Some fear that the idea of citizenship becomes compromised and diluted when people have emotional and cultural attachments to several countries. In fact, there is a flexible notion of what citizenship entails. Furthermore, they view transnationalism as destabilizing as people maintain their ties to their land of origin instead of the country in which they reside. They voice concern that transnationalism might strengthen loyalty to a religion or ideology that might promote the potential for conflict or violence. Finally, some community leaders see transnationalism as promoting conditions that allow for multinational businesses to exploit migrant workers. Laborers with limited skills and lacking fluency in the language of the receiving country may be forced to accept low wages with little benefit to their families or themselves.[4]

Whether transnationalism is favorable or not for Asian Americans is a subject of debate. Some consider transnationalism as a development that is advantageous to immigrants and ethnic minorities in the United States. In contrast, others feel that transnationalism has negative consequences for Asian Americans and their communities. These are some of the propositions that are being discussed pertaining to transnationalism:

1. Transnationalism is harmful to Asian Americans because it promotes the idea that they are perpetual foreigners.
2. As Asian Americans maintain transnational ties, they increase the likelihood that there will be divisions within their communities.
3. To the extent that Asian Americans are interested in their ancestral homelands, these transnational ties lessen community involvement and detract from community-building in the United States.

DOES TRANSNATIONALISM HURT ASIAN AMERICANS BECAUSE IT PROMOTES THE IDEA THAT THEY ARE PERPETUAL FOREIGNERS?

For

It is commonplace to speak of the world as being ever more interdependent. The global economy has led to the integration of economies, and the marketplace seeks out the most efficient use of resources, labor, and capital. Globalization of the economy has strengthened the linkages in communication, transportation, and technology. The interconnectedness of the world allows people to maintain ties with their land of origin or ancestral heritage. Landscapes in the United States are now geographies of cultural diversity, in which immigrants and ethnic groups can have contact with the fashions, trends, and popular culture of Asian societies. Asian Americans can watch Chinese satellite television and Asian Indian videos, listen to Filipino CDs, eat Korean food, and participate in Tet, the Vietnamese New Year celebration. The economy, innovations, and science of the contemporary world have made it possible for people to freely choose and consume what they wish in a global marketplace.

Many observers welcome this transnationalism, in which people can easily cross national borders and keep contact with several geographical sites. Nonetheless, this occurrence does exact a cost from immigrants and ethnic groups. As the public learns about Asian Americans who read newspapers or magazines in the Hmong, Khmer, Korean, Chinese, or Filipino languages, they may doubt that Asian Americans have a stake in the United States. As they look at ethnic landscapes with Lao Buddhist temples, Sikh gurdwara temples, Filipino Iglesia Ni Kristo churches, and Islamic mosques with Asian Muslims, they may be mystified by the heterogeneity of these religious practices. As the public learns about the frequent travel between the United States and Asia by Asian Americans, they may wonder if Asian Americans are more committed to Asia than America.

Asian American community leaders in the late 1960s and early 1970s complained that they were always viewed as exotic, foreign, and not part of the American mosaic. But to the extent Asian Americans maintain their transnational ties, they are perpetuating the notion that Asian Americans are eternal foreigners and perpetual strangers who are staying only temporarily in the United States. Some members of the public may see them as only temporarily anchored in this country, with no deep loyalty to the culture and ideals of the United States. Instead, they see that Asian Americans are like mobile nomads freely traversing borders, who seek economic advantage wherever and whenever it presents itself, and who hold citizenship and residence in this country only because it is convenient. They view Asian Americans as appearing to have no roots in any society.

By failing to integrate themselves into American popular culture and by seeming to be foreign, Asian Americans are marginalizing and isolating themselves from the mainstream of contemporary American life. They may also provoke demands by policymakers to reform immigration laws and impose restrictions, so that those who are admitted to the United States can be assimilated into American society. There can be other consequences, too. During World War II, there was a general perception that Japanese in the United States could not be assimilated and were loyal to Japan. The *kibei,* or second generation Japanese Americans who had lived or studied in Japan, fed the notion that even Japanese born in America continued to have sentimental attachments to their parents' homeland. Because their allegiance was in doubt, the result was a Japanese American internment, in which over 110,000 Japanese on the West Coast were uprooted from their communities and placed in ten different War Relocation Authority camps administered by the United States government.[5]

After World War II, the arrest, trial, and imprisonment of Iva Ikuko Toguri d'Aquino also reinforced the notion that Japanese Americans might be loyal to Japan. While d'Aquino was visiting her aunt in Japan in 1941, World War II broke out between Japan and the United States. Stranded in Japan during the duration of the conflict, she worked with Americans and others as radio announcers on Radio Tokyo. But after the war, she was singled out as "Tokyo Rose," an alleged broadcaster of propaganda against American troops in the Pacific. Although the charges against her were of dubious validity, she was forced to serve a prison term of ten years, starting in 1949. Due to a campaign by Japanese American community leaders, President Gerald Ford finally decided to pardon her in 1977. But the whole episode regarding the alleged Tokyo Rose showed how transnationalism and stereotypes could have devastating consequences for d'Aquino.[6]

Moreover, since the terrorist attacks on the World Trade Center Towers in New York City on September 11, 2001, many governments around the world have tightened controls on immigration. The United States and other nations are regulating immigrants much more tightly and scrutinizing their behavior. This has caused difficulties for international students, tourists, and travelers when they try to enter the United States and other countries. Those who seek visas have to undergo greater delays and must deal with more regulations. Thus, it is misleading to think that transnationalism and the crossing of borders is inevitable and unstoppable. It is premature to think that transnationalism means that states and governments cannot exert control over migrants and the movement of peoples.

Against

It is interesting to see that Asian Americans maintaining relations with Asia is an issue for many "Americans." No one questions the loyalty of people of British ancestry when business is conducted in London or when Americans choose to go to Europe for work. However, when Asian Americans maintain or promote transnational relations, their motives and intentions are questioned. Are they committed to the United States or are they seeking to benefit their "homeland"?

The legacy of the "yellow peril," the idea that Asians are a cultural, ideological, and military threat to the United States, continues to haunt Asian Americans. For regardless of how long they have been in the United States, they are still seen as foreigners. Yet, this perception of being an outsider is not a result of transnationalism, but due to the racism that Asian Americans continue to face in the United States. The nomadic nature of today's global economy, which makes travel fluid and accessible, has actually benefited Asian Americans and Asian immigrants. Speaking Mandarin, Cantonese, Japanese, Korean, Hindi, Tagalog, and other Asian languages, which were once shunned as a characteristic of aliens or immigrants, is now seen as a necessity in a world where fluency in foreign languages is desired. Being bilingual or multilingual is now regarded as a valuable asset in the contemporary world of commerce and finance.

The perception of Asian Americans as foreigners has more to do with the history of racist policies that prevented Asians from actively participating in social, political, and economic aspects of American life than their current transnational status. It was not until World War II and after that people of Asian ancestry were granted the right to naturalize for citizenship. Thus, Asian Americans of the immigrant and refugee generation have only recently been given the opportunity to become citizens of America. But regardless of whether they were foreign-born or American-born, they have been questioned and mistrusted when it came to matters involving U.S. intelligence or the notion of national security.

During World War II, Japanese Americans who were born in the United States were under tremendous suspicion and were questioned about their loyalty and intentions. Over 110,000 Japanese in America, nearly two-thirds of whom were American citizens, were confined to ten different War Relocation Authority camps. After the attacks of September 11, 2001, on the World Trade Tower in New York and the Pentagon in Washington, D.C., Muslims, Arabs, South Asians, and other Asian Americans were suspected of being terrorists. The incidence of hate crimes rose in many locales throughout the country, and those who were believed to be foreign faced the dangers of being the target of verbal abuse to being murdered. Regardless of whether these Asian Americans maintained connections with their "homeland" or not was irrelevant to those who perpetrated these hate crimes. These crimes were committed primarily due to the racial profiling of Asian Americans who fit the description or profile of what people thought to be typical of a terrorist or a foreigner whose loyalty is to another country.

DO TRANSNATIONAL TIES AMONG ASIAN AMERICANS INCREASE THE LIKELIHOOD OF INTERNAL COMMUNITY DIVISIONS?

For

Transnational Asians in the United States maintain links across national boundaries. They cultivate and sustain ties to the homeland that may be political, economic, social, and cultural, even as they reside in the United States. The technological innovations of the modern world have made it easy to maintain connections with distant geographical sites, thanks to the Internet, the phone, fax machines, and contemporary modes of transportation. By

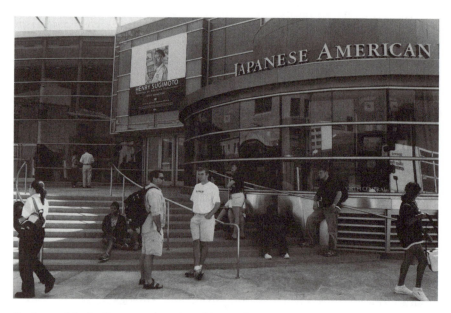

Students visit the Japanese American National Museum in May 2001 in downtown Los Angeles. Even as California's Asian population surged in the 1990s, the number of residents of Japanese descent notably declined. California lost 24,000 residents of Japanese ancestry in the 1990s, according to the U.S. Census data. AP/Wide World Photos.

making use of videos, satellite television, karaoke machines, and computers, people can preserve or strengthen their nostalgic or emotional ties to persons, ideas, memories, practices, and developments in their homeland.

While there may be benefits in this transnational access to the land of origin, the homeland also gains access to the migrants, in this case, Asian Americans. Countries outside the United States can manipulate the sentimental attachments of immigrants for their homeland. They may encourage the sending of remittances or money to help in the development of their economies. They can also nurture feelings of pride and patriotism, so that immigrants display nationalism for the land of origin. For example, during the autocratic rule of Ferdinand Marcos, who imposed martial law in the Philippines from 1972 to 1981, his government officials appealed to Filipinos in the United States to invest in businesses, purchase land, and help in the economic development of the Philippines. The political struggles of the Philippines were reenacted in the United States as there was dissent between his Filipino supporters and opponents. In Hawai'i, it was claimed that officials of the Philippine consulate took photographs of those who were his critics.

When South Korea was under the authoritarian rule of presidents Park Chung Hee and Chun Doo Hwan in the 1960s to 1980s, its KCIA, or Korean Central Intelligence Agency, maintained surveillance of critics and dis-senters in the United States. When the Republic of China on Taiwan was governed by the Kuomintang, or Nationalist Party, its officials and agents kept records on the Chinese in the United States. Nationalist officials on Taiwan channeled money into community organizations, language schools, and cultural events to enlist Chinese Americans to side with it in the com-petition against mainland China, more formally known as the People's Re-public of China.

Transnationalism also can foster conflict with other groups. For example, during World War II, many Chinese, Koreans, and Filipinos in the United States were hostile to Japanese Americans because of Japan's military actions in Asia. The Chinese American communities held Rice Bowl parties to raise money for war relief in China.[7] Koreans in America, under nationalist leaders such as Syngman Rhee, had long protested the Japanese takeover of Korea from 1910 to 1945. Filipinos also protested the Japanese occupation of the Philippines. Or, in another example, after the Vietnam War in 1975, many refugees from Laos and Cambodia were hostile to refugees from South Viet-nam. During the Southeast Asian conflict, Communist Vietnamese troops had invaded Laos and Cambodia, and the refugees from those countries har-bored resentment against all Vietnamese, although the Vietnamese refugees in the United States had also fled from the Communists. Finally, even as India and Pakistan dispute who should have governmental control over Kashmir, there are contrasting views between Asian Indian Americans and Pakistani Americans about which country has a more legitimate claim over this region.

Against

When divisions are explained as being due to transnationalism, this ignores the reality that power struggles and conflict existed before people began trav-eling across geographic boundaries. The common assumption that Asian Americans are a homogeneous group has much to do with the misunder-standing of Asians having just one community. There is heterogeneity among Asian Americans just as there is heterogeneity among Asians in Asia. As a result, Asian American communities are characterized by age, gender, class, religion, politics, and other differences.

The communities that formed before the 1965 immigration act are signifi-cantly different than those that have been developing more recently. In the past, Asian Americans created ethnic enclaves in various metropolitan areas to serve their fellow ethnic Asians. It was a place where Asians could find others like themselves, purchase groceries to maintain their ethnic diets, and have a sense of community in a land that treated them as outsiders. Today, however, ethnic enclaves are slowly disappearing. What was once known as a Chinatown or Japantown has now been transformed into more of a pan-Asian town. For example, the Chinatowns that once were dominated by Chinese in New York, San Francisco, and Hawai'i are now infused with more recent immigrants from Thailand, Vietnam, and other countries of Southeast Asia. This has much to do with the generation of American-born Asian Americans who do not want to maintain their family businesses. Instead, they would rather pursue other professional careers. Often, these careers take them away from their ethnic enclaves. Subsequently, these enclaves have faced many changes; in some instances, one cannot just call an area Chinatown, for there are other ethnic groups who have transformed the landscape. Thus, many Vietnamese have moved into Chinatowns and have set up businesses and restaurants. Furthermore, ethnic communities are no longer in metropolitan cities alone. As more Asian Americans move into suburban neighborhoods, there is a growing number of post-suburban communities that are sprouting up. In Orange County, for example, Vietnamese and Korean Americans have transformed what was once a predominantly White, conservative area into a place with ethnic post-suburban communities, where businesses dominate a portion of the Orange County landscape.[8] In these communities, transnational ties have actually strengthened the communities. The import and export businesses that are commonplace in ethnic communities have made transnational ties an integral part of establishing and building their businesses.

Some may argue, however, that transnational ties can sometimes bring unwanted pressure and stereotypes from the dominant society. The SARS (Severe Acute Respiratory Syndrome) scare of 2003 ignited fear that an untreatable disease was spreading from Asia. SARS is a highly contagious disease that caused great concern when the outbreak occurred. The media had much to do with this misinformed hysteria. Like the AIDS (Acquired Immune Deficiency Syndrome) scare of the 1980s was seen as a "gay" disease, SARS has been viewed by many as an "Asian" disease. The SARS scare also had the unfortunate effect of hurting many Asian American businesses in the United States. Immediately after the SARS outbreak in Asia, a dramatic drop in business was seen in Asian grocery stores and restaurants. Having heard about this contagious disease, people in the United States were afraid of coming into contact with someone who might have been to Asia. For legal Asian residents, the SARS scare, along with the tightened supervision by the Immigration and Naturalization Service after the attacks of September 11, 2001, has made international travel risky. These incidents, however, are few and far between, but they are highlighted in the news. Scapegoating of this kind, not transnationalism, is what separates Asian communities. In fact, transnationalism helps promote better relations between members of the community.

DO TRANSNATIONAL TIES LESSEN COMMUNITY INVOLVEMENT AND WEAKEN COMMUNITY BUILDING IN THE UNITED STATES?

For

Asian Americans as immigrants are naturally interested in their homelands. After all, members of their family, relatives, friends, and acquaintances may still live there. But when there is a strong transnational preoccupation with the land of origin, the effects can be harmful to Asian American communities. By being transfixed with trans-Pacific concerns, Asian Americans may ignore more pressing problems within their communities in the United States.

For example, transnational ties often result in the sending of funds and remittances to relatives or organizations. Whether it is monies to assist family members, aid to finance schools and scholarships, or support for the economy of their homeland, this support leads to an outflow of funds from the United States. This diversion of monies across the Pacific could have been used in a similar manner to help the Asian American communities in the United States. It could have been used by Asian American community organizations and language schools, or it could have paid for scholarships and cultural events. The loss for worthy causes in the United States is a gain for the land of origin.

One example of the diversion of monies is the Indian government's Persons of Indian Origin (PIO) card program. Initiated in 1999, people of Indian descent can purchase a card for $1,000, which will be valid for 20 years. The card allows those in the Indian diaspora, who are citizens of other countries, to travel to India without the need of a visa. It also allows them to purchase and sell property in India. Finally, they can buy government bonds and seek admission to Indian universities. This is an attempt to attract direct foreign investment from the estimated 15 million Indians who are living abroad.[9] Another example is the flow of monies by Asian Indian Americans to militant Hindu organizations in India. Some South Asian scholars and the Human Rights Commission in India have expressed concern about branches of Hindu nationalist groups in the United States that were sending funds to Hindu militants in India. These funds might be supporting religious violence and anti-Muslim activities in India, such as the Hindu attacks on Muslims in the state of Gujarat.[10]

Sometimes the transnational interest in the land of origin leads Asians in the United States to support political movements across the Pacific. Thus, after the fall of mainland China to Communist control in 1949, some Chinese in the United States worked tirelessly to assist in the overthrow of the People's Republic of China. There have been immigrants from China, Taiwan, and Hong Kong who have debated whether American support should be accorded to mainland China or Taiwan. Related to this is the issue of whether Taiwan is a sovereign, independent nation, or whether it is a regional part of a single country known as China. Although the United States eventually established formal diplomatic relations with the People's Republic of China in 1979 and recognized its government in Beijing, it still holds informal relations with the Republic of China on Taiwan. The Taiwan Relations Act of 1979 passed by Congress allowed for the creation of an American Institute on Taiwan to maintain contact with Taiwan. Because of this complex relationship of the United States with China and Taiwan, first- and second-generation Chinese and Taiwanese immigrants have tried to influence Washington to persuade it to support either the government of Beijing or Taipei.

With the fall of South Vietnam, Laos, and Cambodia to communism in 1975, organizations appeared in the United States to carry on resistance movements against the Communist regimes in those countries. One example is the Neo Hom, a Hmong resistance movement against the Communist government in Laos. It receives funds from Hmong refugees in the United States and elsewhere to launch military raids against Laos from Thailand.[11] The Hmong are also opposed to the normalization of trade relations to Laos that would result in lower tariffs on Laotian goods coming into the United States. Hmong organizations such as the Lao Veterans of America and the Lao Family Community thus have lobbied against any new legislation that would allow any change in trade relations with the Laotian Communist government in Vientiane.[12] This is similar to Vietnamese refugees who tried to persuade the American government not to restore diplomatic relations with the Communist government of Vietnam located in Hanoi. But diplomatic relations between the two nations were reestablished in 1995, ambassadors were exchanged in 1997, and bilateral trade relations were regularized in 2001.

Transnational ties may also concern matters besides opposition to communism. For example, Sikhs in America were very disturbed about the Golden Temple incident in India in 1984. Sikhs are a religious group in India, with many of them residing in the province of Punjab. Because of disagreements between the Indian government and the Sikhs, in 1984 government troops were sent to seize the Golden Temple in Amritsar. Thousands of Sikhs died trying to defend this holiest of shrines for the Sikh faith. In retaliation in that same year, Sikh bodyguards for the government killed the Indian prime minister, Indira Gandhi. This, in turn, triggered anti-Sikh rioting by Hindus.[13] Sikhs in America proclaimed solidarity with Sikhs in India and favored the formation of an independent Sikh nation known as Khalistan. In various South Asian communities across the United States, Sikhs posted car stickers that proclaimed "Khalistan Now," an expression of support for an autonomous Sikh nation, separate from India.[14]

But to the extent that attention is devoted to transnational concerns, there is less effort paid to domestic issues and local communities in the United States. For example, Southeast Asians in the United States, as a refugee community, are wrestling with problems of limited English fluency, unemployment, and dependence on welfare. There are troublesome issues of generational conflict, juvenile delinquency, school dropouts, gender conflict, religious conversion, and coping with assimilation and cultural identity. To the extent that some community leaders try to mobilize their fellow Southeast Asians on foreign policy matters, that detracts from efforts at community building and the resolution of pressing domestic problems. By failing to cultivate relations with local groups and not participating in domestic politics, Asian Americans are powerless to effect policies and changes that can benefit their communities, such as increased support for social programs. It also delays efforts to build bridges with other ethnic and racial groups in the United States to address common civic concerns and to promote intercultural understanding.

Against

More so than before, population movements are commonplace in today's world. Migrating to far away places has become the fate of millions, a widespread phenomenon because of the development of modern transportation and communication. Although diasporas are no longer considered exceptional, there are several assumptions about what constitutes a diaspora. For example, organizers of a conference on diaspora and transnational identities write on their Web site, "diasporas are constituted by the collective forced dispersion of a religious, ethnic, or political group. Diasporas are guardians of collective memory that transmits both the historical facts that precipitated the dispersion and a cultural heritage. Diasporas exhibit the will to survive as a minority. Diasporas withstand all the above over time."[15] The conditions that create diasporas have contributed to various groups migrating and creating ethnic communities in new homelands. Diasporic communities try to reconstitute communities that reflect their ethnic culture, politics, and religion.

It is indisputable that diaspora and transnationalism have fostered the creation of new ethnic communities. The very strong sense of cultural memory and attachment to heritage has made it possible for Asian American communities to thrive. In this sense, by preserving and enacting cultural traditions through folk festivals, literature, music, visual art, architecture, and religion, diasporic communities can maintain a sense of place. This reinforces their sense of identity. This collective awareness of their distinctiveness helps to affirm the unique place they have in the new host society.[16] This commonality of shared memory and collective temporal consciousness are common threads in diasporic communities. They have shared history and understanding of where they came from and what they face in the new country. Although this will undoubtedly change as the new generations appear, the transmission of tradition and culture helps a new generation maintain a modified version of their parents' memories. Furthermore, for those who visit their families in Asia, they have a renewed sense of what it means to be Asian and American. The connection they feel with both cultures is what helps to make the communities viable and flourishing.

With the increasing ethnic diversity in the American population, there are more and more visible markers of Asian influence in the United States. From temples and monuments to language schools and restaurants, the Asian American diasporic communities have created a commercial mecca where they are able to successfully navigate the social, political, and economic landscape by capitalizing on their cultures. The communities have made it a business to market their cultural foods, clothes, religions, and cultural practices. For example, sushi has become a common food in many American diets; Chinese patterns have become regular features on purses, jackets, and shirts in some of the finest boutiques; Buddhism is becoming more popular; Feng Shui, Yoga, nose piercing, and henna tattoos are common household practices. The communities market their ethnicity as well as their mythical past, thus while much of what they create in their ethnic communities comes from collective memories of their homeland, it is more a representation of how they view their ethnicity and their communities. Thus transnational ties and diaspora have been an integral part of community formation and transformation.

QUESTIONS

1. What is the definition of transnationalism? Is it something that has occurred only in the contemporary era for immigrants and Asians in the United States?

2. How is transnationalism today similar or different from the experiences of immigrants or Asians in other times? How have changes in transportation and communication played a role?

3. What is the traditional view of migration?

4. Does transnationalism present a different way of looking at migration? Why or why not?

5. Describe the characteristics of transnational migrants.

6. What is globalization? How is migration linked to economics?

7. Is the world more connected and interdependent because of economic changes? Explain.

8. What are the benefits and costs of globalization for Asian Americans?

9. Explain what diaspora is. Why do some people refer to several Asian groups as being diasporic? Cite some examples of Asian diasporas. Are there other examples?

10. Discuss the relationship of transnationalism to globalization, diasporas, and multiculturalism.

11. How might transnationalism promote heterogeneity and cultural diversity? Is this desirable or not? Why?

12. In what ways might transnationalism affect the traditional idea of a homogeneous national culture? How might the concept of citizenship to one country be affected by transnationalism?

13. Which is a more desirable development for Asian Americans—homogeneity or heterogeneity? Explain. Might that also be said for America as a society?

14. Is transnationalism likely to foster division among Asian American groups?

15. Is it a utopian idea to think of a world without national borders where people, goods, and ideas can freely cross territorial boundaries without governmental regulation or obstruction? Or will governments continue to regulate access and seek control of those who move in and out of their countries?

16. Is transnationalism harmful or beneficial to Asian American communities? How does it relate to community involvement and community building? Does it help to preserve cultural traditions and cultural awareness? Does it mean more linkage to political movements and ideologies in Asia and the Pacific?

NOTES

1. Robert E. Park, *Race and Culture* (Glencoe, IL: Free Press, 1949), 150, quoted in Vincent N. Parrillo, *Strangers to These Shores: Race and Ethnic Relations in the United States* (Boston: Allyn and Bacon, 1997), 50.

2. Min Zhou, "'Parachute Kids' in Southern California: The Educational Experience of Chinese Children in Transnational Families," *Educational Policy* 12 (1998): 682–704; Aihwa Ong, *Flexible Citizenship: The Cultural Logics of Transnationality* (Durham, NC: Duke University Press, 1999).

3. Jeff Yang, Dina Gan, and Terry Hong, *Eastern Standard Time: A Guide to Asian Influence on American Culture from Astro Boy to Zen Buddhism* (Boston: Houghton Mifflin Company, 1997).

4. Richard H. Robbins, *Global Problems and the Culture of Capitalism* (Boston: Allyn and Bacon, 2002), 119–122.

5. Roger Daniels, *Prisoners without Trial: Japanese Americans in World War II* (New York: Hill and Wang, 1993).

6. Masayo Duus, *Tokyo Rose: Orphan of the Pacific* (New York: Kodansha International, 1979); Russell Warren Howe, *The Hunt for "Tokyo Rose"* (Lanham, MD: Madison Books, 1990); Rex B. Gunn, *They Called Her Tokyo Rose* (Santa Monica, CA: n.p., 1985).

7. Nancy Abelmann and John Lie, *Blue Dreams: Korean Americans and the Los Angeles Riots* (Cambridge, MA: Harvard University Press, 1995), 20, 78; Amy Ling, "Introduction: What's in a Name?" in *Yellow Light: The Flowering of Asian American Arts* (Philadelphia: Temple University Press, 1999), 7; Parks M. Coble, *Chinese Capitalists in Japan's New Order: The Occupied Lower Yangtze, 1937–1945* (Berkeley: University of California Press, 2003), 205; Judy Yung, *Unbound Feet: A Social History of Chinese Women in San Francisco* (Berkeley: University of California Press, 1995), 239.

8. Linda Trinh Võ and Mary Yu Danico, "The Formation of Postsuburban Communities: The Impact of Immigration on American Institutions," *International Journal of Sociology and Social Policy* 24, no. 7/8 (2004): 15–45.

9. Cecilia W. Dugger, "India Offers Rights to Attract Its Offspring's Cash," *New York Times,* 4 April 1999, A4; Kamala Visweswaran and Ali Mir, "On the Politics of Community in South Asian-American Studies," *Amerasia Journal* 25 (1999/2000): 104.

10. Barbara Crossette, "Indian Starts a Campaign against Cash for Militants," *New York Times,* 16 August 2002, A8.

11. Tim Pfaff, *Hmong in America: Journey from a Secret War* (Eau Claire, WI: Chippewa Valley Museum Press, 1995), 74.

12. Michael Doyle, "Valley Leaders Split on U.S. Trade with Laos," *Fresno Bee,* 30 October 2003, C6.

13. Edward A. Gargan, "Though Sikh Rebellion Is Quelled, India's Punjab State Still Seethes," *New York Times,* 26 October 1993, A1, A4; John F. Burns, "The Sikhs Get Justice Long after a Massacre," *New York Times,* 16 September 1996, A4.

14. Ritu Sarin, *The New Puritans: The Sikhs of Yuba City* (San Francisco: Crosscurrent Media, 1985).

15. "Diasporas and Transnational Identities," http://www.ssc.uwo.ca/polysci/necrg/diaspora/.

16. Ibid.

SELECTED WORKS

Abelmann, Nancy, and John Lie. *Blue Dreams: Korean Americans and the Los Angeles Riots.* Cambridge, MA: Harvard University Press, 1995.

Burns, John F. "The Sikhs Get Justice Long after a Massacre." *New York Times,* 16 September 1996, A4.

Coble, Parks M. *Chinese Capitalists in Japan's New Order: The Occupied Lower Yangtze, 1937–1945.* Berkeley: University of California Press, 2003.

Crossette, Barbara. "Indian Starts a Campaign against Cash for Militants." *New York Times,* 16 August 2002, A8.

Daniels, Roger. *Prisoners without Trial: Japanese Americans in World War II.* New York: Hill and Wang, 1993.

Doyle, Michael. "Valley Leaders Split on U.S. Trade with Laos." *Fresno Bee,* 30 October 2003, C6.

Dugger, Cecilia W. "India Offers Rights to Attract Its Offspring's Cash." *New York Times,* 4 April 1999, A4.

Duus, Masayo. *Tokyo Rose: Orphan of the Pacific.* New York: Kodansha International, 1979.

Gargan, Edward A. "Though Sikh Rebellion Is Quelled, India's Punjab State Still Seethes." *New York Times,* 26 October 1993, A1, A4.

Gunn, Rex B. *They Called Her Tokyo Rose.* Santa Monica, CA: n.p., 1985.

Hirabayashi, Lane Ryo, Akemi Kikumura-Yano, and James A. Hirabayashi, eds. *New Worlds, New Lives: Globalization and People of Japanese Descent in the Americas and from Latin America in Japan.* Stanford: Stanford University Press, 2002.

Howe, Russell Warren. *The Hunt for "Tokyo Rose."* Lanham, MD: Madison Books, 1990.

Hu-DeHart, Evelyn. "Introduction: Asian American Formations in the Age of Globalization." In *Across the Pacific: Asian Americans and Globalization,* ed. Evelyn Hu-DeHart. Philadelphia: Temple University Press, 1999.

Jaret, Charles. "Troubled by Newcomers: Anti-Immigrant Attitudes and Actions during Two Eras of Mass Migration." In *Mass Migration to the United States: Classical and Contemporary Periods,* ed. Pyong Gap Min. Walnut Creek, CA: AltaMira Press, 2002.

Koehn, Peter H., and Xiao-huang Yin, eds. *The Expanding Roles of Chinese Americans in U.S.-China Relations: Transnational Networks and Trans-Pacific Interactions.* Armonk, NY: M.E. Sharpe, 2002.

Lessinger, Johanna. "Class, Race, and Success: Two Generations of Indian Americans Confront the American Dream." In *Migration, Transnationalization, and Race in a Changing New York,* ed. Héctor R. Cordero-Guzmán, Robert C. Smith, and Ramón Grosfoguel. Philadelphia: Temple University Press, 2001.

Ling, Amy. "Introduction: What's in a Name?" In *Yellow Light: The Flowering of Asian American Arts.* Philadelphia: Temple University Press, 1999.

MacDonald, Jeffery L. *Transnational Aspects of Iu-Mien Refugee Identity.* New York: Garland Publishing, 1997.

Okamura, Jonathan Y. *Imagining the Filipino American Diaspora: Transnational Relations, Identities, and Communities.* New York: Garland Publishing, 1998.

Ong, Aihwa. *Flexible Citizenship: The Cultural Logics of Transnationality.* Durham, NC: Duke University Press, 1999.

Parillo, Vincent N. *Strangers to These Shores: Race and Ethnic Relations in the United States.* Boston: Allyn and Bacon, 1997.

Park, Robert E. *Race and Culture.* Glencoe, IL: Free Press, 1949.

Pfaff, Tim. *Hmong in America: Journey from a Secret War.* Eau Claire, WI: Chippewa Valley Museum Press, 1995.

Sarin, Ritu. *The New Puritans: The Sikhs of Yuba City.* San Francisco: Crosscurrent Media, 1985.

Visweswaran, Kamala, and Ali Mir. "On the Politics of Community in South Asian-American Studies." *Amerasia Journal* 25 (1999/2000): 104.

Võ, Linda Trinh, and Mary Yu Danico. "The Formation of Postsuburban Communities: The Impact of Immigration on American Institutions" *International Journal of Sociology and Social Policy* 24, no. 7/8 (2004): 15–45.

Wang, L. Ling-chi. "The Structure of Dual Domination: Toward a Paradigm for the Study of the Chinese Diaspora in the U.S." *Amerasia Journal* 21 (1995): 149–169.

Wong, Sau-ling C. "Denationalization Reconsidered: Asian American Cultural Criticism at a Theoretical Crossroad." *Amerasia Journal* 21 (1995): 1–27.

Wu, Frank H., and Francey Lim Youngberg. "People from China Crossing the River: Asian American Political Empowerment and Foreign Influence." In *Asian*

Americans and Politics: Perspectives, Experiences, Prospects, ed. Gordon H. Chang. Stanford, CA: Stanford University Press, 2001.

Yang, Jeff, Dina Gan, and Terry Hong. *Eastern Standard Time: A Guide to Asian Influence on American Culture from Astro Boy to Zen Buddhism.* Boston: Houghton Mifflin Company, 1997.

Yung, Judy. *Unbound Feet: A Social History of Chinese Women in San Francisco.* Berkeley: University of California Press, 1995.

Zhou, Min. "'Parachute Kids' in Southern California: The Educational Experience of Chinese Children in Transnational Families." *Educational Policy* 12 (1998): 682–704.

6

ASIAN PACIFIC AMERICAN OR ASIAN AMERICAN PANETHNICITY

What does it mean to be an Asian American or part of the Asian American panethnicity? If one looks at race relations and racial categories in the United States, the term Asian American is a recent concept that developed out of the Asian American movement, which, in turn, grew out of the civil rights movement during the 1960s. Thus, in order to fully examine whether this concept in viable, desirable, or tenable, one must first look at the social, political, and historical transformation and construction of Asian American panethnicity, and how the population itself has changed dramatically since the 1970s.

BACKGROUND

Pan-Asian American ethnicity is the process of linking organizations and forging solidarities among different groups of Asians in the United States that have immigrant, refugee, or American-born backgrounds. The development of panethnicity among Asian Americans has a short history. For this reason, scholars and laypersons alike argue that Asian Americans are not a panethnic group because they do not share a common culture. This contrasts with other groups, like Native Americans, who have a common link through their unique relationship to the land. Panethnicity does not equate with affinity between groups, but rather it is an awareness of a shared history and a consciousness of being part of and being perceived as belonging to a larger Asian group. Asian Americans share in their history of oppression, exploitation, and discrimination. It is the socially defined racial distinctiveness of their imposed identity as Asians in the United States that has created a sense of Pan-Asian identity. What it means to be Asian American is very different from how one would define being Asian. Therefore, people of Asian descent have to construct what it means to be Asian American, something different from how they would define their own specific ethnic heritage. Through various social and political situations, Asian Americans have built their own distinct ethnic Asian culture as well as one that is Pan-Asian. People of Asian ancestry have played a vital role in the development of America since the early 1800s.[1] The need for cheap labor in the economic development of the United States led to the recruitment of Asian laborers from China, Japan, Korea, the Philippines, and South Asia, working as miners, railroad builders, farmers, factory workers, and fishermen. The Chinese represented 20 percent of California's labor force by 1870, even though they constituted only .002 percent of the entire U.S. population. By 1885, large numbers of young Japanese laborers, together with smaller numbers of Koreans and Indians, began arriving on the West Coast where they replaced the Chinese as cheap labor in building railroads, farming, and fishing. Once the Philippines were acquired by the United States after the Spanish-American War in 1898, Filipinos came to work in agriculture in Hawai'i and the West Coast. With their legal status as nationals, they could freely immigrate to the United States, unlike the Chinese and Japanese. The laborers from Asia were often pitted against each other due to their cultural and political differences. Ironically, while the Asian laborers were used to threaten each other, they were also perceived as economic threats to Whites.

While the Asian laborers came from very different cultures, they had similar experiences that shaped their shared identity in the United States. Throughout their history in America, Asian immigrants have endured racism, oppression, and institutional barriers barring them from actively participating in mainstream decision-making processes. The foreign miner's tax of 1852 was one of the first laws introduced to restrict equal participation and access to social mobility. This tax collected $3 a month from every foreign miner who did not desire (or was prohibited by law) to become a citizen. During this time, exemptions were given only to European immigrants. The main purpose of this tax was to reduce the number of Chinese immigrating to California and to discourage the Chinese from mining for gold. This was done although the Chinese did not pose a great threat to White miners since they usually worked deserted claims. Despite their not being a real threat to European Americans, the Chinese were seen as a group that was not welcome and not desirable for the United States.

The fear of Chinese reaching close to or equal status with Whites sparked a movement to keep the Chinese out of California and eventually out of the

United States. The Chinese Exclusion Act of 1882 surfaced as a result of perceived Chinese competition with American workers. A growing nativist movement brought pressure for restrictive action, which began with the Exclusion Act of May 6, 1882. Passed by the 47th Congress, this law suspended the immigration of Chinese laborers for ten years. It permitted those Chinese in the United States, as of November 17, 1880, to stay, travel abroad, and return. It also prohibited the naturalization of Chinese and created the Section 6 exempt status for teachers, students, merchants, and travelers. These exempt classes would be admitted upon presentation of a certificate from the Chinese government. However, unlike the Chinese, the Japanese, who immigrated later, were able to bring or sponsor their wives to the United States and Hawai'i.

The next significant exclusionary legislation was the Act to Prohibit the Coming of Chinese Persons into the United States of May 1892 (27 Stat. 25). Referred to as the Geary Act, it allowed Chinese laborers to travel to China and to reenter the United States, but its provisions were otherwise more restrictive than the preceding immigration laws. This act required the Chinese to register and secure a certificate as proof of their right to be in the United States. Imprisonment or deportation were the penalties for those who failed to have the required papers or witnesses.

The Chinese, however, were not the only group that was under the tight rein of U.S. immigration laws. The Japanese government protested to President Theodore Roosevelt when Japanese laborers were not allowed to leave their country legally until after 1884 when an agreement was signed between their government and Hawaiian sugar plantations. From Hawai'i, many Japanese moved to the U.S. mainland. By 1890, 2,038 Japanese resided in the United States. A systematic method of recruiting laborers from regions in Japan for Hawaiian sugar plantations was established. Natives from Hiroshima, Kumamoto, Yamaguchi, and Fukushima were recruited for their skills in agriculture, commitment to hard work, and willingness to travel. Japanese immigration continued until 1907 when agitation from White supremacist organizations, labor unions, and politicians resulted in a "Gentlemen's Agreement" curtailing the immigration of laborers from Japan. Under the Gentlemen's Agreement of 1907–1908, the Japanese government agreed to limit passports issued to Japanese in order to permit wives to enter the United States. Many thought the Gentlemen's Agreement would limit the number of Japanese laborers in the United States. Instead, however, the Japanese population increased as women, many as picture brides, came to the continental United States and Hawai'i.[2]

Beginning in 1909 and continuing until after World War II, anti-Japanese bills were introduced into the California legislature every year. The issue of

U.S. citizenship eventually was decided by the 1922 Supreme Court decision *Takao Ozawa v. United States,* which declared that Japanese immigrants were ineligible for U.S. citizenship. In 1790 Congress had made "Free white persons" eligible for citizenship. Due to some ambiguity about the term "White," some 420 Japanese had been naturalized, but a ruling by a U.S. attorney general to stop issuing papers to Japanese ended the practice in 1906. The Supreme Court ruled that since Takao Ozawa was neither a "free white person" nor an African by birth or descent, he did not have the right of naturalization as a Mongolian. A movement to totally exclude Japanese immigrants eventually led to the Immigration Act of 1924. That legislation curtailed most immigration from Japan until 1952, when 100 immigrants per year were allowed under the provisions of the McCarran-Walter Act. This included a number of Japanese wives of U.S. servicemen who came to this country in the years after the end of World War II.

South Asian Indian immigrants also entered the United States as laborers, following Chinese exclusion. Recruited initially by Canadian-Pacific railroad companies, a few thousand Sikh immigrants from the Punjab region immigrated to Canada, which, like India, was part of the British Empire. Later, many migrated into the Pacific Northwest and California, and became farm laborers. Ironically decried as a "Hindu invasion" by exclusionists and White labor, the "tide of the Turbans" was outlawed in 1917, when Congress declared that India was part of the Pacific-Barred Zone of excluded Asian countries. Efforts were also made to keep the children of Asian Americans away from White children. An amendment to the California State Political Code in 1921 established separate schools for Indian, Chinese, Japanese, or Mongolian children. Chinese, Japanese, and Filipino children in several school districts attended segregated schools until World War II. In 1945 a Japanese American family challenged the constitutionality of segregated schools, and the Los Angeles County Superior Court concurred that segregation on the basis of race or ancestry violated the 14th Amendment. The California legislature finally repealed the 1921 provision in 1947.

By 1924, with the exception of Filipino nationals, all Asian immigrants, including Chinese, Japanese, Koreans, and Indians were fully excluded by law and denied citizenship and naturalization. In some states, such as California, they were also prevented from marrying Caucasians or owning land. With all other Asians excluded, thousands of young, single Filipinos began migrating in large numbers to the West Coast during the 1920s to work in farms and canneries, filling the continuing need for cheap labor. The immigration laws did not legally exclude Filipinos, because the United States, as a result of the 1898 Spanish-American War, had annexed the Philippines. Racism and economic competition, intensified by the depression of 1929, however, led to severe anti-Filipino violence. This was followed by the passage of the Tydings-McDuffie Act of 1934, which placed an annual quota of fifty on Filipino migration. This ended the free migration of Filipinos to the United States, even as it promised independence for the Philippines in ten years.

Other restrictive immigration acts affecting citizens of Chinese ancestry followed. During World War II, when China and the United States were allies, President Franklin D. Roosevelt signed an Act to Repeal the Chinese Exclusion Acts, to Establish Quotas, and for Other Purposes (57 Stat. 600-1). This act of December 13, 1943, also lifted restrictions on naturalization for Chinese immigrants. While this act represented somewhat better treatment for the Chinese, the Japanese in the United States did not fare as well. The most serious discriminatory act toward Japanese Americans had been their internment during World War II from 1942 to 1945. Ten War Relocation Authority camps in several states were hastily established to hold Japanese Americans. The constitutionality of incarcerating more than 120,000 Japanese Americans is still questioned by legal historians and scholars of constitutional law. Some estimate that the losses by Japanese Americans were estimated to be at least $400,000,000 and only 10 percent of this amount was disbursed to former internees. It has been argued that there is no basis for the $400 million figure. What cannot be questioned, however, is that Japanese Americans suffered tremendous losses in property, earnings, and business. Moreover, the Japanese Americans had to endure discrimination in employment, housing, shopping, dining, and recreational activities. To underscore this point, when the remains of the highly decorated 442nd Regimental Combat Team were returned to the United States after World War II, they were refused gravesites in some cemeteries because of their ancestry. Despite the courage and heroism of this Japanese American regiment fighting in Italy and Germany for the United States, they still were not accepted as Americans by the public.

Due to the changing international relations, there were minor changes in immigration after World War II. This allowed for limited numbers of Asians to enter the United States. Nevertheless, these token quotas were so small that they were discriminatory. It was not until 1965, when, in response to the civil rights movement and the Cold War competition with the Soviet Union, that a nonrestrictive annual quota of up to 20,000 immigrants per country in the eastern hemisphere was established. For the first time in U.S. history, large numbers of Asians were able to come to the United States as families. In addition, due to the desire of the United States for competitiveness in technology and science during the Cold War, foreign engineers and scientists were also encouraged to emigrate to the United States. The dramatic changes in the Asian Pacific American landscape in recent decades, particularly with the explosive growth of new Filipino, Korean, South Asian Indian, and Chinese populations are rooted in the liberalization of immigration laws since 1965. The addition of Southeast Asian refugees after 1975 introduced further population growth among Asians in the United States.

In the 1960s, the civil rights movement triggered debates about equity and racial equality. However, while there was a great deal of rhetoric about fairness and the improvement of society, this contrasted with the discrimination experienced by persons of color. The divergence between what was said and what was practiced led to organized struggles against racism, sexism, poverty, war, and exploitation. These social and political struggles caused minority groups to realize that forming coalitions could better advance their interests. In particular, the Black Power movement sensitized minority groups to racial issues and set into motion the Yellow Power, Red Power, and Brown Power movements by Asian Americans, Native Americans, and Hispanic Americans. Furthermore, according to Robert Blauner, the success of anticolonial nationalist movements in Asia, Africa, and Latin America encouraged racial and cultural pride and created an environment for panethnic activism.[3]

As a result of the 1960s movements, ethnicity was institutionalized. This included the implementation of government mandated affirmative action programs designed to ensure minority representation in employment in public programs and in education. Government bureaucracies went on to categorize diverse racial and ethnic minority groups into the four umbrella categories: Blacks, Asian Americans, Hispanics, and Native Americans. In response, members of the different ethnic groups collectively worked to protect and to advance their interests. Thus, panethnic groups emerged as the result of political and social processes, rather than of cultural bonds. For Asian Americans, this movement helped to solidify the Asian American panethnicity, which places all Asian ethnic groups in the United States under one category. Under this model, some Asian American groups have made much progress toward having their voices heard. However, it is less certain how well issues pertaining to gender equality and the Southeast Asians have fared with Asian American panethnicity. While there has been an increasing discussion of Asian American issues, discussions about gender inequality and sexuality in Asian American communities is still lacking. Finally, some community members and activists will also argue that until recently, Pan-Asian issues have only included East Asian American issues, which has created difficulties for Southeast Asian Americans. For example, while the idea of Asian American solidarity is effective when getting issues heard, some would argue that the issues are not necessarily the same for all Asian Americans.

The concept of Asian American panethnicity operates on two general dimensions. One is at the conceptual dimension and relates to Pan-Asian American consciousness. This is linked to self-identification, Pan-Asian residential, friendship, and marriage patterns, and membership in pan-Asian organizations. The second dimension is the organizational one. This is the dimension that focuses on formal organizations and the factors that give institutional force to Pan-Asian consciousness. However, some argue that the strength of panethnicity in the marriage market varies between ethnic groups within the panethnic category.[4] One researcher found that there is a negative association between Filipino men and other Asian women, but a positive association for Chinese men and Filipina women.[5] Thus, even in the conceptual dimension, it is not quite clear whether panethnicity is applicable to all. Aside from marriage, social distance and friendship are other measures of the salience of Asian American panethnicity. Other researchers found that Vietnamese youth are more likely to engage in panethnic friendships, while Koreans and Japanese are the least panethnic in their friendship choices. Asian American panethnicity is less apparent in friendship choices among adolescents.[6]

Hence, whether Asian American panethnicity is viable, desirable, or tenable today is debatable. Scholars and community leaders would argue that panethnicity provides more power through numbers and that the commonality of experiences shared in the past is very similar to those experienced today by the newer Asian immigrants and refugees. However, others would argue that the panethnic label lumps all people of Asian ancestry under one umbrella, not recognizing the uniqueness of each group. These are some of the propositions to Asian American panethnicity that are being discussed:

1. Since the arrival of the post-1965 immigrant and refugee populations, it is desirable that there is a collective Pan-Asian American consciousness to address the needs of this new population.
2. Panethnicity promotes solidarity, especially in communities where Asian Americans are few. Asian groups are more likely to seek out each other for support and solidarity.
3. The struggles today are different versions of past struggles, and people of Asian descent can see the interconnections of this larger Pan-Asian American community.

DOES A COLLECTIVE PAN-ASIAN AMERICAN CONSCIOUSNESS HELP THE POST-1965 IMMIGRANT AND REFUGEE POPULATIONS?

For

Demographic and social changes have altered the meaning of Asian American panethnicity. A majority of Asians in America are now foreign-born. Many were not even in the United States during the protest era of the 1960s.

Neither they nor their children share a direct link to the Asian American movement of the 1960s and 1970s. As a result, their cultural, ethnic, class, and political differences have complicated the possibility for panethnic solidarity. If Asian America was once united on the basis of shared perspectives, there are now jumbles of distinct pieces tenuously held together.

Beginning in 1975, Southeast Asian refugees from Vietnam, Cambodia, and Laos have entered the United States. After escaping from war, social chaos, discrimination, and economic hardship, roughly one million Southeast Asians, including about 30,000 Amerasian children of American servicemen and their families, have entered the United States. Since then, through a variety of refugee resettlement and immigration programs, the Southeast Asians have tried to adjust to American society. But this is not easy, as the refugees from Vietnam, Cambodia, and Laos each have distinct cultures, languages, and contexts of historical development. Although each country shares certain influences from their common history as a French colonial territory for nearly a century until 1954, Vietnam is much more culturally influenced by China while Cambodia and Laos have been more influenced by India. Within each country, there are Chinese and other ethnic minority populations, such as the Hmong, Mien, and Kmhmu from Laos. The experiences of these groups as refugees differ significantly from the immigrant experience. However, as a result of the Asian American label and the institutionalized racism that lingers in most parts of the United States, policy makers, government officials, and average citizens cannot differentiate between someone who is Korean, Japanese, Laotian, or Vietnamese. Thus, the stereotype that all Asians look and act alike works against those who do not conform to the model minority image.

Examining past history, people of Asian ancestry have been pitted against each other at various times. For example, when the Chinese were seen as a threat and legally excluded from entering, the U.S. labor market looked for replacements from the Japanese, Koreans, Filipinos, and South Asians, respectively. It was only when these Asian groups recognized the shared experience of discrimination and racism that they banned together to become a more formidable force that could mobilize for better race relations and social equality. Asian immigrants coming after 1965 and refugees arriving after 1975 are bound to experience similar sentiments from others who see them as a threat or burden to the U.S. economy. Yet, for this same reason it is critical to include the new Asian groups in discussions that pertain to Asian Americans. A shared collective consciousness of being Pan-Asian will bring a louder voice to a group that is invisible in the landscape of U.S. race relations.

Furthermore, while Asian Americans who experienced the struggles of the 1960s and 1970s may see the new groups as outsiders, panethnicity is bound to increase between the first and second generations of Asian Americans. Panethnicity is more likely to occur among immigrants and refugees due to a shared experience of being treated as "Asians." But it is also due to language homogeneity, as virtually all Asian Americans who are second generation and beyond speak English as their primary or only language.[7] The shared experience of growing up in the United States is thought to foster Asian panethnicity.[8] In other words, while refugee and immigrant groups may feel disconnected from each other's experiences, the second- and third-generation Asian youths are more likely to encounter similar experiences growing up in the United States as Asian Americans.

Against

With the significant changes in the Immigration Act of 1965, which opened the door more widely for Asian immigration, the face of Asian America changed dramatically. Greater diversity and complexity were now introduced into the Asian American population. When the Asian American movement began in the 1960s, the major groups at the time were the Japanese and the Chinese. The Japanese were the largest group of Asian Americans in the United States in 1960, with a U.S. Census total of 464,332. The Chinese were second with 237,292, followed by the Filipinos with 176,310. By the time of the 1980 U.S. Census, the Chinese were the largest group with 812,178, the Filipinos ranked second with 781,894, and the Japanese followed in third place with 716,331.[9] Two decades later, in the 2000 U.S. Census, tallies were included for single-race and multiple-race affiliations. Using the combination, the Chinese led with 2,734,841 followed by the Filipinos with 2,364,815, with the Asian Indians ranking third at 1,899,599. Koreans were fourth with 1,228,427, the Vietnamese ranked fifth with 1,223,736, while the Japanese followed with 1,148,932. The effects of the refugee influx from the end of the Southeast Asian conflict were evident, as the Vietnamese had surpassed the Japanese. Cambodians numbered 206,052, the Laotians followed with 198,203, and the Hmong were listed at 186,310. The census also noted 204,309 Pakistani, 150,283 Thai, and 57,412 Bangladeshi. Smaller numbers for Indonesians, Malaysians, Sri Lankans, Burmese, Okinawans, Nepalese, and others were mentioned as well.[10]

Because of the legacy of exclusion, in the 1960s, two of the major Asian groups in the United States, the Japanese Americans and Chinese Americans, were primarily American-born in composition. In the decades that followed, only the Japanese Americans would be a population comprised of those who were mainly born in the United States. The other groups of Asian Americans, such as the Chinese, Filipinos, Koreans, Asian Indians, and Southeast Asians, were primarily foreign-born. (Due to the relatively small size of the American-born Chinese population, the arrival of larger numbers of new immigrants had changed the composition of the Chinese American community by 1980.) The majority in these populations was made up of immigrants and refugees who had scant knowledge of the history of Asians in the United States. They knew little about the legacy of discrimination, prejudice, and exclusion that had been directed against Asians in America in the past. As a result, the goals and objectives of the Asian American movement meant nothing to them. Moreover, coming from Asia and accustomed to their own cultures and heritages, many of the new immigrants and refugees were indifferent, if not in competition, with the other Asian American groups in the United States. The Chinese resented atrocities by Japan against China during World War II, while the Vietnamese harbored memories of attempts by China to rule Vietnam in the past. The Hmong, Laotians, and Cambodians remembered the invasion of their former homelands by Communist Vietnamese, while Asian Indians and Pakistani debated who should control Kashmir.

Without a tradition of interethnic cooperation among the new Asian immigrants and refugees, it is hard to see how Asian American panethnicity can be a reality. At the moment, attempts at Asian American cooperation are led by several activist groups, which are primarily Japanese American and Chinese American in composition. The key examples would be the Japanese American Citizens League (JACL) and the Organization of Chinese Americans (OCA). But the JACL is declining in membership, and Japanese Americans are becoming a smaller percentage of the Asian American population. Beyond these two organizations, many of the other ethnic activist organizations are really focused upon their own ethnicity and do not have much to say about Asian American panethnicity. Asian American panethnicity is thus more a dream and a hope than a reality. Moreover, the notion that Asian Americans should have a collective consciousness and solidarity, presumably because of some imagined primordial tie to Asia is dangerous. It leads to a stereotyping, or a racialization and essentializing, of Asian Americans, leading people to think that all Asian Americans are essentially the same.

DOES PANETHNICITY PROMOTE SOLIDARITY, ESPECIALLY IN COMMUNITIES WHERE ASIAN AMERICANS ARE FEW?

For

When discussing Asian American issues, those who think of multicultural communities like Los Angeles, Seattle, New York, Honolulu, and Chicago will argue that the large concentration of people of various Asian groups has created enclaves, ethnoburbs,[11] or post-suburban neighborhoods.[12] However, since the beginning of Asian immigration, laws and policies have placed and displaced people of Asian ancestry all across the continental United States. While areas like Hawai'i have managed to fuse the diverse cultures of Asia into the local culture, other states have maintained a distinct and separate Asian business community. San Francisco's Chinatown and Japantown started off with predominantly Chinese- and Japanese-owned and run businesses catering to those specific ethnic groups. But with time, the clientele and the businesses have become more Pan-Asian with Korean, Vietnamese, and Thai businesses and restaurants popping up in these ethnic specific enclaves. Some would argue that across the United States, Chinatowns have changed with the increasing numbers of Vietnamese restaurants and stores that are sandwiched in between the Chinese businesses. Still, in these communities, there are distinct markers for the ethnic businesses that one is patronizing. For when one goes into more rural areas or areas that are not heavily populated by Asian Americans, one sees fewer ethnic-specific businesses, and the stores instead sell a wide array of Asian foods or products from a variety of different groups. The attempt at mass appeal to several Asian American groups simultaneously is a response to the limited number of Asian clientele that do not constitute a sizable minority, let alone a majority, in an area. This is the case in areas like Florida or New Mexico, where there are only a small number of Asian groups represented in the population. As a result, they are more likely to associate with each other. Panethnicity thus includes both the willingness to cross ethnic boundaries, and the desire to stay within racial boundaries.

When there are a limited number of Asian Americans in a particular geographical area, there is a higher likelihood that a Pan-Asian American identity surfaces. At universities on the West Coast, where there are large concentrations of Asian American students from diverse backgrounds, other Asian Americans are not as noticeable. In fact, the more there are of a specific ethnic group, the less likely it is that one will seek out one's own ethnic group. In a recent study of adolescent friendship, it was concluded "that interethnic and interracial friendships occur most often among youth who are in settings with few members of their own ethnic group."[13] Thus, those who do not have ethnic options or choices in their communities will align themselves with those with whom they have the most shared interests or experiences. For those Asian Americans who live in areas with few members of their own group, college becomes a focal point in their lives when they realize their Pan-Asian American identity. College therefore provides a space for Asian Americans to come into contact with other Asian Americans who have similar experiences, thus increasing their panethnicity.[14]

Against

Ask people to mention places where there are large Asian American communities, and their responses probably will include the states of Hawai'i, California, and New York. But those three states or their cities of Honolulu, San Francisco, Los Angeles, and New York do not constitute the total picture of Asian America. In the years since the important Immigration Act of 1965, Asian Americans, both natives and foreign-born, have been building new communities outside of the traditional areas of concentration, the West Coast and the East Coast. Today there are many who live in the Midwest, and that is not only Chicago. The Midwest has increasing numbers of Asian Americans who are of East Asian, South Asian, and Southeast Asian descent. Beyond the Japanese and Chinese, the Asian Americans in the Midwest include Asian Indians, Koreans, Filipinos, Asian Indians, Hmong, and other Southeast Asians. In the South, larger numbers of Asian Indians and Southeast Asians, such as Vietnamese, are becoming residents of the Sunbelt states. In general, most regions of the United States are seeing an increase and diversity in the population of Asian Americans who are living there.[15]

But this wider distribution of Asian Americans in other parts of the United States does not necessarily mean that there will be a strengthening of Asian American panethnicity. While these Asian Americans are appearing in regions of the country where there are smaller concentrations of them, this does not mean that there will be more coalition-building or cross-ethnic alliances. True, these Asian Americans will be relegated to the role of being a minority. But minorities do not forge alliances just because they are minorities. The idea of Asian American panethnicity, forging links with other Asian American ethnic groups, is difficult and requires considerable effort to make it work. It is not something that is natural and inevitable. Because Asian Americans are so diverse, it is not obvious that they have common concerns. For example, why should South Asian Americans make common cause with East Asian Americans? South Asian values and history are different from that of East Asia. A Pakistani American is very different from a Japanese American. The former is likely to be a Muslim, while the latter may be a Christian or a Buddhist. The former is likely to be an immigrant, while the latter may be of the third or fourth generation in America. Even within the major regional groupings of Asian Americans—those from East Asia, South Asia, and Southeast Asia, there can be vast differences. For instance, Vietnamese Americans may be Buddhist or Catholic in their religious affiliation. On the other hand, Hmong Americans are likely to be practicing shamanism unless they have converted to Christianity. Within the Asian Indian American community alone, the religious affiliations can be Sikh, Hindu, Muslim, Jain, or Christian.

Beyond the religious differences, there is linguistic diversity as the new Indian immigrants no longer come primarily from the Punjab as in the early part of the twentieth century. How much does a Filipino American know about the cultural and religious background of a Cambodian American and vice versa? Asians in America can claim that they or their ancestors were originally from Asia but that does not in itself help to promote Asian American panethnicity.

DO STRUGGLES TODAY HAVE LINKS WITH PAST STRUGGLES, AND CAN ASIAN AMERICANS SEE THE PAN-ASIAN CONNECTIONS?

For

While there are stark differences between the new refugee populations and the old Asian immigrant groups of the past, there are many cases that link the present to the past. The experiences of personal struggle, economic contribution, racial harassment, and discriminatory legislation targeting Vietnamese fishermen in California's Monterey Bay during the 1980s, for example, are almost identical to those of earlier generations of Japanese and Chinese fishermen who successively fished in Monterey Bay during the late 1800s and early 1900s. The similarities do not end there. The stereotypes of the "yellow peril" or perpetual foreigner have lingered and permeated the U.S. landscape. Regardless of how many generations a Chinese American may have been in the states, he or she may still be seen as an outsider and not as an American. Thus, for those Asian Americans who have internalized racism, they may in turn discriminate against other new Asian immigrants and refugees. These Asian Americans, who are examples of ethnic misidentification, focus on the inability of new immigrants and refugees to speak English, adapt to western pop culture, or the mere fact that they appear to be "FOBs" (Fresh off the Boat). Ironically, these sentiments are identical to those that were expressed by the dominant groups in American society since the eighteenth century. In fact, people of Asian ancestry have had to deal with not only the stereotypes that have stigmatized them, but they have also faced discriminatory actions in relation to jobs, education, and housing. The elements of self-identification, cultural commonality, shared fate, and special interest group participation are important catalysts for Asian American panethnicity. When people of Asian ancestry begin to examine their history, as well as contemporary issues facing Asian Americans today, they will see how the past and the present are connected through the persistent mistreatment and dismissal of the role of Asian Americans in the development of the United States.

Since the terrorist attacks of September 11, 2001, or "9/11," as it is popularly called, there has been an increase in hate crimes against South Asians,

Arabs, and anyone who "looks" like a terrorist. It is difficult to miss the similarities of how Japanese Americans were treated after the bombing of Pearl Harbor. It is similar to how the Arabs, South Asians, Muslims, and Sikh Americans have been treated since the attacks on the World Trade Center and the Pentagon. It may cause one to wonder if the lessons of the past have been lost upon the people of the present. Former Japanese internees have warned against the scapegoating of the innocent members of these stereotyped groups. Yet, these comments notwithstanding, there have been numerous instances of the detainment of Muslims, Arabs, Middle Easterners, South Asians, and others by the Immigration and Naturalization Service (INS) for the sake of national security. Most of those who knew that they were considered to be suspects have gone into the INS offices voluntarily and offered their cooperation. Their fate, however, was only to be tied up in the judicial system and sometimes wound up spending months in jail. Such detainment of these groups is not far from the internment of Japanese Americans during World War II. Although the numbers are smaller for the alleged 9/11 terrorist suspects, nevertheless, the rationale and justification are alarmingly similar. Furthermore, racial profiling has been legitimized again for the sake of security, similar to how Japanese and Chinese were caricatured in the late nineteenth and early twentieth centuries. This type of stereotyping was repeated by the U.S. government during World War II to show the public how to differentiate between the enemy Japanese and the docile Chinese. The message was that to be White was to be a "real American," and this is a struggle that Asian Americans continue to face in the new millennium. Pan-Asian American identity, therefore, is not constrained by nationalism to Asian countries, but rather by shared experiences here that shape what it means to be Asian American in the United States. This creates a panethnic solidarity that continues to strengthen the effort of Asian American communities to attain equality.

Against

The Asian American movement was conceived in struggle. In a time of political turmoil and social change, Asians in the United States made common cause with other minority groups and fought to change their minority status. They were able to get governmental agencies and the public to discard the term "Oriental" for "Asian American," and they promoted a greater awareness of the presence of Asian Americans in the United States. But it is not the sixties anymore.[16] The climate of America has changed, and the Vietnam era and civil rights era of the 1960s is a distant past. Gains have been registered, and changes have taken place.

Representatives from the National Asian Pacific Legal consortium, National Federation of Filipino American Association, and the Philippine American Foundation come together in 1999 to express grief and outrage over the death of a Filipino American by a White supremacist. AP/Wide World Photos.

But to maintain the idea of Asian American panethnicity, a goal of the Asian American movement, is a difficult challenge. One commentator mentions that Asian American panethnicity is tantamount to "constructing a community that (almost) cannot be."[17] It is a collective consciousness that should not be. She lists a variety of roadblocks that should hamper Asian American coalition-building. The mosaic of Asians in America does not share the same immigration experience, they have different lengths of history in this country, and they have diverse ethnic and racial origins. They have a variety of different home languages, their English language proficiency is dissimilar, they subscribe to different religions, and they belong to different socioeconomic classes. They are aware of homeland tensions, frictions between Asian neighbors, and there have been few cases of actual interethnic coalition-building. Finally, when the Asian American movement took place in the 1960s and 1970s, it was confined to a very small constituency, which others might say were predominantly Americans of Japanese and Chinese ancestry, with smaller numbers of Filipinos and Koreans. Asian America, with its Pan-Asian American consciousness, is really an imaginary community yet to be constructed.

Some have suggested that it is continuing discrimination and prejudice that has mobilized Asian Americans into accepting Asian American panethnicity. Certainly, the tragic death of Vincent Chin and other individuals alerted Asian Americans to the need for collective Asian American action, an Asian American panethnicity to address the discrimination and prejudice that still targets Asians in the United States. Vincent Chin was a Chinese American who was mistaken for a Japanese and killed in Detroit in 1982, during a period of Japan-bashing in the United States. Some Americans had felt that Japan had been unfairly taking jobs away from the automobile industry and other manufacturing sectors in the United States through unfair competition.[18] Other Asians who have met tragic deaths include Navroze Mody and Jim Ming Hai Loo. Mody was a South Asian who was senselessly killed by several youth in Hoboken, New Jersey, in 1987. Loo, a college student, was killed by two men in Raleigh, North Carolina in 1989.[19] But, a few years later, aside from Asian American activists, probably few Asian Americans know about Vincent Chin, Navroze Mody, and Jim Ming Hai Loo. While prejudice and discrimination, especially anti-Asian violence and hate crimes, should always be resisted, much more is needed to cement a firm foundation for Asian American panethnicity. Much more interethnic and intercultural communication needs to take place among the different Asian American populations before a true Asian American panethnicity can be realized.

QUESTIONS

1. How did people of Asian ancestry become Asian American? What were the social, political, and cultural factors that helped to create a Pan-Asian American ethnicity?

2. What do Asian Americans today have in common with Asian Americans in the past? Were social situations better or worse for people of Asian ancestry in the past or are racial barriers just as bad today?

3. Since the civil rights movement, has the situation improved for Asian Americans or remained the same? Are there differences for the Asian Americans who are immigrants versus those who are born in the United States?

4. Does Pan-Asian American ethnicity reflect the needs of all the people of Asian descent? How about those who were displaced or fled their homes because of political turmoil? How can Pan-Asian American ethnicity reflect the needs of diverse Asian American groups?

5. Is Pan-Asian American ethnicity only viable when it comes to transforming the political landscape of the country, or is it also helpful when addressing the cultural changes that occur in everyday life?

6. What was the significance of the 1960s for Asian American panethnicity? How was ethnicity institutionalized during this time?

7. Does Asian American panethnicity exist at the levels of consciousness, organization, or social interaction? Explain.

8. Is the potential for Asian American panethnicity different among those who are foreign-born versus those who are American-born? Why or why not?

9. Might joining together in the labor market help to mobilize for social equality and better race relations? Why or why not?

10. Does the size of the Asian American population have an effect upon the likelihood of developing a sense of Asian American panethnicity? For example, is it more likely to be supported in a community with a smaller or larger population of Asian Americans?

11. Does Asian American panethnicity rely upon religious, cultural, or linguistic ties? Why or why not?

12. Is Asian American panethnicity today largely a response to discrimination or stereotypes?

13. Can a collective response against discrimination, stereotyping, or hate crimes provide a firm foundation for Asian American panethnicity?

14. Are the different Asian American groups facing the same degree of discrimination? Might this affect their willingness to join in a Pan-Asian American coalition? Explain.

15. Have Asian Americans forged ties with other groups in American society that have experienced discrimination and racism? Why or why not?

16. Who are Vincent Chin, Navroze Mody, and Jim Ming Hai Loo? Of the Asian Americans that you know, how many of them can identify these individuals?

NOTES

1. In fact, documents record Asian immigration starting as early as the late 1700s (*Asian American Experience in the U.S.: A Chronological History: 1763–1992.* Chronology adapted from LEAP [Leadership Education for Asian Pacific]). The year 1763 marks the first recorded settlement of Filipinos in America. They escaped imprisonment aboard Spanish galleons by jumping ship in New Orleans and fleeing into the bayous. The year 1790 marks the first recorded arrival of an Asian Indian in the United States.

2. Based on the arranged marriage system of Japan and Korea, women exchanged photos with prospective husbands in the United States, had their names entered in the husbands' family registers, and then applied for a passport to join husbands they had never met.

3. Robert A. Blauner, *Racial Oppression in America* (New York: Harper, 1972).

4. Yen Le Espiritu, *Asian American Panethnicity: Bridging Institutions and Identities* (Philadelphia: Temple University Press, 1992).

5. Michael J. Rosenfeld, "The Salience of Pan-National Hispanic and Asian Identities, in U.S. Marriage Markets," *Demography* 38 (2001): 161–175.

6. Grace Kao and Kara Joyner, "Does Race and Ethnicity Matter between Friends? Activities among Interracial, Interethnic, and Intraethnic Adolescent Friends," *Sociological Quarterly* 45, no. 3 (2004): Forthcoming.

7. Alejandro Portes and Rubén Rumbaut, *Immigrant America* (Berkeley: University of California Press, 1996).

8. Zhenchao Qian, Sampson Lee Blair, and Stacey D. Ruf, "Asian American Interracial and Interethnic Marriages: Differences by Education and Nativity," *International Migration Review* 35, no. 1 (2001): 225–247; Larry Hajime Shinagawa and Gin Yong Pang, "Asian American Panethnicity and Intermarriage," *Amerasia Journal* 22, no. 2 (1996): 127–152.

9. Robert W. Gardner, Bryant Robey, and Peter C. Smith, "Asian Americans: Growth, Change, and Diversity," *Population Bulletin* 40 (October 1985): 8.

10. Kimiko Kelly and Daniel Kikuo Ichinose, *Demographic Profile of Asian and Pacific Islanders in Southern California: Census 2000* (Los Angeles: Asian Pacific American Legal Center), 5.

11. Timothy P. Fong, *The Contemporary Asian American Experience: Beyond the Model Minority* (Englewood Cliffs, NJ: Prentice Hall, 1998).

12. Mary Yu Danico and Linda Võ, "'No Lattés Here': Asian American Youth and the Cyber Café Obsession," in *Asian American Youth: Culture, Identity, and Ethnicity*, ed. Min Zhou and Jennifer Lee (New York: Routledge Press, 2004).

13. Grace Kao and Kara Joyner, "Do Hispanic and Asian Adolescents Practice Panethnicity in Friendship Choices?" (presented at 2001 annual meeting of the American Sociological Association, Anaheim, CA, http://people.mw.mediaone.net/drharris1/kaojoyner.pdf).

14. Qian, Blair, and Ruf, "Asian American Interracial and Interethnic Marriages," 557–586.

15. Eric Lai and Dennis Arguelles, eds., *The New Face of Asian Pacific America* (San Francisco and Los Angeles: AsianWeek and UCLA Asian American Studies Center Press, 2003), 122–181.

16. Michael Omi, "It Just Ain't the Sixties No More: The Contemporary Dilemmas of Asian American Studies," in *Reflections on Shattered Windows: Promises and Prospects for Asian American Studies*, ed. Gary Y. Okihiro et al. (Pullman: Washington State University Press, 1988), 31–36.

17. Pei-te Lien, *The Making of Asian America through Political Participation* (Philadelphia: Temple University Press, 2001), 42, 48–50.

18. Helen Zia, *Asian American Dreams: The Emergence of an American People* (New York: Farrar, Straus and Giroux, 2000), 58–61.

19. Ibid., 90–92.

SELECTED WORKS

Aguilar-San Juan, Karin. "Creating Ethnic Places: Vietnamese American Community-Building in Orange County and Boston." Ph.D. thesis. Providence, RI: Brown University, 2002.

Baron, Debra. "Who Are the Pacific Islanders?" In *The Asian American Almanac*, ed. Susan Gall and Irene Natividad. Detroit: Gale Research, 1995.

Bennett, Claudette. "Racial Categories Used in the Decennial Censuses, 1790 to the Present." *Government Information Quarterly* 17, no. 2 (2000): 161–180.

Blauner, Robert A. *Racial Oppression in America*. New York: Harper, 1972.

Brody, Jeffrey. "Garden Grove Seeks to Ring up Business, Tourists for Little Seoul." *The Orange County Register,* 29 September 1986, B1, B3.

Chan, Sucheng. *Asian Americans: An Interpretive History.* Boston: Twayne Publishers, 1991.

Chang, Edward Taehan. "An Emerging Minority Seeks a Role in a Changing America." *Los Angeles Times,* 31 May 1994, B9.

Danico, Mary Yu, and Linda Trinh Võ. "'No Lattés Here': Asian American Youth and the Cyber Café Obsession." In *Asian American Youth Culture, Identity, and Ethnicity,* ed. Min Zhou and Jennifer Lee. New York: Routledge Press, 2004.

Espiritu, Yen Le. *Asian American Panethnicity: Bridging Institutions and Identities.* Philadelphia: Temple University Press, 1992.

———. *Filipino American Lives.* Philadelphia: Temple University Press, 1995.

Fong, Timothy. *The First Suburban Chinatown: The Remaking of Monterey Park, California.* Philadelphia: Temple University Press, 1994.

———. *The Contemporary Asian American Experience: Beyond the Model Minority.* Englewood Cliffs, NJ: Prentice Hall, 1998.

Gardner, Robert W., Bryant Robey, and Peter C. Smith. "Asian Americans: Growth, Change, and Diversity." *Population Bulletin* 40 (October 1985): 8.

Horton, John. *The Politics of Diversity: Immigration, Resistance, and Change in Monterey Park, California.* Philadelphia: Temple University Press, 1995.

Hum, Tarry. "The Promises and Dilemmas of Immigrant Ethnic Economies." In *Asian and Latino Immigrants in a Restructuring Economy: The Metamorphosis of Southern California,* ed. Marta Lopez-Garza and David R. Diaz. Stanford, CA: Stanford University Press, 2001.

Kao, Grace, and Kara Joyner. "Does Race and Ethnicity Matter between Friends? Activities among Interracial, Interethnic, and Intraethnic Adolescent Friends." *Sociological Quarterly* 45, no. 3 (2004): Forthcoming.

Kelly, Kimiko, and Daniel Kikuo Ichinose. *Demographic Profile of Asian and Pacific Islanders in Southern California: Census 2000.* Los Angeles: Asian Pacific American Legal Center, 5.

Kwong, Peter. *The New Chinatown.* New York: Hill Wang, 1987.

Lai, Eric, and Dennis Arguelles, eds. *The New Face of Asian Pacific America.* San Francisco and Los Angeles: AsianWeek and UCLA Asian American Studies Center Press, 2003, 122–181.

Li, Wei. "Anatomy of a New Ethnic Settlement: The Chinese Ethnoburb in Los Angeles." *Urban Studies* 35, no. 3 (1998): 479–502.

Lien, Pei-te. *The Making of Asian America through Political Participation.* Philadelphia: Temple University Press, 2001.

Lin, Jan. *Reconstructing Chinatown: Ethnic Enclave, Global Change.* Minneapolis: University of Minnesota Press, 1998.

Mangiafico, Luciano. *Contemporary Asian American Immigrants: Patterns of Filipino, Korean, and Chinese Settlement in the United States.* New York: Praeger, 1988.

Ng, Franklin, and John Wilson. *The Asian American Encyclopedia.* Volumes 2–5. Philippines, Republic of the U.S.–China Relations. New York: Marshall Cavendish, 1995.

Omi, Michael. "It Just Ain't the Sixties No More: The Contemporary Dilemmas of Asian American Studies." In *Reflections on Shattered Windows: Promises and Prospects for Asian American Studies,* ed. Gary Y. Okihiro, 31–36. Pullman: Washington State University Press, 1988.

Patterson, Wayne. *The Korean Frontier in America: Immigration to Hawai'i, 1896–1910.* Honolulu: University of Hawai'i Press, 1988.

Portes, Alejandro, and Rubén Rumbaut. *Immigrant America*. Berkeley: University of California Press, 1996.

Qian, Zhenchao. "Breaking the Racial Barriers: Variations in Interracial Marriage between 1980 and 1990." *Demography* 34, no. 2 (1997): 263–276.

Qian, Zhenchao, Sampson Lee Blair, and Stacey D. Ruf. "Asian American Interracial and Interethnic Marriages: Differences by Education and Nativity." *International Migration Review* 35, no. 1 (2001).

Rosenfeld, Michael J. "The Salience of Pan-National Hispanic and Asian Identities, in U.S. Marriage Markets," *Demography* 38 (2001): 161–175.

Saito, Leland. *Race and Politics: Asian Americans, Latinos, and Whites in a Los Angeles Suburb*. Chicago: University of Illinois Press, 1998.

Shinagawa, Larry H., and Gin Yong Pang. "Asian American Panethnicity and Intermarriage." *Amerasia Journal* 22, no. 2 (1996): 127–152.

Võ, Linda Trinh. "A Community in Transition: Little Saigon." In *The New Face of Asian Pacific America: Numbers, Diversity & Change in the 21st Century*, ed. Eric Lai and Dennis Arguelles, 126–127. Los Angeles: AsianWeek and UCLA Asian American Studies Center, 2003.

Võ, Linda Trinh, and Mary Yu Danico. "The Formation of Post-Suburban Communities: Little Saigon and Koreatown, Orange County." *The Impact of Immigrants on American Institutions: International Journal of Sociology and Social Policy* 24, no. 7 (2004): 15–45, guest ed. Prema Kurien.

Wong, Morrison G. "Chinese Americans." In *Asian Americans: Contemporary Trends and Issues*, ed. Pyong Gap Min. Thousand Oaks, CA: Sage Publications, 1995.

Yu, Eui-Young. "Korean Communities in America: Past, Present, and Future," *Amerasia Journal* 10, no. 2 (1983): 23–35.

———. *Korean Community Profile*. Los Angeles: Korea Times, 1990, 9–10.

———. "Koreatown in Los Angeles: Emergence of a New Inner-City Ethnic Community." *Bulletin of the Population and Development Studies Center* 14 (1985): 37.

Zhou, Min. *Chinatown: The Socioeconomic Potential of an Urban Enclave*. Philadelphia: Temple University Press, 1992.

Zia, Helen. *Asian American Dreams: The Emergence of an American People*. New York: Farrar, Straus and Giroux, 2000, 58–61.

7

ASIAN AMERICAN STEREOTYPES

Stereotypes about ethnic groups are not new phenomena. In fact, every ethnic group has a stereotype imposed on them that has shaped how others perceive them. A stereotype is an exaggerated belief, image, or distorted truth about a person or group. It is a generalization that allows for little or no individual differences or social variation. Stereotypes are based on images passed on by the media, or beliefs and attitudes passed on by parents, peers, and other members of society. Some would argue that stereotypes could be both positive and negative. Regardless of how one views the impact of stereotypes on ethnic groups, stereotypes affect individual judgments about other groups.

BACKGROUND

Since people of Asian ancestry began to migrate to the United States, there have been numerous stereotypes about them that have lingered to this day. From the yellow peril to the model minority, the media has played a significant role in creating images of Asian Americans for the larger society to digest. The constructed images of Asian Americans vary, however, which helps situate Asian American men and women differently in non-Asian eyes. Asian American men have been portrayed as the foreigner in our midst, threatening our economic survival, who dutifully works for people, who threatens the national security of the United States, and who has mastered the martial arts. Above all, Asian men have been portrayed as having no emotions and as asexual, almost femalelike. They are not seen as a threat to White men, indeed, they are seen as inferior to White men in every way. Asian women, however, have been portrayed as desirable mates to White men, who unlike "American" or White women, are dutiful, obedient, and sexually accessible. The objectification of Asian women comes in the shape of mystery, desirability, and sacrifice.

One of the first stereotypes that emerged about Asian American men began in the 1800s with the flow of Chinese migrant workers as the foreign sojourners. According to one source, "When Asian immigrants appeared in newspapers and magazines in the 1900's, they were depicted with slanted eyes, buck teeth and yellow skin."[1] The emphasis at the time was clearly on what was foreign about them, marking them as unassimilable. The "otherness" of the Chinese laborers, the quality of being distinct or different from that otherwise experienced or known, was created by the media and the government and led to larger societal perceptions of Chinese men as those who were only interested in their own people. They were seen as unwilling to adapt to "American" culture, and as perpetual outsiders who would only deplete the resources for the real Americans and eliminate jobs only to divert them to China. This perception of an economic threat contributed greatly to the anti-Asian sentiment that led to the passage of the 1882 Chinese Exclusion Act. Public sentiments during this time affected how Chinese men were presented in contemporary newspapers and in movies that were produced later. It has been stated that "culturally biased perceptions of the Chinese as uniquely non-Western in dress, language, religion, customs, and eating habits determined that the Chinese were inferior."[2]

While Asian men were perceived as inferior beings due to their "foreignness," they were also seen as the docile and reliable servant who unconditionally worked for their White masters in a surrogate female role. Around the 1920s, brief sightings of the beginning of this stereotype can be found in *Son of Kong* (1933), *San Francisco* (1936), and *The Painted Veil* (1934). The first is a sequel to the famous *King Kong* where Victor Wong plays the loyal servant in coolie attire, who steals guns from the enemy and rows the boat while his White boss stands handsome and helpless. His boss shows his gratitude by saying "Good boy, Charlie."

Public perception of Asians as being foreigners comes in different shapes. During times of war, Asians are seen as the foreign enemy. Many theorists have noted the abundance of films made during times of war that completely vilified the enemy. Films of World War I and II clearly "had a propagandist as well as an entertainment mission," which led them to paint the Americans as good and the other as bad.[3] In terms of war stereotypes, Hollywood representations of Germans, especially the Nazis, may be the most prevalent.

These villains can be recognized by their "German-sounding names or German-style uniforms."[4] For example, in movies, books, or news stories about the Nazis, there were the evil Nazis who brutalized groups of people, but there were also the "good" Germans who provided their homes as safe havens for the displaced groups during the Nazi regime. However, war images of the Japanese were one-dimensional for they were depicted as merciless, cruel, and insensitive military men who were brutal to their captives and cold to the women. The overwhelming negativity with which the Japanese were portrayed had very real consequences. There was little fear and no discussion of the loyalty of people of German descent during World War II. However, the fear of Asian disloyalty and treachery led to President Franklin Roosevelt's Executive Order 9066, which resulted in the internment of thousands of Japanese Americans and their families.

During and after the war, various stereotypes of Asians surfaced. Not only did they all look alike, but they were also identical in their culture, thinking, and behavior. Rather than acknowledging the differences between Asian cultures, American versions of Asians often borrowed haphazardly from all cultures. Even decades later, the situation remained the same. As Renee Tajima comments, "All of the dozens of Asian and Pacific Island cultures are lumped into one homogenous identity, thus Korean and Vietnamese women in the 1950s–70s are commonly called Mama-San despite the Japanese (American) origins of that term."[5] There are some parallels to an earlier female Chinese character that appeared in *Broken Blossoms* (1919). Asian women were prone to be committing hari-kari and were randomly associated with Buddhism, which all Asians were supposed to believe. In the end, the image of both the Chinese and Japanese in the media depended more on the mind-set and perceptions of the dominant Caucasian population of the United States than upon the characteristic behavior or attitudes of either immigrant group."[6]

During the post-1965 era, with the influx of Asian immigrants and refugees, the perceptions of all Asians being the same basically continued. The stereotype of Asians as the model minority surfaced to extol the successes of East Asian immigrants who had made it economically and had for the most part assimilated into the American way of life. The model minority stereotype was highlighted to some extent in the print medium, such as *Newsweek*'s article on "Whiz Kids." However, the movies seized upon this stereotype to devise television programs for comedic relief. As an example, the few Asian Americans who were visible in the movies or on television were often portrayed as nerds or math geeks who had no social skills. They only related to their parents and to school, and they studied all the time to make their family proud. On occasion there were also the stereotypes of Asian boys on the other spectrum, being depicted as gang members who tormented their communities. These gang members are not seen as Asian Americans but rather portrayed as the "Chinese" gang or the "Vietnamese gang" that deals with drugs, harasses storefront owners, and creates havoc in their communities. Thus these gang members are seen as foreigners and not really Asian Americans. In the late 1970s, the Dragon Restaurant in San Francisco's Chinatown fell victim to the violence of a notorious Chinese gang, and in the early 1990s, a Vietnamese gang held Sacramento's Circuit City patrons hostage. While the media has reported these incidents, crimes committed by Asian American gangs are not generally reported as much as African American or Latino gang-related incidents. On the other hand, success stories of African Americans and Latinos are not reported in the media as much as the successes of the Asian American model minorities.

Stereotypes are not only perpetuated in the print media and movies. Most recently, late night talk show hosts and politicians have also been perpetuating negative Asian stereotypes. For example, Jay Leno was under siege for his comments about Koreans eating dogs. Representative Howard Coble, 6th District of North Carolina, who chairs the Judiciary Subcommittee on Crime, Terrorism and Homeland Security, said in an interview on WKZL-FM's "Murphy in the Morning" show on February 4, 2003, that he agreed with Franklin D. Roosevelt's decision to intern Japanese Americans during World War II. Furthermore, Asian American leaders have also been under attack for their alleged lack of loyalty to America. The question of disloyalty continues to haunt Asian Americans to this day. Wen Ho Lee, a scientist for the Los Alamos National Laboratory, spurred widespread suspicions about his being a Chinese scientist who allegedly was stealing information out of his office. After serving nine months in jail, Lee pled guilty to mishandling sensitive materials, but he was found innocent of espionage. The FBI eventually announced that there was not enough information to prosecute Lee of espionage at the Los Alamos National Laboratory. Most recently, Katrina Leung, a Chinese socialite who lives in prestigious San Marino, California, has been indicted for allegedly serving as a double agent for the FBI and the Chinese. While no trial has been conducted, she has already been described as a spy who uses sex to lure men in secured positions to gain access to top-secret information while financially profiting from both countries by being on their payrolls. But it is not just Chinese Americans. Since September 11, 2001, Arab Americans, Muslims, Sikhs, and South Asians have been under suspicion regarding their loyalty and have consequently been under the close scrutiny of the Immigration and Naturalization Service, and the Department of Homeland Security.

There have been, however, attempts to challenge the one-dimensional look of Asian Americans in the media. After the 1992 Los Angeles uprising, *Late*

Protestors outside Abercrombie & Fitch in San Francisco in 2002 showing T-shirts from the store that depict stereotypes of Asians. AP/Wide World Photos.

Night interviewed Angela Oh, a Korean American attorney in Los Angeles. Oh spoke about the racial climate in Los Angeles and the quality of the media coverage on the "Black-Korean conflict." The public was amazed at how Americanized she was. In fact, she was one of the first Korean Americans interviewed who did not have a Korean accent. Her poise and fluency in English as an educated professional helped to alter perceptions about how the public viewed Korean Americans and Asian Americans in general. The independent films have also put forth the voices of Asian Americans from an Asian American perspective. In Hollywood, Filipino filmmakers brought *American Adobo, Flip Side,* and *The Debut* into mainstream theatres, showing the complexities of growing up Filipino in the United States. However, these films were criticized for in some ways playing on the stereotypes of Filipino Americans and making ethnicity the centerpiece of the film. These films, however, did not start a groundswell for Asian American movies in the film industry. Most recently, *Better Luck Tomorrow,* otherwise referred to as *BLT,* has received a lot of publicity in its portrayal of Asian American youths in Orange County. This film is unique in that it features a cast of Asian Americans and is also directed by an Asian American director who cowrote the script. Unlike the other Asian American films before it, there has been a movement in the community to support this Asian American film and show that Asian American audiences will pay to see such movies. The film depicts Asian American characters but their identities are fluid and ambivalent. There are no references to their ethnic background or even to the characters being Asian American for that matter. Instead, the filmmaker portrays a complex group of Asian American youth who have some of the characteristics of the model minority stereotype, such as being overachievers. Yet at the same time, these Asian American youth fall victim to deviant acts of gambling, stealing, drug dealing, and sexual and drug escapades. As a result of this atypical stereotype of Asian Americans, someone at the Sundance Festival blasted the filmmaker by saying, "How could you make a movie that was so denigrating to your race?" Roger Ebert, a noted film critic, rebutted the comment by saying that such criticism would not have even been mouthed if a White director portrayed White actors in such a manner. He voiced the opinion that Asian Americans "have the right to be . . . whoever the hell they want to be!" This controversial film has stirred much discussion, but for Asian American audiences, the pressing question is whether this movie will serve as a catalyst for Hollywood to take Asian American filmmakers and actors more seriously, and whether Asian Americans will be seen in a different light.

The print and visual media provide a framework for some people to form impressions about Asian Americans. It is worth exploring what type of an impact these images have on the general public and on Asian Americans themselves. The following are some of the propositions related to Asian American stereotypes that are being discussed:

1. Stereotypes perpetuate the one-dimensional look of Asian Americans in movies.

2. Stereotypes of Asian American men and women affect how they are treated interpersonally, at work, and in everyday interactions. Demasculinizing Asian American men, while over-sexualizing Asian American women, has become a social problem, e.g., hate crimes, domestic violence with arranged marriages, etc.

3. Stereotypes have an impact on the identity of Asian Americans and may cause them to internalize shame about themselves.

DO STEREOTYPES PERPETUATE THE ONE-DIMENSIONAL LOOK OF ASIAN AMERICANS IN MOVIES?

For

Public stereotypes have played a critical role in perpetuating stereotypes of Asian Americans in the movies. Yet, it is unclear whether public stereotypes sway the media's portrayal of Asian Americans or if it's the other way around. Still, one cannot discount the manner in which Hollywood, and more recently the news media, has bought into the constructed images inherited from history. While portrayals of Asian Americans have not been one-dimensional per se, it has been limited and one-sided. Very rarely will people see images of Asian Americans from the perspective of Asian American communities.

The movies have played a vital role in shaping how the public views various ethnic groups. Although Asian Americans make up the second fastest growing ethnic minority group, there is still a void in the number of movies that reflect Asian American experiences. Movies that have Asian American or Asian leads most often deal with foreigners in the United States or are actually foreign films. Very few films have had Asian American story lines, and when there are Asian Americans depicted in the movies, it usually has to do with their cultural ties to their "homeland" or tradition. *The Joy Luck Club* (1993), for example, was a groundbreaking film for Asian Americans. However, according to some critics, stereotypes associated with three of the Asian American women compromised the movie. The film portrayed an Asian American woman, married to a cold, heartless Asian American man, who later found happiness with a Caucasian man. Such images depict the notion that happiness can not be found with an Asian American man, and that Caucasian men are the saviors, or Prince Charming who comes to the rescue. There was also the Asian American woman who wanted to fulfill what she thought was her White husband's wishes, so she changed herself into a submissive, dutiful wife. And then there was a heartless Asian American woman, who was calculating and manipulative but at the same time alluring and attractive. In short, all of the main actresses in the film personified in some way the stereotypical images of Asian American women. The film also did not do much for Asian American men either. They are either portrayed as cold and heartless, or docile and servile fathers. It is clear that the stereotypical images have not changed much.

Movies in many ways mirror the attitudes and beliefs of contemporary society. When Asian or Asian American women are paired with White men in film, society accepts the interracial relationship between White men and Asian women. Yet, one cannot help but wonder why White men prefer Asian women? In metropolitan areas like San Francisco, one may argue that it has to do with demographics, that there are a large number of White men and Asian American women. However, the interest by White men in Asian and Asian American women existed before the demographic shifts. Oftentimes famous Asian American women writers, newscasters, and actresses are married to White men. There are two possible explanations for this. One, there are some White men who prefer Asian women. This situation is sometimes referred to as the "Asian women syndrome," in which the White men are "Asian-woman-aholics" or "Rice Kings." The phrase "Rice Kings" is a label borrowed from the gay community, where a White man who prefers Asian men is referred to as a "Rice Queen" because they find them physically more attractive than other ethnic or racial groups.[7] Or second, the attraction to Asian women is rooted in fantasies about Asian femininity and submissiveness that has been engrained in the American male psyche through three major wars in the Pacific. Asian women are seen as China dolls or geisha girls who gracefully submit and obediently yield to White males. According to one source, "Since the 1940s, more than 200,000 Asian women have married United States servicemen, helping spread the G.I. gospel that Asians make 'good wives.'"[8] One can see the exotic-erotic appeal of Asian women in American films, from *The World of Suzie Wong* to *Full Metal Jacket* (albeit in stereotypes offensive to most Asians).

As for Asian American men in movies, some would argue that the images have greatly improved. However, if the leading roles or supporting roles of Asian actors are closely examined, there are no real story lines about Asian American men. Chow Yun Fat, Jet Li, and Jackie Chan have all contributed to the success of Asian men in Hollywood, but the movies that they star in all have to do with martial arts and with them being from another country. The few Asian American men who have had leading or supporting roles in Hollywood, such as Keanu Reeves, Rob Schneider, and Dean Cain, are multiracial but are not recognized as Asian Americans. In fact, movies and television continue to depict Asian American men in minor roles or as extras. Their roles today are not much different from those of the past. Asian American men are still portrayed as geeky nerds, the smart quiet "brainiacs," or the silent masters of martial arts. Movies, television, and the print media for that matter have done very little to dismantle Asian American stereotypes. Instead, they have only perpetuated the myths about Asian American men and women on the big screen.

Against

Stereotypes are all-pervasive, and they are hard to avoid. In a world in which time is at a premium, no one has the luxury of knowing about every ethnic group, religion, country, or subject. Lacking information on a topic, people fall back upon first impressions, or stereotypes that they have somehow developed. These stereotypes can be harmful or advantageous for a group. In the past, Asians in the United States were associated with unfavorable stereotypes. In the nineteenth century, the Chinese were seen as a backward people, polluting America with their diseases, opium, and heathen ways. With the American annexation of the Philippines at the end of the Spanish-American War in 1898, Filipinos were seen as benighted, "little brown brothers," colonial wards of the United States. Asian Indians in America, who were hoping for Indian independence from the British Empire, were seen as part of a vast Hindu conspiracy, a "tide of turbans," which this country did not need. On the other hand, after the Russo-Japanese War of 1904–1905, the Japanese were seen as a yellow peril, a military and cultural threat to the United States and its possessions, such as Hawai'i and the Philippines. These negative stereotypes of Asians in the United States led to discriminatory laws and practices, and even the restriction of Asian immigration to this country. Even after World War II, when the doors of immigration were opened once again to Asians, these stereotypes lingered on in motion pictures and television programs.

But times have changed. While there are occasional instances of stereotyping, for the most part the situation has improved for Asian Americans. Asian Americans are not depicted as diabolical Fu Manchu's, author Sax Rohmer's fictional character who plotted to conquer the world. The Asian American movement of the 1960s and 1970s brought about developments that helped to diminish the frequency of negative stereotypes in the movies and television. The East West Players of Los Angeles, the first Asian American theater company in the United States, helped to train actors and scriptwriters to improve the climate for Asian Americans in movies and television.[9] Other theater companies, such as the Asian American Theatre Company of San Francisco, the Pan Asian Repertory Theatre of New York, Theatre Mu of Minneapolis, and the Northwest Asian American Theatre of Seattle have joined in this effort. Actors James Hong, Beulah Quo, and others have worked to develop a stream of professionally trained Asian American actors for motion pictures and television.[10]

Today, the image of Asian Americans in the entertainment industry is much more complex and varied. Actresses like Lucy Liu in *Charlie's Angels, Ally McBeal,* and *Kill Bill,* Ming-Na Wen in *The Joy Luck Club* and *ER,* Tia Carrere in *The Relic Hunter,* and Kelly Hu in *The Scorpion King* and *Martial Law* offer different views of Asian Americans in film and television. Pat Morita in the *Karate Kid* movies, and George Takei in the *Star Trek* series are household names. Asian Americans of mixed ancestry, such as Keanu Reeves in *The Matrix,* Jason Scott Lee in *Dragon: The Bruce Lee Story* and *The Jungle Book,* Lou Diamond Phillips of *La Bamba,* and Kristen Kreuk of *Smallville,* have caught the eye of American viewers. Margaret Cho's television series *All-American Girl* was not a success, but her stand-up comedy performances and her off-Broadway show, *I'm the One that I Want,* have received critical acclaim. The popular response to Asian actors and actresses, such as Jackie Chan, Jet Li, Chow Yun-Fat, and Michelle Yeoh, have contributed to a more favorable climate overall for Asian and Asian American films, actors, actresses, and directors. Even Disney's film for children, *Mulan,* about a young heroine who disguised herself as a man to fight in place of her father, was a popular box office success. In general, the current situation is a vast improvement from the past, when there were almost no Asian American actors or actresses before the American public. Like *Mulan,* actresses like Liu, Wen, Carrere, Cho, and Hu present images of Asian and Asian American women as talented, confident, and assertive; they are more than just China dolls, geisha girls, or femmes fatales cast in the Hollywood films of the past. Moreover, very seldom today are there attempts to use actors and actresses in "yellow face," that is, non-Asians who try to pass themselves off as Asians or Asian Americans through the use of makeup. And if such a situation were to arise, activist and community organizations are likely to mobilize to protest such caricatured depictions of Asians or Asian Americans.

DO STEREOTYPES IMPACT ASIAN AMERICAN MEN AND WOMEN NEGATIVELY, AFFECTING THEIR EVERYDAY LIFE?

For

The stereotype of Asian Americans as hardworking but passive, docile workers has affected Asian Americans in the workforce. Although statistics reflect a great deal of educational and occupational success for Asian Americans, the reality is that there are very few Asian Americans in CEO positions in business and in higher education. Scholar and community activist Bob Suzuki, one of the first to critique the model minority myth, argues that while Asian Americans constitute a large percentage of students in four-year institutions, there are few faculty and even less administrators of Asian American descent. Suzuki suggests that there is a need to have more Asian Americans in the pipeline for leadership positions. However, the stereotypes make it difficult for many Asian Americans to obtain such positions. In law firms, while Asian Americans have been fairly successful in obtaining jobs and positions as associates, they have not been successful gaining partnerships in law firms because they are regarded as team players but not leaders. And even with these accomplishments, they are not representative of the diverse Asian American population. For example, in 1999 the U.S. census reported that Asian Americans received 10 percent of the doctorates conferred by colleges and universities. This included 22 percent of the doctorates in engineering and 21 percent of those in computer science. Furthermore, the census reported that 32.7 percent of Asian and Pacific Islander women had received a bachelor's degree or higher compared to 17.6 percent of the total population. Yet these numbers do not reflect the situation for all Asian American women, for only 3.2 percent of Cambodian American women have received a bachelor's degree or higher. The misreading of the census data, that all Asian Americans are successful, is unfortunate. It misrepresents those Asian Americans who are not like the model minority that is celebrated by the mass media. The reality is that there are many Asian Americans who are living at or below the poverty level, with limited education and occupational opportunities. Hence, the false notion that all Asian Americans are successful in their studies and careers actually hinders those who have achieved limited success as well as those who are far below parity in terms of educational and occupational attainment.

Another stereotype that has been projected on the big screen is the image of Asian women committing suicide. They allegedly do this after they "lose face" when their Caucasian men leave them. Furthermore, in the famous opera *Madame Butterfly,* a Japanese woman kills herself after realizing that her Caucasian lover will not marry her, but will instead take their child back to the United States. Such misleading notions about Asian American women hinder their interpersonal relationships with all men as these images not only affect the psyche of Caucasian men but Asian American men as well. For Caucasian men, these images perpetuate the notion of Asian women as passive, submissive objects who would rather die than confront conflict. For Asian men, these stereotypes facilitate the notion that White men take available Asian American women away from them, or that Asian American women are primarily interested in White men.

For Asian American women who do not fit into this "geisha" mold, they are criticized for being too aggressive, hot tempered, dragon ladies, or even "whitewashed" (losing one's Asianness and acting more White). For the reality is that when they are involved in interracial relationships, they have to combat the preconceived notions that they will be the submissive, domesticated woman in the house. For many women from Asia who marry White Americans, they not only experience culture shock, but the realization that their own images about the White knights rescuing them are far from reality. In a documentary titled *Women Outside* (1995), the lives of Korean sex workers are candidly shared with the viewing audience. Many of those women who marry American servicemen find that their lives in the United States are often characterized by discrimination, racism, sexism, and, in some instances, violence. When these women speak up for their rights and fight for egalitarian relationships that they have seen in the movies, it contradicts the expectations that many White servicemen have about marrying an Asian woman. Consequently, there is a high incidence of domestic violence and divorce in these relationships. When women leave their American husbands, they have difficulty finding jobs because of limited education and language abilities, and having no social support, many turn to the sex industry to support themselves and their children.

Aside from the subservient stereotype that follows Asian American women, they are also seen as the ideal sex partners for White men. The image of the submissive woman who is aggressive in bed appeals to men who are interested in dominating women rather than being involved in an egalitarian relationship. Marrying outside their own race for Asian women continues to soar in comparison to other groups. Yet, the objectification of the Asian American women as the "China doll," "geisha," and "dutiful wife" is something that has lingered.

On the flip side of things, Asian men are seen as asexual and feminine or cold and sexist; they are also seen as not being open to a relationship with an independent woman. Thus, it is no surprise that we have not seen a comparable high number of interracial relationships between White women and Asian men. However, the model minority stereotype and the "dot com" boom made Asian American men visible as those who have good jobs, make good money, and still believe in monogamous relationships. Esther Pan, who wrote a 2000 article in *Newsweek* "Why Asian Guys Are on a Roll," notes that Asian American men are now more desirable to White women, due to changing media perceptions of Asian men and the new generation who looks at race differently. Based on marriage license data in California, second-generation Asian American men are far more likely to marry women who are White (18.9%), of other Asian ethnicity (22.7%), or another racial minority (6%) than more recent immigrants.[11] Pan argues that much of this has to do with recent successful images of Asian Americans and Pacific Islanders. The image of Asian American men has changed from that of laborer or domestic servant to that of dot com mogul. Pan asserts that social position plays a critical role in how someone is evaluated as a partner.[12] However, gender issues affect interracial marriages. An Asian American woman is more likely to find acceptance by marrying a White man than an Asian American man would marrying a White woman. Consequently, divorce rates for interracially married Asian men are much higher than those for Asian women.[13]

The most damaging stereotypes recently have been those of Asian Americans as terrorists and Asian Americans as a disease infested community. Since September 11, 2001, South Asians, along with Arabs, Muslims, Sikh, and others who appear to look Middle Eastern, have been the victims of hate crimes. Hollywood has always presented those from the Middle East as terrorists. This was the case even before planes struck the twin towers of the World Trade Center in New York on September 11, 2001. However, the constant coverage of this incident by the news media fueled the hate that Americans had toward this group. Somehow, this incident made it acceptable for the U.S. government to racially profile citizens of and visitors to the United States at airports, on the streets, in schools, and in public places. The call to secure the rights of "Americans" again made it abundantly clear that those who did not look White were seen as a threat and questioned about their loyalty to America. Most recently, Representative Howard Coble of North Carolina, who serves as chair of the Subcommittee on Crime, Terrorism and Homeland Security, stated that in light of what happened on September 11, 2001, he supported President Franklin Roosevelt's decision to intern the Japanese during World War II. When the Japanese American Citizens League (JACL), along with other Asian American and civil rights organizations, asked for Coble's resignation, he said that he intended no offense, and did not think he said anything wrong. As he put it, "I certainly intended no harm or ill will toward anybody. I still stand by what I said . . . that, in no small part, it (internment) was done to protect the Japanese-Americans themselves."[14] Coble argued that not only did President Roosevelt have to take national security into account, but also he put the Japanese Americans in internment camps for their own protection. Floyd Mori, the national JACL president, said, "Rep. Coble's comments are outrageous and uneducated." He continued, "To suggest that the government locked up 120,000 innocent people for their own protection is not only patronizing and offensive, but it is patently incorrect."[15] The racist views about who is American in this country continue to haunt Asian Americans regardless of how long they have been in the United States.

The Severe Acute Respiratory Syndrome (SARS) epidemic in Asia in 2002 and 2003 not only hurt Asia's economy, but hurt Asian American businesses in the United States as well. The fear of contracting the disease was once again fueled by the news media's portrayal of a disease out of control in all parts of the world but in the United States. Still, Chinese restaurants, Asian grocery stores, and other Asian American businesses were hit hard because of the fear that somehow someone may have traveled to Hong Kong or another part of Asia. The fear, based on the stereotype of Asian Americans as foreigners, hurt the pocketbooks of many small businesses across the nation.

While many realize the danger of overgeneralization in stereotypes, nevertheless, they continue to affect the daily activities and lives of Asian Americans today. Sometimes it is just in very superficial ways, but nonetheless it is affecting how Asian Americans cope with their education, jobs, and interpersonal relationships.

Against

Stereotypes about Asian American men and women exist in American society, but those stereotypes have been changing. One of the most popular stereotypes is that of Asian or Asian American women as desirable sexual objects, a Japanese geisha or a China doll, eager to please her boyfriend or husband. Asian women in Asia or the United States are seen as submissive, compliant, and eager to please their men. But in the United States, Asian American women are now seen more and more as intelligent, resourceful, assertive, and capable of assuming leadership. Television personality Connie Chung, for example, is viewed as one who is skilled at her work and capable of eliciting surprising revelations in her interviews. Another example is Ann Curry, who is a newscaster on NBC's morning program, *The Today Show.* Many other Asian American women serve as news anchors or reporters for local television programs, demonstrating their competence as journalists.

In fact, the images of Asian American men and women should not be focused exclusively on motion pictures and television. In the world of business and economics, names such as Linda Tsao Yang, Andrea Jung, and Helen Young Hayes are altering the image of Asian American women in business. Linda Tsao Yang, for example, was appointed U.S. ambassador to the Asian Development Bank from 1993 to 1999. Prior to that, she was the California Savings and Loans Commissioner from 1980–1982.[16] Andrea Jung assumed the helm of Avon Products, a cosmetics company. As its chief executive officer and president, she took charge, taking it out of its financial difficulties, and steering it back into financial health.[17] Helen Young Hayes graduated from Yale University in economics and later became the manager for the Janus Worldwide Fund. Under her guidance, the Janus Worldwide Fund was a leader among mutual funds in its category, and many were sorry to see her retire in 2003.[18]

In the world of sports, Asian American women are changing the way the public sees them. As figure skaters, Olympic gold winner Kristi Yamaguchi and World champion Michelle Kwan have been dazzling world audiences with their artistry and athletic ability. Amy Chow received a gold medal in the Olympics for gymnastics, while thirteen-year-old Michelle Wie became a sensation as the youngest player to win the U.S. Women's Amateur Public Links in 2003. In 1996, Rell Sunn, an international surfing champion who helped to establish professional women's surfing, was inducted into the Huntington Beach Surfing Walk of Fame, joining another Hawai'i native, Duke Kahanamoku.[19]

Asian American men have not fared so badly either.[20] In advertisements and commercials, Asian American men are portrayed positively. For example, while it does seem that there are more ads targeting women, at the same time, businesses are aware of the changing demographics of a rapidly growing Asian American population and they do not want to neglect its male segment either. These days, one finds ads with Asian American male models displaying fashions that department stores hope will sell to its clientele. Furthermore, individuals such as Jerry Yang, a creator of Yahoo!, an Internet Web site, and Charles B. Wang, the founder of Computer Associates, have helped to popularize the idea that Asian Americans have entrepreneurial ability and can lead successful businesses. The success of the computer and software industry in Silicon Valley and other parts of the United States has added appeal and luster to the image of Asian American men. They are seen as upwardly mobile, educated, and likely to live in suburban homes.

In sports, the images of Asian American males are also changing. In the 2002 Winter Olympics, downhill racer Apolo Anton Ohno, the defending World Cup champion, thrilled audiences with his exciting performances. Golfer Tiger Woods's remark that he was "Cablinasian," a combination of Caucasian, Black, Indian, and Asian, heralded the fact that he was also part Thai and Chinese in his mixed racial ancestry. Tennis player Michael Chang, baseball player Benny Agbayani of the New York Mets, and football player Dat Nguyen of the Dallas Cowboys, are among the growing number of Asian American males who are represented in a variety of different sports. By cracking into this area, they are helping to dispel the impression that Asian Americans are only intent on academic study and are inept as athletes. Ichiro Suzuki, a baseball player for the Seattle Mariners, and Yao Ming, a basketball player for the Houston Rockets, are showing that Asians are endowed with athletic ability. In a wide variety of arenas, a vast array of multidimensional images are now being generated about Asian American men and women, and they are helping to erase the old negative stereotypes of the past.

DO STEREOTYPES IMPACT ASIAN AMERICAN COMMUNITIES, ETHNIC IDENTITY, AND INTERETHNIC RELATIONS?

For

The model minority stereotype has damaging consequences for Asian Americans, but especially for youths. The idea of the perfect minority, as one that is smart, family oriented, loyal, and dedicated is something that is difficult for anyone to achieve. It is unrealistic to expect someone to be the model anything. High- and low-achieving Asian American students have expressed concern about the high level of anxiety they feel to meet the expectations of the model minority stereotypes.

Dispelling the academic success myth, the Educational Testing Service has found that twelfth grade students from six major ethnic groups (Chinese, Japanese, Korean, Filipino, South Asian, and Southeast Asian) had significantly varied educational backgrounds and achievements.[21] Stereotyping has led to neglect in developing student services and support for many Asian

American students who are undereducated and have low socioeconomic status. Some of the stereotypes identify Asian Americans as "geniuses," "overachievers," "nerdy," "great in math or science," competitive, uninterested in fun, and having 4.0 GPAs.[22] Personality stereotypes categorize Asian Americans as "submissive," "humble," "passive," "quiet," "compliant," "obedient," "stoic," "devious," "sneaky," and "sly," and describe them as those who "tend to hang out in groups," "stay with their own race," "condescend to other races," "are not willing to mesh with American culture," "want to be like Americans," "want to be Caucasian," and "act FOB [Fresh off the Boat, like immigrants]."[23] Socioeconomic status stereotypes identify them "as stingy, greedy, rich, poor, liquor storeowners, dry cleaners, restaurant owners."[24] Asian Americans experience school, social, and familial stresses to maintain their model minority image.[25] One study found that although Asian American students did better academically and had fewer delinquent behaviors than Caucasians, Asian American youth reported more depressive symptoms, withdrawn behavior, and social problems.[26] They also had poorer self-images and reported more dissatisfaction with their social support. In an informal study conducted by the Orange County Asian Pacific Island Community Alliance (OCAPICA), it was found that Asian American young women had the highest suicide attempts.

In addition to the model minority stereotype of success that Asian Americans feel they have to live up to, they are also faced with social and psychological struggles. These struggles stem from model minority stereotypes that foster discrimination and anti-Asian sentiments from peers.[27] In another study, it was found that 63 percent of Vietnamese, Hmong, and Korean elementary and secondary students reported that American students were mean to them.[28] The students complained of being insulted and teased by classmates, which resulted in alienation and having few friends at school. Moreover, Vietnamese, Chinese, and Cambodian refugee children of school age faced constant physical altercations with peers in school and in other social interactions. The model minority stereotype can also backfire on Asian Americans. Due to the image of what it means to be "American," Asian American youth often stay away from new Asian immigrants. It is a form of disidentification with Asians. Asian American youth fear that association with Asian immigrants might make them the target of teasing and ridicule by others. In Hawai'i, 1.5 generation Korean Americans have recounted how they did not want to be associated with FOBs and made sure they were seen as Japanese or Filipino. It was important to be seen as "local," meaning they were born or had lived for a long time in Hawai'i. Asian American youth have internalized shame from being associated with foreigners, so they often discriminate against immigrant Asian groups.[29] In another study, Korean students distanced themselves from Southeast Asian students because they did not want to be associated and be perceived as "welfare sponges."[30] Because many Southeast Asian students are from refugee families, their parents may not be in the middle or upper classes. Instead, their parents may be holding jobs with low salaries that place them in the lower class. For the new Asian immigrants, then, they are faced with combating discrimination and racism from those outside and inside their ethnic group. Consequently, it is not surprising that suspensions for fighting and troubled behavior were cited as common problems for immigrant groups. These fights were attributed to cultural barriers and prejudice against Asians, especially Southeast Asians. Such racial tensions and hostile school environments may divert the focus of students from their studies to less productive and more destructive activities, such as joining gangs.[31]

Against

While negative stereotypes have the potential to hurt a group, those about Asian Americans are not necessarily of that category. If anything, Asian Americans today are often typecast as being successful in their studies. They have a reputation of being a model minority—hardworking, talented, and highly intelligent. Many Asian Americans even find that this perception, misleading though it might be, sometimes works in their favor. Teachers give them the benefit of the doubt, and if the grading is subjective, the Asian American students may find that the grades are weighted in their favor. But many Asian Americans also do work very hard, with the help of their parents and families, and they are able to gain admission into colleges and universities in large numbers.

Because there is a general impression that Asian Americans should do well in school, it can add impetus for Asian American students to succeed in their educational endeavors. Rather than being labeled negatively, with the adverse consequences of being categorized as not being academically able, a model minority stereotype encourages Asian American students to try harder and to study conscientiously. Educational success, after all, often depends on the mastery of learning, and, according to noted theorist Benjamin Bloom, given time and dedication, most students should be able to do it.[32] Whether this application of time and effort is described as a Confucian ethic or Asian work ethic, or even the Protestant ethic, the fundamental principle is perseverance.

Asian students who immigrate to the United States may have benefited from the educational systems in Asia. Those who arrive from Taiwan, Hong Kong, China, Singapore, Japan, South Korea, India, Pakistan, Bangladesh, and other countries are aware of the importance of education as the route to professional success. While immigrant and refugee students may have difficulties with the English language, the strangeness of American culture, and other barriers, many will strive to overcome these hurdles to realize their dreams. Others will face great obstacles. Poverty, intergenerational conflict, cultural conflict, the clash between immigrants and American-born natives, lack of parental supervision, and juvenile delinquency are problems that immigrants and refugees entering the United States from other countries may experience as well. But these are difficulties not based on stereotypes but factors such as class and cultural adjustment. The stereotypes of Asian Americans as a model minority are really secondary or tertiary in determining their success in the United States or in their communities.

QUESTIONS

1. What are stereotypes? What are some of the stereotypes about Asian Americans that you have heard? If you are Asian, how did that affect how you felt about yourself and other Asian Americans? If you are not Asian, how did it affect how you viewed Asian Americans in general?

2. Have the stereotypes about Asian Americans changed over the years?

3. Do other minority groups hold stereotypes about Asian Americans? Do Asian Americans hold stereotypes about other groups? Explain.

4. What impact has the media had on the images of Asians and Asian Americans? Think about comic strips, cartoons, magazines, television, or the movies you have seen. How are Asian Americans depicted?

5. Where have you seen Asian Americans in popular culture? Is it in comic strips, cartoons, magazines, television, the movies, or video/computer games? Do you think there have been changes over time?

6. How have periods of war and conflict affected the perception of Asian Americans? Can examples be cited from the Philippine-American War of 1898, World War II, the Korean War, and the Vietnam War?

7. Who is Wen Ho Lee? How have national security concerns affected the images and perceptions of Asian Americans? Are there examples that can be cited after the September 11, 2001, terrorist attacks against the United States?

8. Does the public develop stereotypes, which the media and entertainment industry then perpetuate, or is it the reverse?

9. How have Asians been portrayed in movies and television? In your experience, have you thought of Asians as different from Asian Americans? Or do you see them as a single group?

10. Do Asian or Asian American actors have greater or lesser prominence in the motion picture and television industry? Are the roles that they portray diverse or limited? Are they cast in stereotypical or predictable roles? Can stereotypes influence the scripts in their portrayals of Asians or Asian Americans? Why do you think this is so?

11. Has there been any improvement in the images of Asian Americans in the entertainment industry? Why or why not?

12. Are stereotypes about Asian Americans similar or different from those of other ethnic groups? Are there common characteristics or differences? Explain.

13. Are Asian American men stereotyped in different ways than Asian American women? Explain. Do you think it affects Asian American men and women in the same way or not?

14. Do Asian American women have a more favorable image than Asian American men? Why? Was this always so? Do you think this has an impact on interracial dating and marriage?

15. Stereotypes are generalizations about a group. Why do you think people believe in stereotypes and think they are true? Are there ways to mitigate the effect of stereotypes?

NOTES

1. Christine Choy, "Cinema as a Tool of Assimilation: Asian Americans, Women and Hollywood," in *Color: 60 Years of Images of Minority Women in Film: 1921–1981*, a project of the Exhibition Program of 3rd World Newsreel (Santa Cruz, CA: UC Santa Cruz Library, 1993), 23.

2. Eugene Franklin Wong, *On Visual Media Racism: Asians in the American Motion Pictures*, Ph.D. diss., University of Denver, 1978, ii.

3. Daniel J. Leab, "Deutschland, USA: German Images in American Film," in *The Kaleidoscopic Lens: How Hollywood Views Ethnic Groups*, ed. Randall M. Miller (Englewood, NJ: Ozer, 1980).

4. Ibid.

5. Renee Tajima, "Asian Women's Images in Film: The Past Sixty Years," in *Color: Sixty Years of Minority Women in Film: 1921–1981*, a project of the Exhibition Program at 3rd World Newsreel (Santa Cruz, CA: UC Santa Cruz Library, 1993), 26.

6. Wong, *On Visual Media Racism*.

7. Joan Walsh,. "Asian Women, Caucasian Men: It's a Growing Trend in the Bay Area's New Multicultural World. But These Relationships Can Bring with Them Social and Psychological Complications," *San Francisco Examiner*, 2 December 1990.

8. Ibid.

9. Yuko Kurahashi, *Asian American Culture on Stage: The History of the East West Players* (New York: Garland Publishing, 1999).

10. Ibid., 16, 182.

11. Esther Pan, "Why Asian Guys Are on a Roll," *Newsweek*, 21 February 2000, http://newsweekparentsguide.com/nw-srv/printed/us/so/a16374-2000feb13.htm.

12. Ibid.

13. Ibid.

14. Nick Maheras, "Groups Call on Coble for Apology," *Archdale (North Carolina) Trinity News*, 7 February 2000, www.modelminority.com.

15. Ibid.

16. "Ambassador Linda Tsao Yang," *California-Asia Business Council*, http://www.calasia.org/Ambassador%20Linda%20Tsao%20Yang_v2.pdf (accessed 3 July 2003).

17. Katrina Brooker, "It Took a Lady to Save Avon," *Fortune*, 1 October 2001,

http://www.fortune.com/fortune/women/articles/0,15114,367458,00.html (accessed 3 July 2003).

18. Russel Kinnel, "What Helen Young Hayes' Departure Means to Janus," *Forbes.com,* 21 April 2003, http://www.forbes.com/finance/feeds/mstar/2003/04/21/mstar1_2_10211_132.html (accessed 3 July 2003).

19. Greg Ambrose, "Sunn Gets Her Chance to Shine," *Honolulu Star-Bulletin,* 6 August 1996, http://starbulletin.com/96/08/06/sports/index.html (accessed 3 July 2003).

20. Colleen Fong and Judy Yung, "In Search of the Right Spouse: Interracial Marriage among Chinese and Japanese Americans," *Amerasia Journal* 21 (winter 1995/1996): 92.

21. Educational Testing Service, "Stereotyping Shortchanges Asian American Students," http://modelminority.com/academia/ets.html; Angela Kim and Christine J. Yeh, "Stereotypes of Asian American Students," *ERIC Digest* (New York: ERIC Clearinghouse on Urban Education, 2002), http://www.ericfacility.net/databases/ERIC_Digests/ed462510.html.

22. Stacey J. Lee, *Unraveling the "Model Minority" Stereotype: Listening to Asian American Youth* (New York: Teachers College Press, 1996).

23. Ibid.

24. Kim and Yeh, "Stereotypes of Asian American Students."

25. C. B. Fisher, S. A. Wallace, and R. E. Fenton, "Discrimination Distress during Adolescence," *Journal of Youth and Adolescence* 29, no. 6 (2000): 679–695.

26. M. K. Lorenzo, A. K. Frost, and H. K. Reinherz, "Social and Emotional Functioning of Older Asian American Adolescents," *Child & Adolescent Social Work Journal* 17, no. 4 (2000), 289–304.

27. Sau Fong Siu, *Asian American Students at Risk: A Literature Review,* Report No. 8 (Baltimore, MD: Johns Hopkins University, Center for Research on the Education of Students Placed at Risk, 1996).

28. Mary Yu Danico, *The 1.5 Generation: Becoming Korean American in Hawai'i* (Honolulu: University of Hawaii Press, 2004).

29. Siu, *Asian American Students at Risk.*

30. Lee, *Unraveling the "Model Minority" Stereotype.*

31. Siu, *Asian American Students at Risk.*

32. Benjamin S. Bloom, Bertram B. Mesia, and David Krathwohl, *Taxonomy of Educational Objectives,* 2 vols. (New York: 1964).

SELECTED WORKS

Atkinson, D. R., G. Morten, and D. W. Sue, eds. *Counseling American Minorities: A Cross-Cultural Perspective.* 4th edition. Madison, WI: Brown and Benchmark, 1993.

Bloom, Benjamin S., Bertram B. Mesia, and David Krathwohl. *Taxonomy of Educational Objectives.* 2 vols. New York: 1964.

Choy, Christine. "Cinema as a Tool of Assimilation: Asian Americans, Women and Hollywood." In *Color: 60 Years of Images of Minority Women in Film: 1921–1981.* A project of the Exhibition Program of 3rd World Newsreel. Santa Cruz, CA: UC Santa Cruz Library, 1993, 23.

Danico, Mary Yu. *The 1.5 Generation: Becoming Korean American in Hawai'i.* Honolulu: University of Hawaii Press, 2004.

Fisher, C. B., S. A. Wallace, and R. E. Fenton. "Discrimination Distress during Adolescence." *Journal of Youth and Adolescence* 29, no. 6 (2000): 679–695.

Fong, Colleen, and Judy Yung. "In Search of the Right Spouse: Interracial Marriage among Chinese and Japanese Americans." *Amerasia Journal* 21 (winter 1995/1996): 92.

Kurahashi, Yuko. *Asian American Culture on Stage: The History of the East West Players.* New York: Garland Publishing, 1999.

Leab, Daniel J. "Deutschland, USA: German Images in American Film." In *The Kaleidoscopic Lens: How Hollywood Views Ethnic Groups,* ed. Randall M. Miller. Englewood, NJ: Ozer, 1980.

Lee, S. J. *Unraveling the "Model Minority" Stereotype: Listening to Asian American Youth.* New York: Teachers College Press, 1996.

Lorenzo, M. K., A. K. Frost, and H. Z. Reinherz. "Social and Emotional Functioning of Older Asian American Adolescents." *Child & Adolescent Social Work Journal* 17, no. 4 (2000): 289–304.

Nakamura, David. "They're Hot, They're Sexy . . . They're Asian Men." *Seattle Times Northwest Life,* 7 May 2000.

Nguyen, Trieuduong. "Better Luck Tomorrow Creates New Asian Perspective." *The Johns Hopkins Newsletter,* 7 March 2003.

Pan, Esther. "Why Asian Guys Are on a Roll." *Newsweek,* 21 February 2000, http://newsweekparentsguide.com/nw-srv/printed/us/so/a16374-2000feb13.htm.

Siu, Sau Fong. *Asian American Students at Risk: A Literature Review.* Report No. 8. Baltimore, MD: Johns Hopkins University, Center for Research on the Education of Students Placed at Risk, 1996.

Tajima, Renee. "Asian Women's Images in Film: The Past Sixty Years." In *Color: Sixty Years of Minority Women in Film: 1921–1981.* A Project of the Exhibition Program at 3rd World Newsreel, Santa Cruz, CA: UC Santa Cruz Library, 1993.

Walsh, Joan. "Asian Women, Caucasian Men: It's a Growing Trend in the Bay Area's New Multicultural World. But These Relationships Can Bring with Them Social and Psychological Complications." *San Francisco Examiner,* 2 December 1990.

Wong, Eugene Franklin. *On Visual Media Racism: Asians in the American Motion Pictures.* Ph.D. dissertation, University of Denver, 1978.

8

GENERATIONAL DIFFERENCES

The concept of a generation gap has been a consistent topic of discussion for social scientists and laypersons alike. Yet, what does generation gap really mean? One could very well be engaged in a conversation about generational differences but end up talking about several different things. There are the generational differences between parents and their children, there are the differences between immigrants, refugees, and American-born children, and there is also the generation as historical period, just to name a few. When discussing Asian American generational issues, one not only has to consider the ambiguity of the concept, but also how the concept of generation has been used in reference to Asian Americans.

BACKGROUND

There are multiple meanings that describe a generation, employing concepts involving kinship, cohort, life stage, and/or a historical period.[1] Social scientists frequently discuss and/or analyze more than one way of thinking about generation. For example, kinship descent is a concept of generation that refers not only to parent-child relationships, but also to larger kinship relationships, such as the blood ties of aunts, uncles, cousins, grandparents, and so on. It also describes the population replacement from one generation to another, such as the baby boomer generation, born during the late 1950s to the early 1960s, who replaced the war-baby generation of the 1940s and 1950s. However, others may apply the phrase "baby boom" generation to refer to those who were conceived after the Korean War and before the civil rights movement of the late 1960s. There is also Generation X, which refers to those who were born in the 1970s, while Generation Y refers to those born in the 1980s. While these labels do not cite a particular time in history, per se, they are devised to help frame and place a generation in a particular time and place. On the other hand, generation as a cohort is commonly used to describe people moving from one age group to another, such as preteens, teenagers, college age generation, and so on. The idea of generation as a life stage, in contrast, is often attributed to the conflicts between younger and older generations. Finally, the use of a historical period as a generational category is used more commonly by historians.

While the discussion about generations applies to all groups, for Asian Americans the most commonly discussed generational issues are those concerning generations at a specific time in history. Examples might be the generational differences between immigrants, refugees, and American-born Asian Americans. This is usually linked with parent-child generational conflict compounded by cultural, social, and political clashes. Furthermore, for some of the immigrant or refugee families who have second- or third-generation children, they are also simultaneously dealing with generational and class differences as a result of changes due to migrating to the United States.

The history of Asian Americans in the United States spans more than 200 years. Those who immigrated before the 1965 Immigration Act came voluntarily in most cases. There was the indentured servant generation, the picture bride generation, the war bride generation, and the orphan/adoptee generation. Each of the generations was specific to a particular time in history that pushed them to migrate to the United States. In some cases, the new land pulled the immigrants away from or kept them from returning to their homeland. The indentured servant generation was recruited during American efforts to conquer the continental United States and Hawai'i. Among the first Asians to come to America were a small number of Chinese who ventured to California in the 1850s. They had arrived upon learning that gold had been discovered on John Sutter's property in California. Most were poor peasants from southeastern China who had received loans for their voyage to the United States. By the end of 1850, there were 4,000 Chinese in California. By 1860, the United States had a Chinese population of about 35,000, most of whom lived in California. With the discriminatory treatment associated with the introduction of the foreign miner's tax, Chinese laborers turned to other employment, such as building the transcontinental railroads.

While Hawai'i did not become a state until 1959, American businessmen played a critical role in recruiting Asian laborers to Hawai'i, who later migrated west to California for work. While the earliest record of Asian immigration was to Louisiana, the largest number of Asian immigrants landed first in Hawai'i to work on the sugar plantations. The Chinese were the first to arrive; however, a changing political climate made it difficult for plantation owners to recruit Chinese laborers to Hawai'i, so they turned to Japanese laborers. Unlike the Chinese, some Japanese families were able to migrate together. Between 1885 and 1894, an association of owners of Hawaiian sugar plantations recruited almost 29,000 Japanese as contract laborers, workers imported under an agreement to work for a particular employer. The conditions for the Japanese were harsh, and in some cases unbearable. Japanese workers, while excellent workers, were not the docile, submissive group that plantation owners expected. Instead, they were outspoken about the low wages and harsh working conditions in the plantations, and they were able to organize numerous strikes demanding better pay and work conditions.

To offset the Japanese, the plantation owners turned to Korean laborers to serve as strikebreakers. The majority of the Korean laborers were recruited with the help of the Methodist Church, which had conducted missionary work in the northern portion of Korea. Unlike the southern part of Korea, which was mostly agriculture based and had generally been able to avoid major crises, the northern part of Korea was severely impacted by the Russo-Japanese war. Its people were suffering from hunger, famine, and disease, and they were more desperate for change. The political and social climate made Hawai'i an attractive option for those who were seeking better lives for themselves and their families.

Like the Japanese laborers, Korean women also migrated to Hawai'i. While some of them left their homelands with their husbands and children, most of the women immigrated as "picture brides." Women in Korea would participate in a pen pal-type correspondence with Korean men in Hawai'i. They would exchange pictures and information about themselves. Since arranged marriages were common in Asia, many women saw the opportunity to leave their homeland as a way to support their families, pursue better education, and leave the difficult environmental, political, and social conditions at home. For some women, however, they found that the pictures they received of their picture husbands did not quite match with the men they met when they landed on shore. Many men who wrote these letters ended up sending old photographs of themselves when they had been younger. Sometimes they sent pictures that were 20 years old to their potential picture brides. Needless to say, the women were shocked to find a man 20 years older than they had expected waiting for them. For some women, they married the men and found themselves in happy relationships, while others ran away from their old husbands for younger men working in the plantations. There were other social problems that surfaced for the picture bride generation. There were instances of domestic violence, and some of the women who ran away from their husbands could only find limited options for employment. Without any other alternatives available, they turned to working in brothels to survive economically. Overall, the conditions for Koreans were arguably not much better than the Japanese or their homeland. As soon as they were able to pay off their voyage expenses to Hawai'i, they turned to entrepreneurship or migrated to the Pacific coast states of California, Oregon, and Washington. When United States immigration policies restricted the immigration of people from China, Japan, and Korea, there were increased opportunities for Filipinos to fill the labor shortage in the United States. As nationals, they had the right of free migration to the United States and its territories. Consequently, in Hawai'i and along the West Coast, employers eagerly recruited Filipinos to fill their labor needs.

The "war bride" and "orphan" generation were the next to immigrate in the 1950s before the Immigration Act of 1965. The Korean War affected the lives of Koreans in multiple ways. The 48th Parallel not only divided a country that was once united, but it also introduced the U.S. military as a foreign presence in their lives. The U.S. military played a vital role in shaping and transforming both South and North Korea, but its influence in the South was more extensive and more sustained. One of the ways in which South Korea's culture was changed was through the relationships that were formed between military men and Korean women. The military bases became focal points or sites of opportunity for the sex industry. Various brothels, strip clubs, and hostess bars opened up to cater to the soldiers.[2] The U.S. military, while cognizant of their presence, did nothing to eliminate these establishments. Instead, it countenanced the existence of the sex industry, seeing it as a means of raising the morale of soldiers stationed in a foreign country.

The women who worked in the sex industry entered for various reasons, but none of them chose their careers willingly. As a result of war, families suffered at all levels. For some women who were torn from their families as a result of the Korean War, they had few options for work. Others had been forced or tricked into the sex industry. While many soldiers frequented these establishments for a long period of time, others found meaningful relationships that they pursued into marriage. The marriages resulted in an increasing number of war brides who later immigrated to the United States to join their military husbands. On the other hand, other men had sexual relationships with Korean women, had children with them, but did not pursue marriage. Instead, the women were left to either raise a child on their own or give them up for adoption. There were two big problems for orphans in Korea. With people holding firmly to the idea of "blood ties,"[3] the idea of adoption was not warmly received in Korean society. Moreover, if a child was mixed (part

White or Black and Korean), they were not only ostracized from the community outside of the orphanage, but they were also alienated from and ostracized by the other fully ethnic Korean children in the orphanage. Biracial children had to endure discrimination and hostility from Korean children and adults, for they physically symbolized the presence of the military and neo-colonialism. Consequently, American families wanting to adopt children went to Korea to adopt both Korean and biracial Korean children. Thus prior to the 1965 Immigration Act, a significant number of immigrants were war brides and adopted children.

Besides the use of generation as a historical marker, there are the generational differences between refugees and immigrants and American-born children. The distinctions between these groups are commonly discussed in terms of the first and second generation, and more recently, the phrase "the 1.5 generation" has also been included. Immigrants are those who migrate to the United States voluntarily in search of better education, jobs, and opportunities. Much has been written about Asian immigrants, however, very few articles and books are devoted to the experiences of the children of immigrants and refugees. Since 1975, over 1.5 million Vietnamese were forced to leave their homeland shortly after the fall of Saigon. The first wave of refugees consisted mainly of South Vietnamese government officials, army officers, and employees of the U.S. government. In 1975, approximately 120,000 of the first wave of refugees were initially housed and processed through Camp Pendleton, California, and several other military bases. The next wave of refugees came during the late 1970s to late 1980s; they escaped by boats to the sea and by land routes to neighboring countries. These refugees faced traumatic conditions and had to live in refugee camps, where they stayed for months or years before finding sponsors. Additional groups arrived as immigrants through the Orderly Departure Program (ODP), an organized immigration process. The ODP was created in 1980 in response to half of the boat people dying at sea through drowning or death at the hand of pirates. The program was an agreement between the Socialist Republic of Vietnam and 29 participating countries to create a legal and safe means of emigration from Vietnam, as opposed to the illegal and life threatening flight by sea. In its nearly 20 years of operation, the ODP made possible the departure of well over 500,000 people, mainly to the United States, which was the major country involved in the venture.[4] The images of "boat people" fleeing South Vietnam, of Khmer refugees fleeing the genocidal policies in Cambodia, and the political turmoil in Laos aroused humanitarian concern.[5] Many countries around the world responded by offering asylum and a haven to the Southeast Asian refugees. Other refugees arrived through the Humanitarian Operation Program, which was created in the early 1980s. Through this program, the

U.S. government asked Vietnam's government to send former prisoners of the Communist "re-education" camps to the United States. The United States also created the Amerasian Programs for multiracial Vietnamese with American fathers. In addition to the children among the refugees, there was also a growing number of immigrant children because of the immigration changes in 1965.

Social scientists and historians define the first generation as being made up of immigrants or refugees, the first to live in the United States. The 1.5 generation,[6] or *ilchom ose,* was a term first used by members of the Korean community. The 1.5 generation refers to the children who immigrated with their parents as youths, having received some education in their home country, but receiving most of their education in the United States. They are bilingual and bicultural, and they have the ability to negotiate generational and ethnic boundaries.[7] They are often referred to as the in-between generation, and have been characterized as confused and marginalized. However, they have also been described as the "bridge" between the first and second generations. They can communicate and translate for different generations, and act, as well, as intermediaries between the immigrant group and non-Koreans.[8] Finally, the second generation consists of those who are American-born, having received all of their education and socialization in the United States.

The differences in the generations are not always clear, largely due to a general perception that Asian Americans are all alike or that they are all really foreigners. Some would argue that the generational differences are very slight and not significant, while others would suggest that there are clear demarcations between the first generation and subsequent generations. The following are some of the propositions related to generational differences that are being discussed in the community:

1. The "generation gap" between children, parents, and grandparents is relevant to all households. However, in Asian American families, there are social, political, and cultural differences that emerge as a result of age and time.

2. There are differences between the immigrant, 1.5, second, and subsequent generations. These generational groups have different experiences, which are largely shaped by their family, community, and social connections. There are more visible distinctions between immigrants and American-born Asian Americans in terms of their roles in the family, and how they are perceived by the larger society.

3. While generational differences are evident in Asian American communities, it is desirable to recognize the diversity that exists. Issues of social class impact the experiences and expectations of the different generations, as does gender.

Hence, while generational differences affect how Asian Americans see themselves, so do their class and gender statuses.

CAN A "GENERATION GAP" AFFECTING CHILDREN, PARENTS, AND GRANDPARENTS BE FOUND IN ASIAN AMERICAN FAMILIES?

For

Discussions of the generation gap are not a new phenomenon, but when we factor culture gaps into the equation, the conflicts or issues that arise between children, parents, and grandparents change significantly. For Asian American families, age is not the only obstacle between generations. Social and political views that arise because of cultural differences create generational barriers that contribute to the generation gap. The cultural gaps between Asian American children and their parents mostly impact those children whose parents are first generation or immigrants. Because these parents have been socialized in Asia, their value systems may differ from their children who have been socialized in the United States. Their children have been raised under a different set of circumstances; they were exposed not only to their parents' influence, but the influence of the media, school, peers, and community organizations. These various settings influence the way Asian American youths view society, politics, and even culture. For example, these children will most likely experience their parents speaking their ethnic language at home, eating ethnic foods, and interacting with other Asian immigrants. They are also more likely to have parents who maintain connections to family and friends in their homeland. Their families remain connected to homeland affairs by watching Asian ethnic television shows and reading newspapers.

What Asian American youths observe and experience at home is a significant contrast from what they observe in the mainstream media and at school. For example, in a British film *Bend It Like Beckham* (2003), a South Asian Indian young woman, Jess, is much like what an Asian American teen might relate to. Jess is confronted with the dilemma of pursuing her dream of becoming a soccer player. This is contrary to the wishes of her parents, who want her to attend college and learn how to cook Indian food so that she can marry a nice Asian Indian man. As a result, Jess ends up lying to her parents so that she can sneak away to play soccer. Jess does this because she fears that her parents would never understand. For Asian Americans, the cultural differences are what define the "gap," because unlike their Caucasian friends who rarely face culture wars with their parents, Asian American children are confronted with negotiating between two cultures and the age gaps that exist between the generations.[9]

The young Asian American generation is represented by the hosts and content of the TV show *Stir* in San Francisco, 2003. Left to right, Tony Wang, Sabrina Shimada, Jeannie Mai, and Brian Tong. AP/Wide World Photos.

For Asian American children who have parents and grandparents in their lives, they are confronted with various social, cultural, and political issues. Although Japanese and Chinese Americans have lived in the United States for over four generations, most Asian Americans today are immigrants, or have one parent who is an immigrant.[10] For these children, the cultural gaps they experience at home and outside in the community and larger society significantly impact the relationships they have with their parents and grandparents. Many Asian American youths face communication barriers at home. For example, while their parents speak a foreign language fluently, they have a hard time mastering English. For the youths, they are fluent in English, but often struggle with their ethnic language. Therefore, it becomes increasingly difficult for parents and children to communicate in a language in which both are equally fluent. For immigrant adults, the community and solidarity they experience with other immigrants helps them to cope and adjust to a new environment that is often very foreign to them. Being able to speak their ethnic language and to talk about the shared experiences of growing up helps them to solidify their ethnic identity. There are also differences between immigrant and refugee experiences in adjusting to Western culture. Immigrants, for example, came to the United States voluntarily, and for most of the post-1965 immigrants, they came with professional degrees, and were able to reunite with family members already in the United States. For refugees, however, most did not have professional degrees or a support system in place to help them adjust. At the same time, both of the groups faced racism and discrimination due to a lack of English language proficiency and a lack of cultural knowledge about the new host society.

While the larger society creates many cultural, social, and political barriers for immigrants and refugees, the growing number of post-suburban communities and ethnoburbs has made a significant difference in the lives of immigrant/refugee families. In places like California, Hawai'i, and New York, where there are large concentrations of Asian Americans, Asian American families have an opportunity to find groceries that allow them to continue cooking ethnic foods, newspapers that keep them in touch with events in Asia, and media that delivers the news in their ethnic language.

While the cultural familiarity allows parents and grandparents to adjust and gain a sense of community, the children encounter a different set of obstacles bridging the gap between what they experience at home and what they encounter at school and in the mainstream media. The pressure to fit in is immense for all children, but for children of immigrant families, they find themselves comparing their own families to what they see on television. Currently, there are no Asian American families on television and there are a mere handful of Asian American characters on various programs. Popular culture informs youths that friends are supposed to be White, thin, and living in glamour. Families are also supposed to be White with various idiosyncrasies. Somehow they manage to work through these idiosyncrasies in a 30-minute period. When they do see those who look like them, they most often are foreigners with distinctive accents. With very few exceptions, Asian Americans on television and on the large screen are dominated by the images of Asians, not Asian Americans. While Lucy Liu's role in *Charlie's Angels Full Throttle* does not have an accent, she is also portrayed as *hapa* or having mixed ancestry, with a White father and a Chinese mother. The Asian Americans who are represented in the media are either portrayed as half White, or not Asian at all. Actors like Dean Cain, Keanu Reeves, Rob Schneider, and Ellen Barkin, to name a few, are not even referred to as Asian Americans. In fact this ethnic heritage is ignored all together.

The generation gap affects social conditions as well. While immigrant parents expect their children to behave much as their own parents expected of them, the children in the United States are faced with peer pressure and cultural pressures to fit in and assimilate. Socially, family is not the focal point of attention, largely due to the fragmentation of families that occurs as a result of immigration. For example, in immigrant families that may have one parent working and the other at home, there may be economic hardship. As a result, it is difficult for a one-income earner to support an immigrant family and pay for education, housing, and other necessities. As a result, both immigrant parents are often working one and often two jobs, leaving their children to attend to themselves and their siblings. For these youths, they find that their social life is concentrated around their friends, and in public spaces, such as malls, cyber cafes, and movie theatres. Some turn to organized activities run by church groups, youth organizations, and after-school programs. But regardless of the venue, children's social life is often unsupervised by their parents and self-monitored. The economic reality of living in America has transformed the traditional one-income Asian family, where parents had a stronghold on the progress of their children's education, social life, and everyday activities. It has changed to one where parents, in the quest for economic security, have limited interactions with their children's daily activities.[11]

Against

Many of the writings in Asian American literature deal with the second generation and their differences with the immigrant or first generation. Examples are Pardee Lowe's *Father and Glorious Descendant* (1943), Jade Snow Wong's *Fifth Chinese Daughter* (1950), and Monica Sone's *Nisei Daughter* (1953).[12] The first generation is foreign born, and they enter the United States knowledgeable in the language and culture of their homeland. The second generation, however, growing up in the United States, is less fluent in the parents' native language and is more fluent in the English language. Moreover, they may have conflicts with the culture and expectations of their parents, as the second generation is more familiar with the culture of the United States. This causes what many have termed the "generation gap" between the first and second generations. For example, in Pardee Lowe's book, his father asks him if he would like to study in China. While Lowe replies no, his father hires a tutor to teach him the Chinese language. In Jade Snow Wong's account, she wonders why it is that her father and brothers demand unquestioning obedience from her, because she is a daughter and a sister. In Monica Sone's case, her father was not receptive to her desire to take ballet lessons because of the scanty costuming.

Some observers predicted that subsequent generations were likely to abandon their parents' cultural heritage and assimilate into that of the host society. However, historian Marcus Lee Hansen challenged that idea. He suggested that the third generation would show an interest in the culture and heritage of the grandparents. Hansen's Principle, as it is sometimes called, says that "what the son wishes to forget the grandson wishes to remember."[13] While the second generation may feel insecure and ambivalent because they inhabit two worlds—the world of the immigrant parents and the world of the larger American society—the third generation does not share that feeling. They are raised in a second-generation environment, which is more similar to American society. Moreover, their second-generation parents are more fluent in the English language and very likely will communicate with them in English. With this type of background, the third generation feels no insecurity, only curiosity, in examining the heritage of their family. More recently, scholars have been suggesting different ways to look at the different generations within families. Some have talked about "segmented assimilation," noting that immigrant children may have partial or fragmented, not total, assimilation, and it may be in the direction of the adversarial stance of a minority group rather than that of the majority group.[14] Others have posited the idea of "selective assimilation," pointing out that immigrant children may retain certain aspects of their parents' culture even as they adopt positive values from the host society.[15] Thus, boys may believe that females are subordinate to males, even as they adopt the idea that education is a path for economic advancement and social success. Recent research has also emphasized that modern technology in communication and transportation has made it easier to maintain contacts, or transnational ties, with the first-generation's homeland. As a result, the second generation and the first generation are not necessarily destined to have a generational gap over cultural values. Context and geographical location will always be important factors as to whether there will be a generation gap. The title of Eleanor Wong Telamaque's 1978 book, *It's Crazy to Stay Chinese in Minnesota* puts it well.[16] If Telamaque's family was almost alone in a Midwestern town, what does it mean to be culturally Chinese if everyone else is culturally something else? On the other hand, if one were living in Monterey Park or the San Gabriel Valley in Southern California, where there is a dense concentration of Asian American residents, it would be easier to maintain connections with the cultural values of one's parents or grandparents.

Moreover, the outlook and response of people may be more tied to their personality than to their generation. Some people may be of the first generation, but they are able to assimilate into a new society very quickly. They easily learn to adopt the novel ways of their host society and come to prefer them to those of their former homeland. On the other hand, some people of the second generation may be more comfortable with their immigrant parents' values and practices and therefore try to emulate first-generation behavior. In short, environment or social setting and personality factors may be more important than generation in dictating a particular outlook or mode of behavior.[17]

DOES WHETHER THEY ARE IMMIGRANT, 1.5, OR SECOND GENERATION INFLUENCE LATER GENERATIONS AND SOCIETAL PERCEPTIONS?

For

Research on Asian Americans, until recently, has been dominated largely by immigrant experiences. Various scholars have paid more attention to the issues that 1.5 and second generations (emerging generations) have with their families, their experiences at school, and how they negotiate or deal with their identity.[18] While there has been a stark contrast between first generation/ immigrants and their second-generation children, until recently little attention has been given to the unique characteristics of the 1.5 generation.[19] The experiences of the 1.5- and second-generation Asian Americans shed new light into how they are different from their first-generation immigrant or refugee parents. Families, communities, and social connections largely shape the differences between immigrants and the 1.5, second, and subsequent generations.

Family is a key factor in maintaining one's ethnic culture and identity. At home, immigrant parents will most likely speak their native language, cook their ethnic foods, and expose their families to the various cultural rituals passed on to them by their own parents. Home is where the foundations are made and where children learn about the role they play in the family as a result of immigration. For example, immigrant children are often given adult roles at home. As a result of their parents' inability to speak, read, or write English and/or because of their busy work schedules, immigrant and second-generation children frequently take on the role of translator for their parents, bill sorter, child care provider for younger siblings, and overall house maintainer (cooking and cleaning). Consequently, children often complain that they do not have a childhood, but instead are forced into adult roles.[20] As a result, a barrier is created between parents and children in terms of what constitutes an Asian American family. While immigrant parents hold on to their own perceptions of what a family is supposed to be, with children obeying their parents without question, the children are forced to create a new version of a family where they are an integral part of its function. Their new roles put them in a position where they talk to their parents about finances, problems with their siblings, and questions that other adults, such as teachers or bill collectors, may have. Consequently, these children have access to adult information early on and, therefore, they shoulder many of the responsibilities and worries. The cultural barriers that are created have much to do with the cultural expectations and barriers that are built as a result of economic and social conditions after immigration.

The cultural barriers experienced by immigrant parents and their children have much to do with language. It is difficult to transmit emotions, feelings, and culture without language. For Asian families, there are feelings, thoughts, and emotions that are difficult to translate and, as a result of the generational differences, these things are often left out in parent-child relationships. In other words, parents have a hard time communicating with their children because of their limited English-speaking abilities, and children struggle with their parents due to their limited language abilities in their ethnic tongue. Many of the youths, having been socialized in the United States, have limited fluency of their native language, forget their native language, or never learned it to begin with. Working-class immigrant and refugee parents, who speak limited English, find that lack of communication with their children is one of the biggest obstacles. Often Asian American youth will speak a combination of English and their native tongue to communicate with their parents, but in many cases, they have a difficult time communicating their feelings and thoughts with their parents. While the language problem exists for many Asian immigrant families, it is less of a problem for those with 1.5-generation children. The 1.5-generation children are bicultural and bilingual and, as a result, serve as a bridge between their parents and their second- and third-generation siblings and the larger society. The 1.5 generation speaks a combination of their ethnic language and English. For example, Koreans and Filipinos refer to the fusion of English and their ethnic language as Konglish and Taglish, respectively. This often resolves the problem of children not being able to find the appropriate word when conversing with their parents or other immigrant adults.

Like other youths, the 1.5 generation experiences cultural gaps with their first-generation parents. The sociocultural experiences of the parents vary significantly from the emerging generation for they do not have a shared understanding of the workings of the school system, the political climate, the social climate, or what it means to grow up in America. Furthermore, Asian American youths complain that their parents often treat them as their own parents had treated them, not recognizing that the external influences in the United States have altered their perceptions. For example, first-generation parents enforce strict rules and guidelines on their children, yet these same children observe how their friends' parents treat them. The differences in how immigrant parents and their children have been socialized contribute to the conflict and misunderstanding between them. Furthermore, the differences also create misconceptions about who Asian Americans are by the larger society.

Perceptions of Asians are largely shaped by the idea that they are a homogenous immigrant population. This misconception creates hurdles and barriers for both parents and their children. For the parents, the immigrant image isolates them and makes it difficult for them to blend into mainstream society. Largely due to their limited English proficiency or their accents, they are immediately perceived as foreigners, and not truly American. For their children, the immigrant image sometimes contributes negatively to their own identity formation. The idea of being an immigrant foreigner is something the children try to shy away from and consequently they too begin to discriminate against other immigrants and treat them as foreigners. For Asian American youth, they are most harsh on "FOBs" or immigrants Fresh Off the Boats. Immigrants are seen as FOBs because of their accents and because their clothes are different from what American children wear. The 1.5- and second-generation Asian Americans make fun of "FOBs," as if to say that they are not like them. The internalized shame of being an immigrant affects the interpersonal relationships that Asian American youths have with other Asian Americans. Furthermore, the shame and embarrassment they feel affect their home life as well. Many youths are reluctant to bring their American friends to their homes, afraid of being embarrassed by their parents' accents, their cultural foods, and the overall way they live. For example, Korean children may feel embarrassed to bring friends to their home with the smell of *kim-chee* (spicy fermented cabbage) lingering in the air. Or Filipino children may be worried about the large wooden spoons and forks on the wall with the smell of *bago-ong* (fermented shrimp and fish used for seasoning or dipping), while Chinese children may not want to invite friends for dinner, afraid of the reaction they would get from shark fin soup or marinated chicken feet. Thus the denial of their ethnic heritage, or what social scientists call ethnic disidentification, is one way in which Asian American children cope with being ostracized from the larger society. Immigrant adults do not have the option of ethnically switching from immigrant to Asian American, for they are labeled as the former. Thus, in the eyes of the larger society, they are forever foreigners and their children do not want to stick out as much as their parents do to "Americans."

Against

In much of the literature about Asian Americans, there is a great deal of discussion about the differences among the immigrant (or first), the 1.5, the second, and the third generations. The first and second generations have a major difference, because the latter is more acculturated into American society and has a greater familiarity with the English language and the host culture. The 1.5 generation receives much notice, though, because it is a novel term invented by Korean Americans. The 1.5 generation, or *il-chom-*

o-se, essentially refers to young children who were born abroad but who came to the United States at an early age. As a result, although they are foreign-born, they are almost like the second generation because they receive the socialization, schooling, and wealth of experiences similar to that of the second generation. With the third and subsequent generations, the traditional way of thinking has been that they are much more assimilated into American life.

Because so many of the Asian Americans are foreign-born and have either 1.5- or second-generation children in the United States, social scientists have been especially interested in researching the characteristics of the different generations. The results have been fascinating. According to one study, Hmong American high school students of the 1.5 generation were not as Americanized or acculturated as expected. While many of them had adapted to the United States, they held on to Hmong culture to a greater degree and with more complexity than was expected. They were neither traditional nor assimilated, as they made adjustments to American culture without being assimilated. Moreover, whether or not there is a context of racism and discrimination against them is important in determining how they will fare in their studies at school.[21]

These results suggest that the first- and second-generation distinctions are of limited usefulness. Acculturation or assimilation into American society is nonlinear. The experience of the second generation is influenced by numerous factors. For example, one area that should receive greater attention from researchers is the issue of *hapa* identity. *Hapa* is a Hawaiian word referring to mixed racial identity. With interracial marriage being a frequent occurrence among Asian Americans, there is increasing complexity in the matter of personal and cultural identity. According to the 2000 United States Census, 14.9 percent of the 12.5 million Asian Pacific American population is multiracial. Another 1.5 percent of the Asian Pacific American population is multiethnic.[22] The examples of racial blending and hybridization in the Asian American population are evident when one considers some of the prominent names in the news and the media. Some of the more notable mixed racial Asian Americans are golfer Tiger Woods, television journalist Ann Curry, movie stars Lou Diamond Phillips, Dean Cain, Kristin Kreuk, Keanu Reeves, and downhill racer Apolo Ohno.[23] Given that this is an increasing trend, it is likely that multiracial and multiethnic identities will have a major impact on the status of the second and subsequent generations of Asian Americans in the future.

Mixed marriages and a population of hybrid, multiethnic Asian Americans are important indicators of interethnic and interracial relations. The manner in which different groups interact with each other impacts how immigrants, refugees, and their children react with each other and the dominant society. If there are prejudicial and discriminatory attitudes toward Asian Americans, Asian American youth of the second generation may disassociate from the first generation. On the other hand, if society holds a favorable view of Asian Americans, the second generation may retain pride in their cultural heritage and feel less compelled to separate themselves from their parents and the immigrant generation. Related to this is the economic and social status of the parents and the immigrant or ethnic group. If the parents and the ethnic group command respect because of their higher income, or elevated educational level, or prestigious occupational status, the second generation may feel less of a need to separate themselves from their parents' ethnic heritage.

Contemporary researchers seem to be questioning the differences that are often linked to the various generations. Some believe it is desirable to avoid the discussion of a generation gap because it recycles the theme of parent-child conflict and misses the larger picture of how society may exclude or differentiate different groups.[24] The cultural politics of the larger society "is an important crucible for shaping future choices" and it is "important to pay attention to cultural forms and narratives that youth create in order to make meaning of their worlds."[25] For this reason, it is critical to examine the experiences of the youths themselves and not necessarily in relation to their parents. This focus would help move away from the intergenerational conflict focus that comes out of studying Asian American youth.[26] The world of youth, after all, is not only confined to relations with their parents and siblings and deserves to be studied in broader terms.

CAN CATEGORIZATION BY GENERATIONS REMAINS USEFUL AS A WAY TO UNDERSTAND THE ASIAN AMERICAN EXPERIENCE?

For

Most Asian Americans are of the first or second generation. This is because the Asian American population in the United States increased significantly after the Immigration Act of 1965. That being the case, it is still convenient to refer to the immigrant or refugee generation as the first generation. Their children are American-born or the second generation. There are obviously several differences between the first and second generation. For instance, the first generation may have citizenship through naturalization or they may have permanent resident status. The second generation, on the other hand, possesses U.S. citizenship by virtue of having being born in this country. The first and second generation also have different levels of understanding about the ancestral homeland versus the United States. The first generation undoubtedly is more familiar with their Asian homeland, its culture, and its practices. They are somewhat less familiar with that of the United States. Conversely, the second generation is more familiar with the culture and history of the United States, but they have less knowledge about the homeland from which their parents arrived. In addition, because of this divergence in knowledge about the parents' homeland versus that of the United States, it is fairly common to have a cultural gap or even conflict between the first and second generations. The second generation often prefers to speak English and emulate the practices of the United States, unlike the first generation that frequently seeks to maintain more of the traditional cultural traditions and customs of their ancestral homeland. As one observer puts it, "Generational conflicts arise because Asian families rely on traditional hierarchical authority, demanding respect and audience from their children." But the Asian American children, who are acculturating to U.S. norms, "also learn the competing values of independence and assertiveness and begin to challenge their parents, causing increased conflict within the family."[27]

The third generation, however, presents an enigma. If one subscribes to the theory of Marcus Lee Hansen, the third generation has an interest in ethnic awareness. Simple stated, it is the idea that "what the son wishes to forget, the grandson wishes to remember." Thus, it has been labeled the principle of third-generation interest.[28] Whereas Hansen's idea was discounted in the past, in recent years it has generated a great deal of interest among scholars. The research findings have been fascinating. Some findings indicate that the third generation experiences greater acculturation than the previous generations and appears to be integrating and assimilating more into American society. On the other hand, other findings suggest that there can be an "ethnicity paradox," that even while the process of Americanization is taking place, the third generation is interested in their ancestral culture.[29] Even if there is no residence in an ethnic neighborhood, there can be a sense of social cohesion and ethnic group identity through organizations and relations with other ethnic members.[30] Assimilation and ethnic group identity can be maintained simultaneously.[31]

In his article "The Problem of Generations," scholar Karl Mannheim discussed several ways to think about generations.[32] First, there is "generational status." People locate themselves in a common age group with which they were born and experience the same historical and social forces. But the members of this same generation may not all share a common destiny. So he introduces the "actual generation" as a second concept. The actual generation experiences the same historical and social dynamics. But within the actual generation, there is a third concept, the "generational unit," which shared the same response to the sociohistorical forces it faced.[33] The analytical concepts introduced by Mannheim suggest that it is possible to refine thinking about generational constructs to accommodate the dynamics of a sociohistorical context. Thus, one might analyze different generations of Asian Americans today and their shared responses to multiculturalism, pan-Asian American ethnicity, transnational relations with Asia, and other variables. In any event, there can be little doubt that Asian Americans refer to themselves in terms of generations. The Japanese American community, for example, employs the term *Issei* for the first generation, *Nisei* for the second generation, *Sansei* for the third generation, *Yonsei* for the fourth generation, and *Gosei* for the fifth generation. The Korean community, in a similar vein, refers to the first generation as *Ilse* and the second generation as *Ise*. These examples suggest that Asian American communities still find references to different generations to be convenient and useful.

Against

In the early 1970s, the common perception of Asian Americans was that they were either Chinese or Japanese. Despite the fact that there were growing numbers of Koreans, Filipinos, Vietnamese, Cambodians, South Asians, and Hmong, the perception was that all Asians were the same. In fact, people of Asian descent were actually referred to as "orientals," objectified as a homogeneous group. In the 1990s, growing interest in the new Asian immigrant groups emerged, educating many to recognize the complexities of Asian American communities. Still, discussions of Asian Americans continue to homogenize them, linking Chinese, Cambodians, Vietnamese, and others as if they had the same social, political, and economic issues. What has been missing is the discussion of social class, gender, and the sexuality of Asian Americans.

Clearly, generation gaps and differences greatly affect the experiences of Asian Americans. Yet, social class issues are often ignored due to the model minority stereotype that pigeonholes Asian Americans as the successful minority. Yet, there are growing numbers of Asian Americans who are at or below the poverty line. There are several reasons for this. While the initial immigrant groups during the 1965 reunification act consisted of professionals and their families, the 1970s refugees were escaping political turmoil on their home soil. In the 1980s, the rapid transnational economy created a need for migrant workers who worked in the United States and other parts of the world through various sponsorships. The 1990s continued to bring in the migrant workers, along with a small number of wealthy people from Hong Kong and Taiwan, yet there were also growing numbers of domestic workers. Unlike other ethnic groups, there has been a constant flow of Asian migration to the United States, contributing to Asians being the second fastest growing ethnic population in the United States. The flow of Asian immigrants has much to do with the global economy and the struggles that many Asians face in their homelands. As a result, we have seen more poor Asian immigrants settling in the U.S. landscape. Despite the diverse Asian population, the stereotype of the model minority continues to plague our society. Little attention is given to the large number of Asian Americans on welfare, or at or below the poverty line. Nor is the number of homeless Asian Americans ever spoken about. Social class greatly affects the interactions between generations. Middle-class families are more likely to have one parent at home when the children come to school, speak English, and have more contact with their children. Working-class parents are more likely to have dual employment, speak broken English, and due to their work hours have less contact with their children.[34] Consequently, the social class of the family impacts the parent-child relationship, but it also impacts the relationship that children have with each other. Older children are left to care for their younger siblings while their parents work and, as a result, the children develop a different set of roles in the home.

Another factor that is often ignored in discussions of Asian Americans is the issue of gender. While we have various stereotypes of Asian men as being feminine and Asian women as either the docile, passive ingénue or the dominant dragon lady, little attention is given to gender politics or issues facing Asian immigrants and families. As generational differences affect Asian Americans, gender also contributes to how Asian Americans see themselves and each other. Many of the anecdotal perceptions are shaped by the stereotypes that are perpetuated by the media. However, the reality is that Asian American men and women have had to reconstruct their gender roles in the United States. While working-class men and women worked in Asia as they do in the United States, women find that they have an easier time finding jobs as domestic workers, factory assemblers, and hotel housekeepers. The men, on the other hand, find it more difficult to find a job that they may have once held in Asia. Professionals have difficulty finding jobs due to the language barriers and cultural obstacles that impede their ability to advance economically. This shift in occupational attainment changes the gender dynamics between Asian American men and women. While it may appear that men and women have more of an egalitarian relationship, the reality for women is that they have a double shift, working at the job and then coming home to work their second shift. Despite the hours women put in at their jobs, they still perform most of the household duties when they get home, including taking care of the children. Some Asian American men, having a difficult time finding a job in today's difficult market, become househusbands while their wives work in working-class pink-collar jobs in the garment district, the computer chip assembly line, and in housekeeping. Consequently, children observe a different set of gender roles in the family. In short, then, class and gender issues must be considered as they may be more important than the factor of generational identity.

QUESTIONS

1. Conflicts between parents and children have been a part of U.S. society, but Asian American families face an additional set of circumstances that contribute to the conflict. What are some of the ways in which families can resolve these conflicts?

2. How are the experiences of the children of immigrants different from that of American-born children? What is the root of the conflict, and how can that problem be addressed?

3. Think about the obstacles and difficulties that immigrant families face. What are the differences between working-class and middle-class families?

4. Why is it important to discuss the impact of gender on different generations? How critical is it to consider the consequences of gender reversal on Asian American families?

5. In school, are there differences between Asian American students for whom English is their native language versus those for whom English is a second language? What are the interactions like between these groups? Why might this be?

6. The term 1.5 generation is a relatively new concept. What does it mean and how did the term originate? Can you think of friends or acquaintances that fit into this category?

7. Are the experiences of the 1.5 generation different from those of American-born children? Are there conflicts, and, if so, how can they be addressed?

8. Who is Marcus Lee Hansen and what is Hansen's Principle? Is there any validity to this principle?

9. What is a generation gap? Is it likely to be greater if the parents do not speak English well? Why or why not?

10. What does the term FOB mean? Which generation does this term refer to? Are there any connotations associated with the usage of the phrase?

11. How important is language in causing a gap or cultural barrier between generations? What are Konglish and Taglish, and how did they develop?

12. Can the media play a role in fostering a generation gap? As children watch television and movies, do they look for references to their culture? If they fail to find any examples, does that have any consequences for how they view their cultural heritage or ethnic identity?

13. Conflicts between parents and children have frequently been alluded to in American society. What are some of the ways that families can resolve these conflicts?

14. Social scientists use the terms "segmented assimilation" and "selective assimilation." What do these terms mean? Cite some examples.

15. In addition to the usage of generational categories, are there other ways to look at Asian Americans? Consider class, gender, and *hapa* identity. Are there differences between working-class and middle-class families? How is gender affected in these families?

NOTES

1. David Kertzer, "Generation as a Sociological Problem," *Annual Review of Sociology* 9 (1983): 125–149.

2. *The Women Outside* documentary by J. T. Takagi and Hye Jung Park. Distributed by Third World Newsreel. 53 minutes.

3. Blood ties refer to the idea that only people who are related by blood are family. Thus, if there are no blood ties, one could never be a family member.

4. United States Consulate General, Ho Chi Minh City, Vietnam, Refugee Resettlement Section, usembassy.state.gov/posts/vn2/wwwhref.html.

5. Mary Danico and Linda Võ, "'No Lattés Here': Asian American Youth and the Cyber Café Obsession," in *Asian American Youth Culture,* ed. Min Zhou and Jennifer Lee (New York: Routledge Press, 2004).

6. Pronounced one point five.

7. Mary Yu Danico, *The 1.5 Generation: Becoming Korean American in Hawaii* (Honolulu: University of Hawaii Press, 2004).

8. Ibid.

9. While most Caucasians face little or no cultural obstacles, there has been a recent wave of new White immigrants from Russia and other Eurasian countries who may initially face cultural obstacles.

10. 2000 United States Census.

11. Danico and Võ, "'No Lattés Here.'"

12. Pardee Lowe, *Father and Glorious Descendant* (Boston: Little, Brown and Company, 1943); Jade Snow Wong, *Fifth Chinese Daughter* (New York: Harper and Row, 1950); Monica Sone, *Nisei Daughter* (Boston: Little, Brown and Company, 1953).

13. Marcus Lee Hansen, "The Third Generation in America," *Commentary* 14 (November 1952): 493–500.

14. Min Zhou, "Segmented Assimilation: Issues, Controversies, and Recent Research on the New Second Generation," *International Migration Review* 31 (1997): 975–1008.

15. Sharmila Rudrappa, "Disciplining Desire in Making the Home: Engendering Ethnicity in Indian Immigrant Families," in *The Second Generation: Ethnic Identity among Asian Americans,* ed. Pyong Gap Min (Walnut Creek, CA: AltaMira Press, 2002), 102.

16. Eleanor Wong Telamaque, *It's Crazy to Stay Chinese in Minnesota* (New York: Thomas Nelson, 1978).

17. For a useful discussion, see Laura Uba, *Asian American Personality Patterns, Identity, and Mental Health* (New York: Guilford Press, 1994).

18. See Danico, *The 1.5 Generation.*

19. Danico; this is the first book on the 1.5 generation.

20. Danico, *The 1.5 Generation*.

21. Stacey Lee, "More than 'Model Minorities' or 'Delinquents': A Look at Hmong American High School Students," *Harvard Educational Review* 71 (fall 2001): 511.

22. Teresa Williams-Leon, "Census/Consensus? APAs and Multiracial Identity," in *The New Face of Asian Pacific America*, ed. Eric Lai and Dennis Arguelles (San Francisco and Los Angeles: AsianWeek and UCLA Asian American Studies Center Press, 2003), 18.

23. Ibid., 18.

24. Sunaina Maira, *Desis in the House: Indian American Youth in New York City* (Philadelphia: Temple University Press, 2002), 17.

25. Lisa Lowe, *Immigrant Acts: On Asian American Cultural Politics* (Durham, NC: Duke University Press, 1996), 63.

26. Ibid., 18.

27. Uma A. Segal, *A Framework for Immigration: Asians in the United States* (New York: Columbia University Press, 2002), 197–198.

28. Richard T. Schaefer, *Racial and Ethnic Groups* (Upper Saddle River, NJ: Pearson Prentice Hall, 2004), 143.

29. Ibid., 144.

30. Ibid., 146.

31. Stephen S. Fugita and David J. O'Brien, *Japanese American Ethnicity: The Persistence of Community* (Seattle: University of Washington Press, 1991), 184; Eileen H. Tamura, *Americanization, Acculturation, and Ethnic Identity: The Nisei Generation in Hawaii* (Urbana: University of Illinois Press, 1994), 238–239.

32. Karl Mannheim, "The Problem of Generations," in *Essays on the Sociology of Knowledge*, ed. Paul Kecsdemeti (London: Routledge and Kegan Paul, 1972).

33. Jere Takahashi, *Nisei/Sansei: Shifting Japanese American Identities and Politics* (Philadelphia: Temple University Press, 1997), 10–11; Judy Yung, *Unbound Feet: A Social History of Chinese Women in San Francisco* (Berkeley: University of California Press, 1995), 333.

34. Danico, *The 1.5 Generation*.

SELECTED WORKS

Cho, Lee-Jay, and Moto Yada. *Tradition and Change in the Asian Family*. Honolulu: University of Hawaii Press, 1994.

Danico, Mary Yu. *The 1.5 Generation: Becoming Korean American in Hawai'i*. Honolulu: University of Hawaii Press, 2004.

Danico, Mary, and Linda Võ. "'No Lattés Here': Asian American Youth and the Cyber Café Obsession." In *Asian American Youth Culture*, ed. Min Zhou and Jennifer Lee. New York: Routledge Press, 2004.

Elder, G. H., Jr. "Families, Kin and the Life Course: A Sociological Perspective." In *Review of Child Development Research*, ed. R. D. Park. Chicago: University of Chicago Press, 1984.

Erikson, Erik H. *Childhood and Society*. New York: Norton Press, 1950.

Espiritu, Yen Le. "The Intersection of Race, Ethnicity, and Class: The Multiple Identities of Second-Generation Filipinos." *Identities* 1 (1994): 1–25.

Fawcett, Early G., ed. *Lure and Loathing: Essays on Race Identity and the Ambivalence of Assimilation*. New York: Penguin, 1993.

Fugita, Stephen S., and David J. O'Brien. *Japanese American Ethnicity: The Persistence of Community.* Seattle: University of Washington Press, 1991.

Gans, Hans J. "Symbolic Ethnicity: The Future of Ethnic Groups and Cultures in America." *Ethnic and Racial Studies* 2 (1979): 1–20.

Gans, H. "Symbolic Ethnicity and Symbolic Religiosity: Towards a Comparison of Ethnic and Religious Acculturation." *Ethnic and Racial Studies* 17 (1994): 577–592.

Garbarino, James, and Robert H. Abramowitz. "The Family as a Social System." In *Children and Families in the Social Environment,* ed. James Garbarino. New York: Aldine de Gruyter, 1992.

Gardner, Robert W., Bryant Robey, and Peter C. Smith. "Asian Americans: Growth, Change and Diversity." *Population Bulletin* 40 (October 1985): 8.

Germain, Carol B. "Emerging Conceptions of Family Development over the Life Course." *Families in Society: Journal of Contemporary Human Services* 42 (1994): 259–268.

Hansen, Marcus Lee. "The Third Generation in America." *Commentary* 14 (November 1952): 493–500.

Hurh, Won Moo, Hei Chu Kim, and Kwan Chung Kim. *Assimilation Patterns of Immigrants in the United States: A Case Study of Korean Immigrants in the Chicago Area.* Washington, DC: University Press of America, 1979.

Kertzer, David. "Generation as a Sociological Problem." *Annual Review of Sociology* 9 (1983): 125–149.

Kibria, Nazli. *Family Tightrope: The Changing Lives of Vietnamese Americans.* Princeton, NJ: Princeton University Press, 1993.

Kim, Kwang Chung, Shin Kim, and Won Moo Hurh. "Filial Piety and Intergeneration Relationship in Korean Immigrant Families." *International Journal of Aging and Human Development* 33, no. 3 (1991): 233–245.

Koh, Tong-He. "Ethnic Identity in First, 1.5, and Second Generation Korean-Americans." In *Korean Americans: Conflict and Harmony,* ed. Ho-Youn Kwon. Chicago: North Park College and Theological Seminary, 1994, 43–54.

Lee, Stacey. "More than 'Model Minorities' or 'Delinquents': A Look at Hmong American High School Students." *Harvard Educational Review* 71 (fall 2001): 511.

Lee, Yoon Mo. "Interorganizational Context of the Korean Community for the Participation of the Emerging Generation." In *The Emerging Generation of Korean-American.* Korea: Kyung Hee University Press, 1993.

Lowe, Lisa. *Immigrant Acts: On Asian American Cultural Politics.* Durham, NC: Duke University Press, 1996.

Lowe, Pardee. *Father and Glorious Descendant.* Boston: Little, Brown and Company, 1943.

Maira, Sunaina. *Desis in the House: Indian American Youth in New York City.* Philadelphia: Temple University Press, 2002.

Mannheim, Karl. "The Problem of Generations." In *Essays on the Sociology of Knowledge,* ed. Paul Kecsdemeti. London: Routledge and Kegan Paul, 1972.

Phinney, Jean. "Ethnic Identity in Adolescents and Adults: Review of Research." *Psychological Bulletin* 108, no. 3 (1991): 499–514.

Phinney, Jean, and Linda Alipuria. "Ethnic Identity in Older Adolescents from Four Ethnic Groups." *Journal of Adolescence* 13 (1990): 156–176.

Phinney, Jean S., Victoria Chavira, and Lisa Williamson. "Acculturation Attitudes and Self-Esteem among High School Students." *Youth & Society* 23, no. 3 (1992): 299–313.

Portes, Alejandro. *The New Second Generation.* New York: Russell Sage Foundation, 1996.

Rudrappa, Sharmila. "Disciplining Desire in Making the Home: Engendering Ethnicity in Indian Immigrant Families." In *The Second Generation: Ethnic Identity among Asian Americans,* ed. Pyong Gap Min. Walnut Creek, CA: AltaMira Press, 2002.

Ryu, Charles. *1.5 Generation: Asian American.* Boston: Twayne Publishing, 1990.

Schaefer, Richard T. *Racial and Ethnic Groups.* Upper Saddle River, NJ: Pearson Prentice Hall, 2004.

Segal, Uma A. *A Framework for Immigration: Asians in the United States.* New York: Columbia University Press, 2002.

Sone, Monica. *Nisei Daughter.* Boston: Little, Brown and Company, 1953.

Takahashi, Jere. *Nisei/Sansei: Shifting Japanese American Identities and Politics.* Philadelphia: Temple University Press, 1997.

Tamura, Eileen H. *Americanization, Acculturation, and Ethnic Identity: The Nisei Generation in Hawaii.* Urbana: University of Illinois Press, 1994.

Telamaque, Eleanor Wong. *It's Crazy to Stay Chinese in Minnesota.* New York: Thomas Nelson, 1978.

Uba, Laura. *Asian American Personality Patterns, Identity, and Mental Health.* New York: Guilford Press, 1994.

Verkuyten, Maykel. "Self-Esteem, Self-Concept Stability, and Aspects of Ethnic Identity among Minority and Majority Youth in the Netherlands." *Journal of Youth and Adolescence* 24, no. 2 (April 1995): 155–175.

Williams-Leon, Teresa. "Census/Consensus? APAs and Multiracial Identity." In *The New Face of Asian Pacific America,* ed. Eric Lai and Dennis Arguelles. San Francisco and Los Angeles: AsianWeek and UCLA Asian American Studies Center Press, 2003.

Wong, Jade Snow. *Fifth Chinese Daughter.* New York: Harper and Row, 1950.

Wong, Morrison. "Post 1965 Asian Immigration: Where Do They Come From, Where Are They Now and Where Are They Going?" *Annals of the American Academy of Political and Social Science* 487 (1986).

Yung, Judy. *Unbound Feet: A Social History of Chinese Women in San Francisco.* Berkeley: University of California Press, 1995.

Zhou, Min. "Segmented Assimilation: Issues, Controversies, and Recent Research on the New Second Generation." *International Migration Review* 31 (1997): 975–1008.

RESOURCE GUIDE

SUGGESTED READING

Abelmann, Nancy, and John Lie. *Blue Dreams: Korean Americans and the Los Angeles Riots.* Cambridge, MA: Harvard University Press, 1995.

Aguilar-San Juan, Karin. "Creating Ethnic Places: Vietnamese American Community-Building in Orange County and Boston." Ph.D. thesis. Providence, RI: Brown University, 2002.

Alquizola, Marilyn. "Subversion or Affirmation: The Text and Subtext of *America Is in the Heart.*" In *Asian Americans: Comparative and Global Perspectives,* ed. Shirley Hune, Hyun-chan Kim, Stephen Fugita, and Amy Ling. Pullman: Washington State University Press, 1991.

"Ancestors in the Americas: Series Overview." *Ancestors in the Americas,* 1988, http://www.cetel.org/ancestors_overview.html.

Atkinson, D. R., G. Morten, and D. W. Sue, eds. *Counseling American Minorities: A Cross-cultural Perspective.* 4th edition. Madison, WI: Brown and Benchmark, 1993.

Azuma, Eiichiro. "Interethnic Conflict under Racial Subordination: Japanese Immigrants and Their Asian Neighbors in Walnut Grove, California, 1908–1941." *Amerasia Journal* 20 (1994): 27–56.

Baron, Debra. "Who Are the Pacific Islanders?" In *The Asian American Almanac,* ed. Susan Gall and Irene Natividad. Detroit: Gale Research, 1995.

Barringer, Herbert R., Peter Xenos, and David T. Takeuchi. "Education, Occupational Prestige, and Income of Asian Americans." *Sociology of Education* 63 (1990): 27–43.

Beauregard, Guy. "Reclaiming Sui Sin Far." In *Re-collecting Early Asian America: Essays in Cultural History,* ed. Josephine Lee, Imogene L. Kim, and Yuko Matsukawa. Philadelphia: Temple University Press, 2003.

Bennett, Claudette. "Racial Categories Used in the Decennial Censuses, 1790 to the Present." *Government Information Quarterly* 17, no. 2 (2000): 161–180.

Blair, John G. "Asian American Writing as Culture Studies: The Difference That Distance Makes." *Hitting Critical Mass: A Journal of Asian American Cultural Criticism* 4 (fall 1996), http://ist-socrates.berkeley.edu/~critmass/v4n1/blair1.html.

Blauner, Robert A. *Racial Oppression in America.* New York: Harper, 1972.

Bonacich, Edna. "A Theory of Middleman Minorities." *American Sociological Review* 38 (1973): 585–594.

Bonacich, Edna, and John Modell. *The Economic Basis of Ethnic Solidarity.* Berkeley: University of California Press, 1980.

Borromeo, Gelly. "Born for Business." In *The New Face of Asian Pacific America,* ed. Eric Lai and Dennis Arguelles. San Francisco: AsianWeek and UCLA Asian American Studies Center, 2003, 41.

Bow, Leslie. "Betrayal and Other Acts of Subversion: Feminism, Sexual Politics, Asian American Women's Literature." Princeton University Press, 11 May 2001, http://pup.Princeton.edu/chapters/17066.html.

Breton, Raymond. "Institutional Completeness of Ethnic Communities and the Personal Relations of Immigrants." *American Journal of Sociology* 70 (September 1964): 103–205.

Bulosan, Carlos. *America Is in the Heart.* Seattle: University of Washington Press, 1973.

Campomanes, Oscar V. "The New Empire's Forgetful and Forgotten Citizens: Unrepresentability and Unassimilability in Filipino-American Postcolonialities." *Sentenaryo/Centennial: The Philippine Revolution and Philippine-American War,* ed. Jim Zwick, 1995, http://www.boondocksnet.com/centennial/sctexts/newempir.html.

Chan, Jeffery Paul, and George J. Leonard. "Asian American Literary Pioneers." In *The Asian Pacific American Heritage,* ed. George J. Leonard. New York: Garland Publishing, 1999.

Chan, S., and L. Wang. "Racism and the Model Minority: Asian-Americans in Higher Education." In *The Racial Crisis in American Higher Education,* ed. P. G. Altbach and K. Lomotey. Albany, NY: SUNY Press, 1991.

———. "European and Asian Immigration into the United States in Comparative Perspective, 1820s to 1920s." In *Immigration Reconsidered: History, Sociology, and Politics,* ed. Virginia Yans-McLaughlin. New York: Oxford University Press, 1990.

Chan, Sucheng. *Asian Americans: An Interpretive History.* Boston: Twayne Publishers, 1991.

Chang, Edward Taehan. "Koreans: Entrepreneurs par Excellence." In *The New Face of Asian Pacific America,* ed. Eric Lai and Dennis Arguelles. San Francisco: AsianWeek and UCLA Asian American Studies Center, 2003, 61.

Chang, M. J., and P. N. Kiang. "New Challenges of Representing Asian American Students in U.S. Higher Education." In *The Racial Crisis in American Higher Education: Continuing Challenges for the Twenty-first Century,* ed. W. A. Smith, P. G. Altbach, and K. Lomotey. Albany: State University of New York Press, 2002.

Chang, Mitchell J. "Growing Pains." *Journal of Asian American Studies* (1999): 183–206.

Chang, Robert S. "Legal Implications of the Model Minority Myth." *Model Minority: A Guide to Asian American Empowerment*, 14 April 2003, http://model minority.com/article368.html.

Chen, Rita, and Pegg Wu. "Asian Americans Often Deemed Foreigners." *The Emory Wheel on the Web*, 21 November 2000, www.emory.edu/WHEEL/Issue/ 00Nov21/column1.html.

Chen, Yong. *Chinese San Francisco, 1850–1943: A Trans-Pacific Community*. Stanford, CA: Stanford University Press, 2000.

Cheung, King-Kok. "*The Woman Warrior* versus *The Chinaman Pacific*: Must a Chinese American Critic Choose between Feminism and Heroism?" In *Conflicts in Feminism*, ed. Marianne Hirsch and Evelyn Fox Keller. New York: Routledge, 1990.

Cheung, King-Kok, ed. *An Interethnic Companion to Asian American Literature*. New York: Cambridge University Press, 1997.

Chin, Andrew. "A Brief History of the 'Model Minority' Stereotype." *Model Minority: A Guide to Asian American Empowerment*, 21 April 2001, http://model minority.com/modules.php?name = News&file = article&sid = 72.

Choy, Christine. "Cinema as a Tool of Assimilation: Asian Americans, Women and Hollywood." In *Color: 60 Years of Images of Minority Women in Film: 1921– 1981*. A project of the Exhibition Program of 3rd World Newsreel. Santa Cruz, CA: UC Santa Cruz Library, 1993, 23.

Chung, Sue Fawn. "Fighting for Their American Rights: A History of the Chinese American Citizens Alliance." In *Claiming America: Constructing Chinese American Identities during the Exclusion Era*, ed. K. Scott Wong and Sucheng Chan. Philadelphia: Temple University Press, 1998.

Crystal, David. "Asian Americans and the Myth of the Model Minority," *Journal of Contemporary Social Work* 70, no. 7 (1989): 405–413.

Danico, Mary Yu. *The 1.5 Generation: Becoming Korean American in Hawai'i*. Honolulu: University of Hawaii Press, 2004.

Danico, Mary Yu, and Linda Trinh Võ. "'No Lattés Here': Asian American Youth and the Cyber Café Obsession." In *Asian American Youth Culture, Identity, and Ethnicity*, ed. Min Zhou and Jennifer Lee. New York: Routledge, 2004.

———. *Coming to America: A History of Immigration and Ethnicity in American Life*. New York: HarperCollins, 1990.

Daniels, Roger. "Asian American History's Overdue Emergence." *Asian-Nation: The Landscape of Asian America*, 2001, http://www.asian-nation.org/academic. shtml.

del Rosario, Carina A., ed. *A Different Battle: Stories of Asian Pacific American Veterans*. Seattle: Wing Luke Asian Museum and University of Washington Press, 1999.

Douglas, Christopher. "Review of *Flexible Citizenship: The Cultural Logics of Transnationality*, by Aihwa Ong." *Bryn Mawr Review of Comparative Literature* (summer 2000), http://www.brynmawr.edu/bmrd/winter2000/ongreview.html.

Educational Testing Service. 1997. "Stereotyping Shortchanges Asian American Students." http://modelminority.com/academia/ets.html.

Espiritu, Yen Le. *Asian American Panethnicity: Bridging Institutions and Identities*. Philadelphia: Temple University Press, 1992.

———. *Filipino American Lives*. Philadelphia: Temple University Press, 1995.

Feng, Jianhua. "Asian American Children: What Teachers Should Know." Eric Digest, June 1994. http://www.ericfacility.net/ericdigests/ed369577.html/.

Fisher, C. B., S. A. Wallace, and R. E. Fenton."Discrimination Distress during Adolescence." *Journal of Youth and Adolescence* 29, no. 6 (2000): 679–695.

Foer, Franklin. "Reorientation: Asian Americans Discover Identity Politics." *The New Republic Online*, 21 June 2001, http://www.asianamerican.net/article1.html.

Fong, Colleen, and Judy Yung. "In Search of the Right Spouse: Interracial Marriage among Chinese and Japanese Americans." *Amerasia Journal* 21 (winter 1995/1996): 92.

Fong, Tim. *The First Suburban Chinatown: The Remaking of Monterey Park, California*. Philadelphia: Temple University Press, 1994.

Fong, Timothy P. *The Contemporary Asian American Experience: Beyond the Model Minority*. Englewood Cliffs, NJ: Prentice Hall, 1998.

Fujikane, Candice L. *"Blu's Hanging*: The Responsibilities Faced by Local Readers and Writers." *Hawaii Herald,* 16 January 1998, A9–A11.

Gardiner, Debbie. "Donuts Anyone? Cambodians Own Some 90 Percent of California's Donut Shops." *Asian Week,* 22–28 June 2000.

Gardner, Robert W., Bryant Robey, and Peter C. Smith. "Asian Americans: Growth, Change, and Diversity," *Population Bulletin* 40 (October 1985): 8.

Gillenkirk, Jeff, and James Motlow. *Bitter Melon: Stories from the Last Rural Chinatown in America*. Berkeley, CA: Heyday Books, 1987.

Hing, Bill Ong, and Ronald Lee, eds. *The State of Asian Pacific America: Reframing the Immigration Debate*. Los Angeles: LEAP Asian Pacific Public Policy Institute and UCLA Asian American Studies Center, 1996.

Hirabayashi, L. R., and M. C. Alquizola. "Asian American Studies: Reevaluating for the 1990s." In *The State of Asian America: Activism and Resistance in the 1990s*, ed. K.A.-S. Juan. Boston: South End Press, 1994.

Hirabayashi, Lane Ryo, Akemi Kikumura-Yano, and James A. Hirabayashi, eds. *New Worlds, New Lives: Globalization and People of Japanese Descent in the Americas and from Latin America in Japan*. Stanford, CA: Stanford University Press, 2002.

Ho, Fred Wei-han, ed. *Legacy to Revolution: Politics and Culture of Revolutionary Asian Pacific America*. San Francisco: AK, 2000.

Horton, John. *The Politics of Diversity: Immigration, Resistance, and Change in Monterey Park, California*. Philadelphia: Temple University Press, 1995.

Hsia, J., and M. Hirano-Nakanishi. "The Demographics of Diversity: Asian Americans and Higher Education." *Change,* November/December 1989, 20–27.

Hu-DeHart, Evelyn. "Beyond Black and White." *IGS: Crosscurrents in Culture, Power & History,* Spring 1996. http://www.jhu.edu/~igscph/spr96ehd.htm.

———. "Introduction: Asian American Formations in the Age of Globalization." In *Across the Pacific: Asian Americans and Globalization,* ed. Evelyn Hu-DeHart. Philadelphia: Temple University Press, 1999.

Huang, Betsy. "The Redefinition of the 'Typical Chinese' in Gish Jen's *Typical American.*" *Hitting Critical Mass: A Journal of Asian American Cultural Criticism* 4 (summer 1997). http://ist-socrates.berkeley.edu/~critmass/v4n2/huang1.html.

Hum, Tarry. "The Promises and Dilemmas of Immigrant Ethnic Economies." In *Asian and Latino Immigrants in a Restructuring Economy: The Metamorphosis of Southern California,* ed. Marta Lopez-Garza and David R. Diaz. Stanford, CA: Stanford University Press, 2001.

Hune, S., and K. S. Chan. "Special Focus: Asian Pacific American Demographic and Educational Trends." In *Minorities in Higher Education,* ed. D. Carter and R. Wilson. Vol. 15, 39–107. Washington, DC: American Council on Education, 1997.

Hune, Shirley, Hyng-chan Kim, Stephen Fugita, and Amy Ling. *Asian Americans: Comparative and Global Perspectives.* Pullman: Washington State University Press, 1991.

Ichioka, Yuji. *The Issei: The World of the First Generation Japanese Immigrants, 1885–1924.* New York: Free Press, 1988.

Im, Soyon. "About Face." *Seattle Weekly,* 14 Aug 2000, http://www.seattle weekly.com/features/0034/arts-im.shtml.

"Immigrant Temporalities: Transnationalism, the Diaspora, Exiles and Refugees." http://www.ncela.gwu.edu/pathways/immigration/transnationalism.htm.

James, Jamie. "This Hawaii's Not for Tourists." *Atlantic Monthly,* February 1999, 90–94.

Jaret, Charles. "Troubled by Newcomers: Anti-Immigrant Attitudes and Actions during Two Eras of Mass Migration." In *Mass Migration to the United States: Classical and Contemporary Periods,* ed. Pyong Gap Min. Walnut Creek, CA: AltaMira Press, 2002.

Kao, Grace, and Kara Joyner. "Do Hispanic and Asian Adolescents Practice Panethnicity in Friendship Choices?" Presented at 2001 annual meeting of the American Sociological Association, Anaheim, CA. http://people.mw.mediaone.net/drharris1/kaojoyner.pdf.

Kasindorf, Martin with Paula Chin, Diane Weathers, Kim Foltz, Daniel Shapiro, and Darby Junkin. "Asian Americans: A 'Model Minority,'" *Newsweek,* 6 December 1982, 39ff.

Keenan, Sally. "Crossing Boundaries: The Revisionary Writing of Maxine Hong Kingston." *Hitting Critical Mass: A Journal of Asian American Cultural Criticism* 6 (spring 2000). http://ist-socrates.berkeley.edu/~critmass/v6n2/keenan.pdf.

Kelly, Kimiko, and Daniel Kikuo Ichinose. *Demographic Profile of Asian and Pacific Islanders in Southern California: Census 2000.* Los Angeles: Asian Pacific American Legal Center, 5.

Ketrak, Ketu H. "South Asian American Writers: Geography and Memory." *Amerasia Journal* 22 (1996): 121–138.

Kidder, William C. "Situating Asian Pacific Americans in the Law School Affirmative Action Debate: Empirical Facts about Thernstrom's Rhetorical Acts." *Asian Law Journal* 7, no. 29 (2000): 43.

Kim, Angela, and Christine J. Yeh. "Stereotypes of Asian American Students." ERIC Digest. New York: ERIC Clearinghouse on Urban Education, 2002. http://www.ericfacility.net/databases/ERIC_Digests/ed462510.html.

Kim, Elaine H. *Asian American Literature: An Introduction to the Writings and Their Social Context.* Philadelphia: Temple University Press, 1982.

———. "Dangerous Affinities: Korean American Feminisms (En)counter Gendered Korean and Racialized U.S. Nationalist Narratives." *Hitting Critical Mass: A Journal of American Cultural Criticism* 6 (Fall 1999), http://ist-socrates.berkeley.edu/~critmass/v6n1/ekim.pdf.

Kim, Elaine H., and Eui-Young Yu, eds. *East to America: Korean American Life Stories.* New York: New Press, 1996.

Kim, Kwang Chung, and Won Moo Hurh. "Korean Americans and the 'Success' Image: A Critique." *Amerasia Journal* 10, no. 2 (1983): 3–21.

Kitano, Harry, and Stanley Sue. "The Model Minorities." *Journal of Social Issues* 29, no. 2 (1973): 1–10.

Kitano, Harry H. L., and Roger Daniels. *Asian Americans: Emerging Minorities.* Englewood Cliffs, NJ: Prentice Hall, 1995.

Kobayashi, Fukuko. "Producing Asian American Spaces: From Cultural Nation to the Space of Hybridity as Represented in Texts by Asian American Writers." *Japanese Journal of American Studies* 13 (2002). http://wwwsocnii.ac.jp/jaas/periodicals/JJAS/PDF/13/No.13–04.pdf.

Koehn, Peter H., and Xiao-huang Yin, eds. *The Expanding Roles of Chinese Americans in U.S.-China Relations: Transnational Networks and Trans-Pacific Interactions.* Armonk, NY: M.E. Sharpe, 2002.

Kotkin, Joel. *Tribes: How Race, Religion, and Identity Determine Success in the Global Economy.* New York: Random House, 1993.

Kurahashi, Yuko. *Asian American Culture on Stage: The History of the East West Players.* New York: Garland Publishing, 1999.

Kwong, Peter. *The New Chinatown.* New York: Hill Wang, 1987.

Lai, Eric. "Business and Hi-Tech." In *The New Face of Asian Pacific America,* ed. Eric Lai and Dennis Arguelles. San Francisco: AsianWeek and UCLA Asian American Studies Center, 2003, 236.

Lai, Eric, and Dennis Arguelles. *The New Face of Asian Pacific America: Numbers, Diversity & Change in the 21st Century.* San Francisco: AsianWeek and UCLA Asian American Studies Center Press, 2003.

Lai, Him Mark, Genny Lim, and Judy Yung, eds. *Island: Poetry and History of Chinese Immigrants on Angel Island, 1910–1940.* San Francisco: Hoc Doi, 1980.

Le, C. N. "The Model Minority Image." *Asian-Nation: The Landscape of Asian America,* n.d. http://www.asian-nation.org/model_minority.shtml.

———. "Writers, Artists, and Entertainers." *Asian-Nation: The Landscape of Asian America,* 2003. http://www.asian-nation.org/artists.shtml.

Leab, Daniel J. "Deutschland, USA: German Images in American Film." In *The Kaleidoscopic Lens: How Hollywood Views Ethnic Groups,* ed. Randall M. Miller. Englewood, NJ: Ozer, 1980.

Lee, Rachel C. *The Americas of Asian American Literature: Gendered Fictions of Nation and Transnation.* Princeton, NJ: Princeton University Press, 1999.

Lee, Stacey J. *Unraveling the "Model Minority" Stereotype: Listening to Asian American Youth.* New York: Teachers College Press, 1996.

Lessinger, Johanna. "Class, Race, and Success: Two Generations of Indian Americans Confront the American Dream." In *Migration, Transnationalization, and Race in a Changing New York,* ed. Héctor R. Cordero-Guzmán, Robert C. Smith, and Ramón Grosfoguel. Philadelphia: Temple University Press, 2001.

Li, Wei. "Anatomy of a New Ethnic Settlement: The Chinese Ethnoburb in Los Angeles." *Urban Studies* 35, no. 3 (1998): 479–502.

———. "Ethnoburb versus Chinatown: Two Types of Urban Ethnic Communities in Los Angeles." *Cybergeo,* no. 70: 1998. http://www.cybergeo.presse.fr/culture/weili/wili.htm.

Lien, Pei-te. *The Making of Asian America through Political Participation.* Philadelphia: Temple University Press, 2001.

Lien, Pei-te, Christian collet, Janelle Wong, and Karthick Ramakrishnan. "Asian Pacific-American Public Opinion and Political Participation." *PS: Political Science & Politics* 34, no. 3 (September 2001): 625–630.

Light, Ivan Hubert. *Ethnic Enterprise in America: Business and Welfare among Chinese, Japanese, and Blacks.* Berkeley: University of California Press, 1972.

Lim, Shirley Geok-lin. "Asian American Literature: Leavening the Mosaic." *U.S. Society and Values,* 5 (February 2000). http://usinfo.state.gov/journals/itsv/0200/ijse/shirley.htm.

Lim, Shirley Geok-lin, and Amy Ling, eds. *Reading the Literatures of Asian America.* Philadelphia: Temple University Press, 1992.

Lin, Jan. *Reconstructing Chinatown: Ethnic Enclave, Global Change.* Minneapolis: University of Minnesota Press, 1998.

Ling, Amy. "Teaching Asian American Literature." *Essays on Teaching the American Literatures,* 17 April 1996. http://www.georgetown.edu/tamlit/essays/asian_am.html.

Ling, Amy, ed. *Yellow Light: The Flowering of Asian American Arts.* Philadelphia: Temple University Press, 1999.

Liu, John M., and Lucie Cheng. "A Dialogue on Race and Class: Asian American Studies and Marxism." In *The Left Academy: Marxist Scholarship on American Campuses,* ed. Bertell Ollman and Edward Vernoff. Vol. 3, 139–163. New York: Praeger, 1986.

Liu, Lily. "All Asian Asians Are Good At . . . " *Diversity and the Bar,* May 2001. http://www.mcca.com/site/data/inhouse/minorityattorneys/asianamerican.htm.

Lorenzo, M. K., A. K. Frost, and H. Z. Reinherz. "Social and Emotional Functioning of Older Asian American Adolescents." *Child & Adolescent Social Work Journal* 17, no. 4 (2000): 289–304.

Louie, Steve, and Glenn Omatsu, eds. *Asian Americans: The Movement and the Moment.* Los Angeles: UCLA Asian American Studies Center Press, 2001.

Low, Victor. *The Unimpressible Race: A Century of Educational Struggle by the Chinese in San Francisco.* San Francisco: East/West Publishing Company, 1982.

Lydon, Sandy. *Chinese Gold: The Chinese in the Monterey Region.* Capitola, CA: Capitola Book Company, 1985.

MacDonald, Jeffery L. *Transnational Aspects of Iu-Mien Refugee Identity.* New York: Garland Publishing, 1997.

Macedo, Ana Gabriela, and Ana Maria Machado-Chaves. "Amy Tan's *The Joy Luck Club:* Translation as a 'Trans/Cultural' Experience." *Hitting Critical Mass: A Journal of Asian American Cultural Criticism* 4 (fall 1996). http://istsocrates.berkeley.edu/~critmass/v4n1/macedo.html.

Mangiafico, Luciano. *Contemporary Asian American Immigrants: Patterns of Filipino, Korean, and Chinese Settlement in the United States.* New York: Praeger, 1988.

Marquis, Christopher. "Woman in the News: A Washington Veteran for Labor–Elaine Lan Chao." *New York Times,* 12 January 2001.

McKeown, Adam. "The Sojourner as Astronaut: Paul Siu in Global Perspective." In *Re-Collecting Early Asian America: Essays in Cultural History,* ed. Josephine Lee, Imogene L. Lim, and Yuko Matsukawa. Philadelphia: Temple University Press, 2002.

"The Model Minority Image." *Asian-Nation: The Landscape of Asian America,* April 2003. http://www.aian-nation.org/model_minority.shtml.

Mura, David. "Re-Examining Japanese Americans: From Honorary Whites to Model Minority." *Model Minority: A Guide to Asian American Empowerment.* 17 May 1996. http://modelminority.com/article286.html.

Nakamura, David. "They're Hot, They're Sexy . . . They're Asian Men." *Seattle Times Northwest Life,* 7 May 2000.

Nakanishi, Don. "A Quota on Excellence? The Asian American Admissions Debate." In *The Asian American Educational Experience,* ed. Don Nakanishi and Tina Yamamoto Nishida. New York: Routledge Kegan Paul, 1995.

Nash, Philip Tajitsu. "The Terrors of Terminology." *AsianWeek Archives,* 16–21 March 2001. www.asianweek.com/2001_03_16/feature_washj.html.

Natividad, Irene, ed. *The Asian American Almanac.* Farmington Hills, MI: Gale Group, 1995.

Nepstad, Peter. "Chinatown." *The Illuminated Lantern: Revealing the Heart of Asian Cinema,* December-January 2002. http://www.illuminatedlantern.com/cinema/features/chinatown.html#top.

Ng, Franklin. "The Sojourner, Return Migration, and Immigration History." In *Chinese America: History and Perspectives.* San Francisco: Chinese Historical Society of America, 1987.

Ng, Franklin, and John Wilson. *The Asian American Encyclopedia.* Vols. 2–5. Philippines, Republic of the U.S.–China Relations. New York: Marshall Cavendish, 1995.

Nguyen, Trieuduong. "Better Luck Tomorrow Creates New Asian Perspective." *The Johns Hopkins Newsletter,* 7 March 2003.

Nguyen, Viet Thanh, and Tina Chen. "Editors' Introduction to Special Issue: Postcolonial Asian America." *Jouvert: A Journal of Postcolonial Studies* 4 (spring/summer 2000), 8 May 2002. http://social.chass.ncsu.edu/jouvert/v4i3/ed43.htm.

Nishioka, Joyce. "Socioeconomics: The Model Minority?" In *The New Face of Asian Pacific America: Numbers, Diversity & Change in the 21st Century,* ed. Eric Lai and Dennis Arguelles. San Francisco: AsianWeek and UCLA Asian American Studies Center, 2003, 32.

Nyíri, Pál. "The 'New Migrant': State and Market Constructions of Modernity and Patriotism." *China Inside Out,* ed. Pál Nyíri and Joana Breidenbach. 2001. http://cio.ceu.hu/courses/CIO/modules/Modul01Nyiri/pn1_index.html.

Okamura, Jonathan Y. *Imagining the Filipino American Diaspora: Transnational Relations, Identities, and Communities.* New York: Garland Publishing, 1998.

Okihiro, Gary Y. *Margins and Mainstreams: Asians in American History and Culture.* Seattle: University of Washington Press, 1994.

Omi, Michael. "It Just Ain't the Sixties No More: The Contemporary Dilemmas of Asian American Studies." In *Reflections on Shattered Windows: Promises and Prospects for Asian American Studies,* ed. Gary Y. Okihiro. Pullman: Washington State University Press, 1988, 31–36.

Orfield, G., and D. Whitla. "Diversity and Legal Education: Student Experiences in Leading Law Schools." In *Diversity Challenged: Evidence on the Impact of Affirmative Action,* ed. G. Orfield and M. Kurlaender. Cambridge, MA: Harvard Education Publishing Group, 2001.

Osajima, Keith. "Pedagogical Consideration in Asian American Studies." *Journal of Asian American Studies* (October 1998): 269–292.

Osumi, Megumi Dick. "Asians and California's Anti-Miscegenation Laws." In *Asian and Pacific American Experiences: Women's Perspectives,* ed. Nobuya Tsuchida. Minneapolis: Asian/Pacific American Learning Resource Center, University of Minnesota, 1982.

Ovando, Carlos J. "Interrogating Stereotypes: The Case of the Asian 'Model Minority.'" Indiana University, Asian Culture Center Newsletter, 7 November 2000. http://www.iub.edu/~acc/newsletter/ovando.html/.

Pan, Esther. "Why Asian Guys Are on a Roll." *Newsweek,* 21 Feb 2000. http://news weekparentsguide.com/nw-srv/printed/us/so/a16374-2000feb13.htm.

Patterson, Wayne. *The Korean Frontier in America: Immigration to Hawai'i, 1896–1910.* Honolulu: University of Hawai'i Press, 1988.

Peffer, George Anthony. *If They Don't Bring Their Women Here: Chinese Female Immigration before Exclusion.* Urbana: University of Illinois Press, 1999.

Petersen, William. "Success Story: Japanese American Style." *New York Times Magazine,* 9 January 1966, 26ff.

Portes, Alejandro, and Rubén Rumbaut. *Immigrant America.* Berkeley: University of California Press, 1996.

Qian, Zhenchao. "Breaking the Racial Barriers: Variations in Interracial Marriage between 1980 and 1990." *Demography* 34, no. 2 (1997): 263–276.

Qian, Zhenchao, Sampson Lee Blair, and Stacey D. Ruf. "Asian American Interracial and Interethnic Marriages: Differences by Education and Nativity." *International Migration Review* 32, no. 1 (2001): 557–586.

Quan, Tracy. "Time to Celebrate Asian Diaspora Month." *AlterNet Mobile Edition,* 21 May 2003. http://www.alternet.org/mobile/story_mobile.html?StoryID= 15969.

Rardin, Sue. "The Professors Revisit, Rewrite and Revise: The Religious Realities of America Today Have Shaken the Scholars." *Religion and the New Immigrants,* 2001. http://newimmigrants.org/classroom/research/rardin3.php3.

Rose, Peter I. "Asian Americans: From Pariahs to Paragons." In *Clamor at the Gates: The New American Immigration,* ed. Nathan Glazer. San Francisco: Institute for Contemporary Studies Press, 1985.

Rosenfeld, Michael J. "The Salience of Pan-National Hispanic and Asian Identities, in U.S. Marriage Markets," *Demography* 38 (2001): 161–175.

Saito, Leland. *Race and Politics: Asian Americans, Latinos, and Whites in a Los Angeles Suburb.* Champaign: University of Illinois Press, 1998.

Sakurai, Patricia A. "The Politics of Possession: Negotiating Identities in *American in Disguise, Homebase,* and *Farewell to Manzanar." Hitting Critical Mass: A Journal of Asian American Cultural Criticism* 1 (fall 1993). http://ist-socrates. berkeley.edu/~critmass/v1n1/sakurai.html.

Samson, Frank L. "Indicators of Asian American Panethnicity: Variation between Ethnic Origin Groups." 2002. http://www.stanford.edu/~flsamson/essays.

Shankar, Lavina Dhingra. "Activism, 'Feminisms' and Americanization in Bharati Mukherjee's *Wife* and *Jasmine." Hitting Critical Mass: A Journal of Asian American Cultural Criticism* 3 (winter 1995). http://ist-socrates.berkeley.edu/ ~critmass/v3n1/shankar1.html.

Shinagawa, Larry H., and Gin Yong Pang. "Asian American Panethnicity and Intermarriage." *Amerasia Journal* 22, no. 2 (1996): 127–152.

Simba, Malik. "*Gong Lum v. Rice:* The Convergence of Law, Race, and Ethnicity." In

American Mosaic: Selected Readings on America's Multicultural Heritage, ed. Young I. Song and Eugene C. Kim. Englewood Cliffs, NJ: Prentice Hall, 1993.

Siu, Paul C. P. "The Sojourner." *American Journal of Sociology* 58 (July 1952): 34–44.

Siu, S. F. *Asian American Students at Risk: A Literature Review*. Report No. 8. Baltimore, MD: Johns Hopkins University, Center for Research on the Education of Students Placed at Risk, 1996.

Skeldon, Ronald. "The Chinese Diaspora or the Migration of Chinese Peoples?" In *The Chinese Diaspora: Space, Place, Mobility, and Identity*, ed. Laurence J. C. Ma and Carolyn Cartier. Lanham, MD: Rowman and Littlefield Publishers, 2003.

Smith-Hefner, N. J. "Language and Identity in the Education of Boston-area Khmer." *Anthropology and Education Quarterly* 21, no. 3 (1990): 250–268.

Sowell, Thomas. *Ethnic America: A History*. New York: Basic Books, 1981.

Srikanth, Rajini. "Gender and the Image of Home in the Asian American Diaspora: A Socio-Literary Reading of Some Asian American Works." *Hitting Critical Mass: A Journal of American Cultural Criticism* 2 (winter 1994). http://ist-socrates.berkeley.edu/~critmass/v2n1/srikanth1.html.

Straub, Deborah Gillan, ed. *Voices of Multicultural America; Notable Speeches Delivered by African, Asian, Hispanic and Native Americans, 1790–1995*. Farmington Hills, MI: Gale Research, 1995.

Sumida, Stephen H., and Sau-ling Cynthia Wong, eds. *A Resource Guide to Asian American Literature*. New York: Modern Language Association of America, 2001.

Sung, Betty Kee. "Chinese Immigrants Create Their Own Jobs." *New Texans*, Institute of Texan Cultures, 1998. http://www.texancultures.utsa.edu/newtexans/jobs.htm.

Suzuki, B. H. "Asian Americans as the 'Model Minority': Outdoing Whites? Or Media Hype?" *Change*, November/December 1989, 2–19.

———. "Asians." In *Shaping Higher Education's Future: Demographic Realities and Opportunities, 1990–2000*, ed. A. Levine. San Francisco: Jossey-Bass, 1989.

———. "Revisiting the Model Minority Stereotype: Implications for Student Affairs Practice and Higher Education." In *Working with Asian American College Students*, ed. Marylu K. McEwen, Corinne Maekawa Kodama, Alvin N. Alvarez, Sunny Lee, and Christopher T. H. Liang. New Directions for Student Services, no. 97. San Francisco: Jossey-Bass, 2002.

Tajima, Renee. "Asian Women's Images in Film: The Past Sixty Years." In *Color: Sixty Years of Minority Women in Film: 1921–1981*. A project of the Exhibition Program at 3rd World Newsreel. Santa Cruz, CA: UC Santa Cruz Library. 1993.

Takagi, D. Y. *Retreat from Race: Asian-American Admissions and Racial Politics*. New Brunswick, NJ: Rutgers University Press, 1992.

Takaki, Ronald. *Strangers from a Different Shore: A History of Asian Americans*. Boston: Little, Brown and Company, 1989.

Takeda, Okiyoshi. "One Year after the Sit-in: Asian American Students' Identities and Their Support for Asian American Studies." *Journal of Asian American Studies* 4, no. 2 (2001): 147–164.

Teraguchi, Maho. "Visiting/Sojourning Japanese Business People in Silicon Valley." *E-ASPAC: An Electronic Journal in Asian Studies*, February 2002. http://mcel.pacificu.edu/Aspac%20%C6%92/Aspac/scholars/Teraguchi/maho.html.

Thrupkaew, Noy. The American Prospect, Inc. Preferred Citation: "The Myth of the Model Minority," *The American Prospect* 13, no. 7 April 8, 2002. www.prospect.org/authors/thrupkaew-n.html.

———. "The Myth of the Model Minority." *The American Prospect Online*, 8 April 2002. http://www.prospect.org/print/V13/7/thrupkaew-n.htm/.

Trask, Haunani-Kay. "Settlers of Color and 'Immigrant' Hegemony: 'Locals' in Hawai'i." *Amerasia Journal* 26, no. 2 (2000): 1–24.

Trueba, H., L. Cheng, and K. Ima. *Myth or Reality: Adaptive Strategies of Asian Americans in California*. Washington, DC: Falmer Press, 1993.

UCLA Asian American Studies Center. "Census Highlights about Asian Pacific Americans with Links." AASC announcement, 18 April 2002. http://www.sscnet.ucla.edu/aasc/change/may02census.html.

Umemoto, Karen. "'On Strike!' San Francisco State College Strike, 1968–69: The Role of Asian American Students," *Amerasia Journal* 15 (1989): 3–41.

United States Commission on Civil Rights. *Civil Rights Issues Facing Asian Americans in the 1990s*. Washington, DC: United States Government Printing Office, 1992.

Uyematsu, Amy. "The Emergence of Yellow Power in America." In *Roots: An Asian American Reader,* ed. Amy Tachiki, Eddie Wong, and Franklin Odo. Los Angeles: UCLA Asian American Studies Center, 1971, 9–13.

Vaidhyanathan, Siva. "Inside a 'Model Minority': The Complicated Identity of South Asians." *The Chronicle Review*, 23 June 2000. http://www.chronicle.com/free/v45/i42/42b00401.htm.

Vandercook, Chris. "Twenty Questions with Garrett Hongo, Author of *Volcano*." *Planet Hawaii*. http://64.75176.15/hfiles/questionsbody.shtml.

Visweswaran, Kamala. "Family in the U.S. Indian Diaspora." *South Asian Women's Forum* 19 (March 2001). http://www.sawf.org/newedit/edit03192001/womensociety.asp.

Võ, Linda Trinh, and Mary Yu Danico. "The Formation of Post-Suburban Communities: Little Saigon and Koreatown, Orange County." *The Impact of Immigrants on American Institutions: International Journal of Sociology and Social Policy* 24, no. 7/8 (2004): 15–45, guest ed. Prema Kurien.

Walsh, James. "The Perils of Success: Asians Have Become Exemplary Immigrants, but at a Price." *Time*, Fall 1993, 55–56.

Walsh, Joan. "Asian Women, Caucasian Men: It's a Growing Trend in the Bay Area's New Multicultural World. But These Relationships Can Bring with Them Social and Psychological Complications." *San Francisco Examiner*, 2 December 1990.

Wang, L. Ling-chi. "Asian American Studies." *American Quarterly* 33, no. 3 (1981): 339–354.

———. "The Structure of Dual Domination: Toward a Paradigm for the Study of the Chinese Diaspora in the U.S." *Amerasia Journal* 21 (1995): 149–169.

Wei, William. *The Asian American Movement*. Philadelphia: Temple University Press, 1993.

White-Parks, Annette. *Sui Sin Far/Edith Maude Eaton: A Literary Biography*. Urbana: University of Illinois Press, 1995.

Wing, Bob. "'Educate to Liberate!': Multiculturalism and the Struggle for Ethnic Studies." *ColorLines* 2, no. 2 (1999). www.arc.org/C_Lines/Story2_2_01.html.

Wong, Eugene Franklin. *On Visual Media Racism: Asians in the American Motion Pictures.* New York: Arno Press, 1978.

Wong, Morrison G. "Chinese Americans." In *Asian Americans: Contemporary Trends and Issues,* ed. Pyong Gap Min. Thousand Oaks, CA: Sage Publications, 1995.

Wong, Sau-ling C. "Denationalization Reconsidered: Asian American Cultural Criticism at a Theoretical Crossroad." *Amerasia Journal* 21 (1995): 1–27.

Woo, Deborah. *Glass Ceilings and Asian Americans: The New Face of Workplace Barriers.* Walnut Creek, CA: AltaMira Press, 2000.

Wu, Frank H. "The Perpetual Foreigner." *Asian American Village,* 2002. http://www.imdiversity.com/villages/asian/article_detaile.asp?Article_ID = 3547.

Wu, Frank H., and Francey Lim Youngberg. "People from China Crossing the River: Asian American Political Empowerment and Foreign Influence." In *Asian Americans and Politics: Perspectives, Experiences, Prospects,* ed. Gordon H. Chang. Stanford, CA: Stanford University Press, 2001.

Yamanaka, Keiko, and Kent McClelland. "Earning the Model Minority Image: Diverse Strategies of Economic Adaptation by Asian American Women." *Ethnic and Racial Studies* 17 (1994): 79–114.

Yanagisako, Sylvia. "Transforming Orientalism: Gender, Nationality, and Class in Asian American Studies." In *Naturalizing Power: Essays in Feminist Cultural Analysis,* ed. Sylvia Yanagisako and Carol Delaney. New York: Routledge, 1995.

Yang, Philip Q. "Sojourners or Settlers: Post-1965 Chinese Immigrants." *Journal of Asian American Studies* 2 (February 1999): 61–91.

Yep, Laurence, ed. *American Dragons: Twenty-Five Asian American Voices.* New York: HarperCollins, 1995.

Yin, X. H. "The Two Sides of America's 'Model Minority.'" *Los Angeles Times,* 7 May 2000, part M, p. 1.

Yin, Xiao-huang. *Chinese American Literature since the 1850s.* Urbana: University of Illinois Press, 2000.

Yong-Jin, Won. "Model Minority Strategy and Asian Americans' Tactics." *Korea Journal* 57 (1994).

Yu, Eui-Young. "Korean Communities in America: Past, Present, and Future," *Amerasia Journal* 10, no. 2 (1983): 23–35.

———. "Koreatown in Los Angeles: Emergence of a New Inner-City Ethnic Community." *Bulletin of the Population and Development Studies Center* 14 (1985), 37.

———. *Korean Community Profile.* Los Angeles: Korea Times, 1990, 9–10.

Yu, Henry. *Thinking Orientals: Migration, Contact, and Exoticism in Modern America.* New York: Oxford University Press, 2001.

Yun, Grace, ed. *A Look beyond the Model Minority Image: Critical Issues in Asian America.* New York: Minority Rights Group, Inc., 1989.

Zhou, Min. *Chinatown: The Socioeconomic Potential of an Urban Enclave.* Philadelphia: Temple University Press, 1992.

Zhou, Min, and James V. Gatewood. "Mapping the Terrain: Asian American Diversity and the Challenges in the Twenty-First Century." *Asian American Policy Review Online,* 10 April 2001. http://www.ksg.harvard.edu/aapr/volume9.htm.

Zhou, Xiaojing. "Possibilities Out of an Impossible Position: Myung Mi Kim's *Under Flag.*" *Electronic Poetry Center,* June 2002. http://epc.buffalo.edu/authorss/kim/xiaojing.html.

Zia, Helen. *Asian American Dreams: The Emergence of an American People.* New York: Farrar, Straus and Giroux, 2000, 58–61.

FICTION

Betancourt, Jeanne. *More than Meets the Eye.* New York: Bantam, 1990.

Chin, Frank, Jeffrey Paul Chan, Lawson Fusao Inada, and Shawn Wong, eds. *Aiiieee! An Anthology of Asian-American Writers.* Washington, DC: Howard University Press, 1974.

Hagedorn, Jessica. *Charlie Chan Is Dead.* New York: Penguin Books, 1993.

Irwin, Hadley. *Kim/Kimi.* New York: Puffin, 1988.

Karlin, Wayne, Le Minh Khue, and Vu Truong. *The Other Side of Heaven: Post-War Fiction by Vietnamese and American Writers.* St. Paul, MN: Curbstone Press, 1995.

Kingston, Maxine Hong. *The Woman Warrior: Memoirs of a Girlhood among Ghosts.* New York: Vintage, 1989.

Lee, C. Y. (Ching-Yang Lee). *The Second Son of Heaven: A Novel of Nineteenth-Century China.* New York: Harper Collins, 1990.

———. *Gate of Rage: A Novel of One Family Trapped by the Events at Tiananmen Square.* Morrow, 1991.

———. *Flower Drum Song.* New York: Penguin, 2002.

Tan, Amy. *Women of the Silk.* New York: St. Martin's, 1991.

———. *The Kitchen God's Wife.* New York: Ivy, 1992.

———. *The Joy Luck Club.* New York: Ivy, 1994.

———. *The Hundred Secret Senses.* New York: G.P. Putnams Sons, 1995.

Watanabe, Sylvia, and Carol Bruchac, eds. *Into the Fire; Asian American Prose.* New York: Greenfield Review Press, 1996

Yamanaka, Lois-Ann. *Blu's Hanging.* New York: Farrar, Straus and Giroux, 1997.

FILMS AND VIDEOS

Documentaries

Act of War: The Overthrow of the Hawaiian Nation (1993) 58 min. Na Maka o Ka'Aina production in collaboration with the Center for Hawaiian Studies, University of Hawaii, Manoa. Documents the events surrounding the overthrow of the Hawaiian monarchy in 1893 from the point of view of the Native Hawaiians. Explores how colonialism and the conquest of a Pacific island by western missionaries and capitalists have devastated the lives of the indigenous peoples.

American Sons (1995) 41 min. Based on interviews with Asian American men, this film addresses issues such as hate, violence, the stereotypes placed on Asian men, and psychological damage that racism causes over generations.

Ancestors in the Americas; Chinese in the Frontier West: An American Story (1998) 60 min. Berkeley: Center for Educational Telecommunications.

Ancestors in the Americas: Coolies, Sailors, Settlers (1996) 64 min. San Francisco: Center for Educational Telecommunications.

Banana Split (1991) 37 min. Director Kip Fulbeck interweaves narratives, stories, and media clips to focus on biracial ethnicity exploration and Asian self-identity. He examines the relationship between his father who is Caucasian and his mother who is Asian and also explores ethnic dating patterns and media stereotypes of Asian American men.

Becoming American (1982) 58 min. Follows a Hmong refugee family from northern Laos awaiting resettlement in a refugee camp in northern Thailand, from the time they learn of their acceptance as immigrants to the time they are settled in Seattle, Washington.

Bhangra Wrap (1994) 20 min. Focuses on South Asian youth subculture that fuses hip-hop, rap, and Bhangra music. Based in Toronto, Canada and New York City, Bhangra is a mix of old and new and is symbolic of universal cultural transformation for new generations.

Blue Collar and Buddha (1987) 57 min. Documents local attitudes toward Laotian refugees living in Rockford, Illinois, and raises issues related to acculturation.

Carved in Silence (1987) 45 min. Documents Chinese immigration to the United States and discriminatory policies toward Asians.

The Color of Honor: The Japanese American Soldier in World War II (1987) 90 min. Focuses on the dilemma of Japanese Americans incarcerated during the war who chose to fight for their country.

Effects of War: The Indochina Refugee Experience (1989) 58 min. A brief historical overview of Cambodia, Laos, and Vietnam and the transitional stages common to the refugee experience.

Forbidden City, U.S.A. (1989) 56 min. Documents America's first all-Chinese American nightclub, one of San Francisco's landmark hot-spots for locals and tourists alike in the 1930s and 1940s.

My America or Honk if You Love Budda. (1993) 87min. Renee Tajima-Peña travels through the United States capturing the complexity of Asian American experiences, identities, and communities.

Sa-i-gu, 4.29 (1993) 39 min. Examines the effects of the Los Angeles uprisings on April 29th from the perspective of women shopkeepers. Based on interviews with Korean women in Los Angeles, issues of racism, ethnic relations, and how mainstream media portray Korean-Black relationships is revealed.

7th Train (2001) 30 min. Follows the lives of immigrants in New York City who take the 7th train to work.

Silence Broken: Korean Comfort Women (1999) 57 min. Based on interviews with comfort women, Japanese soldiers, recruiters, and contemporary scholars, this film documents the lives of women forced into sexual servitude by the Japanese Imperial Army during World War II.

Slaying the Dragon (1987) 60 min. The roles and images of Asian women in the film and television industry are analyzed over the past 50 years.

South Central (1993) 45 min. Filmmakers provide video cameras to a multicultural community in the South Central area of Los Angeles to depict their lives after the uprisings. The voices of Latinos, African Americans, Koreans, and a police officer are documented to show how their lives have been affected by the uprisings.

The Stories of Maxine Hong Kingston (1994) 60 min. Princeton, NJ: Films for the Humanities.

Who Killed Vincent Chin? (1988) 83 min. Documents the violent murder of Vincent

Chin by a laid-off automobile worker in Detroit and the Asian American community's fight to bring his murderers to justice.

Yuri Kochiyama: A Passion for Justice (1993) 57 min. Chronicles Yuri Kochiyama's story from her internment as a young woman during World War II, her dedication to Malcom X and the Black Liberation movement, and her work as an international and domestic political activist.

Feature Films/Short Films

American Adobo (2002) 102 min. Follows the lives of five Filipino American friends who, in a period of a year, share their struggles with finding a "man," losing a loved one to AIDS, and finding out that relationships are more than a one-night stand. They gather to dine on American Adobo, which makes them feel at home.

Bend It Like Beckham (2003) 112 min. Two 18-year-old British women strive to make it as professional soccer players. One of the women comes from an Indian family who would like her to find a nice boy to settle down with and cook Indian food, while the other English girl is confronted with her mother's anxiety over her sexuality.

Better Luck Tomorrow (2003) 80 min. Features the lives of middle-class, intelligent, young Asian American men in Southern California who get caught up in a web of drugs, violence, and lies.

Chan Is Missing (1981) 80 min. In this comedy, a Chinese American taxi driver and his nephew are seeking their friend, Chan, who has apparently disappeared with their savings.

The Debut (2002) 60 min. A young man is confronted with what it means to be Filipino American. He struggles with pleasing his parents versus pursuing his own goals as an artist.

Dim Sum—A Little Bit of Heart (1987) 88 min. A comedy about a Chinese American mother and daughter in San Francisco and their attempts to preserve their cultural heritage.

Heaven & Earth (1994) 142 min. Story of an American soldier and a Vietnamese woman during the Vietnam War.

Joy Luck Club (1993) 139 min. Based on the novel by Amy Tan, this film examines the lives of four Chinese immigrant mothers in San Francisco and their relationships with their daughters.

Mississippi Masala (1992) 118 min. In this interracial love story, an African American businessman falls for a beautiful Indian immigrant, only to encounter shock and outrage from both families.

The Wedding Banquet (1993) 109 min. Highlights the stress of a New Yorker–Taiwanese gay man's effort to hide his sexuality from his parents in Taiwan. In hopes of ending his mother's matchmaking efforts, he announces he is engaged to a woman. His parents, elated by the news, travel to New York to meet the bride and plan the wedding.

WEB SITES

Asian American Arts Alliance. http://www.aaartsalliance.org/
Asian American Film. http://www.asianamericanfilm.com/

Asian American Net. http://www.asianamerican.net/
Asian American Parent Association. http://aapa.net/
Asian American Resources. http://www.ai.mit.edu/people/irie/aar/
Asian Americans for Community Involvement. http://www.aaci.org/index.html
Asian Americans for Community Outreach. http://www.aaco-sf.org/
Asian Pacific American Heritage Association. http://www.apaha.org/
Asian Pacific American Women's Leadership Institute. http://www.apawli.org/
Asian Pacific Women's Center. http://www.apwcla.org/
Asian Women in Business. http://www.awib.org/
Association for Asian American Studies. http://www.aaastudies.org/opening.html
Boat People SOS. http://www.bpsos.org/
Bridge to Asia. http://www.bridge.org/
Hapa Issues Forum. http://www.hapaissuesforum.org/
Japan America Society of Alabama. http://www.jasaweb.net/
Japanese American Citizens League. http://www.jacl.org/
Japanese American National Museum. http://www.janm.org/main.htm
Korean Immigrant Workers Advocate. http://www.kiwa.org/
Leadership in Action Program. http://www.leap.org/
Media Action Network for Asian Americans. http://www.manaa.org
National Asian American Telecommunications Association (NAATA). http://www.
    naatanet.org/
National Association of Asian American Professionals. http://www.naaap.org/
National Japanese American Historical Society. http://www.nikkeiheritage.org/
Second Generation. http://www.2g.org/news/
Thai USA Association. http://www.thai-usa.org/
Vietnamese American Council. http://www.viet-nam.org/

INDEX

ABOUT THE AUTHORS

MARY YU DANICO is Assistant Professor in the Behavioral Studies Department at California Polytechnic State University, Pomona.

FRANKLIN NG is Professor of Anthropology at California State University, Fresno.